Family and Kin in Urban Communities, 1700–1930

Family and Kin in Urban Communities, 1700–1930

EDITED WITH AN INTRODUCTION
BY TAMARA K. HAREVEN

NEW VIEWPOINTS

A Division of Franklin Watts
New York | London | 1977

New Viewpoints
A Division of Franklin Watts
730 Fifth Avenue
New York, New York 10019

Library of Congress Cataloging in Publication Data
Main entry under title:

Family and kin in urban communities, 1700–1930.

Earlier versions of most of the articles in this volume
were first presented at the National Conference on the
Family, Social Change, and Social Structure, which was
held at Clark University in April, 1972.
Includes biographical references and index.
1. Family—United States—History—Addresses, essays, lectures. I. Hareven, Tamara K. II. National Conference on the Family, Social Change, and Social Structure, Clark University, 1972.
HQ535.F33   301.42'0973   76–25596
ISBN 0–531–05388–1
ISBN 0–531–05592–2 pbk.

Contents

Acknowledgments

Earlier versions of all the articles in this volume, except those by Hall and myself, were first presented at the National Conference on the Family, Social Change and Social Structure, which was held at Clark University in April, 1972, and which I organized and directed under the sponsorship of the Department of History and the Cultural Affairs Program at Clark University. The essays by Blumin, Glasco, Griffens, Rutman, and myself and earlier versions of the Introduction to this volume first appeared in a special issue of the *Journal of Urban History* on "The History of the Family in Urban Society," which I guest-edited. I am grateful to the editors of the *Journal of Urban History*, Raymond Mohl and Blaine Brownell, for their encouragement and assistance in the preparation of the special issue of the journal, to Peter Laslett and Daniel Scott Smith for earlier critical reading of the conference essays, and to Howard Chudacoff for constructive criticisms on the Introduction. Also, I appreciate the invaluable editorial assistance of Howard Litwak, and the devoted typing of Annette Slocombe and Laurel Rosenthal.

I am also indebted to Sage Publications, Inc., for permission to reprint the articles that originally appeared in the *Journal of Urban History* and to the National Council on Family Relations for permission to reprint the article by Modell and myself.

T.K.H.

Family and Kin in Urban Communities, 1700–1930

1

Introduction

Prior to the development of psychoanalytic theory, internal experiences of the family were considered private and intimate, best explored by artists and poets. Psychoanalysis legitimized the search into interpersonal dynamics in the family, and placed this search in a scientific framework. It focused, however, on relationships between individuals, especially mothers and children, during the formative years, rather than on the entire family unit. On the other hand, sociology and anthropology have identified the family as a social and economic entity and investigated its organization and interaction with the larger society, but have not accounted sufficiently for historical complexities. Until recently, economics concentrated on family consumption and expenditure patterns, and on the relationship between demographic processes and labor force participation, but paid less attention to the household and the family as economic units, and to the economic participation and the process of decision-making among different family members.[1]

Current research in family history has been trying to combine many of these approaches in order to examine family development in the context of past societies, and to evaluate patterns of change over time. As a rapidly developing field, family history has excited the imagination of historians, sociologists, and psychologists, bringing a variety of new methods into play. Research has developed in such categories as:

analysis of demographic processes (marriage, fertility, and mortality), study of household and family structure, investigation of stages of the life cycle in the past, particularly childhood and adolescence in relationship to the family, and analysis of sex roles and sexuality in their impact on family behavior. Other ongoing work has related family behavior to societal processes such as migration, work, economic organization, mobility, and education. While most research still focuses on the internal organization of the family and the household, or on demographic processes, some effort is under way to link family behavior to such social institutions as schools, reformatories, and welfare. Scholars have devoted less attention to the relationship between the family and religious institutions, and to the interaction between the family and its ecological context in urban and rural environments.[2]

Research into family history has generally considered the question of change in familial organization and demographic behavior in Western society, or, more specifically, the impact of industrialization, urbanization, and modernization on demographic behavior and family change. The counterpart of this issue, the impact of family and demographic behavior on social change and the interaction of the family with other institutions, has been neglected in historical and sociological research.

In the following pages, I will attempt to discuss some of the major findings in recent studies in the history of the family and to relate them to the study of the family in urban society and to the specific essays in this volume.

One of the most important contributions of the new work in the field has been to dispel myths about family and household structure in the past. Recent studies of populations in preindustrial Europe and America have shown that households were *nuclear* rather than *extended,* and that their membership was generally limited to the conjugal couple and to its children.[3] In a most impressive collection of essays analyzing household structure in different societies over different time periods, Peter Laslett presents what he calls "the null hypothesis in the history of the family, which is that the present state of evidence forces us to assume that its organization was always and invariably nuclear unless the contrary can be proven."[4] This work has had a profound impact, resulting in a revision of the myths about the existence of what William Goode called "the great family of Western nostalgia."[5] These findings have already modified the standard assumptions that industrialization broke down traditional extended families and caused the emergence of the "modern" nuclear family.

A real danger still exists that the revision of old stereotypes might generate new ones. The conclusion that industrialization has not caused major changes in household structure over the past two centuries has led historians to the assumption that little change has occurred in family behavior in general. It is important to stress that household structure, although a commonly studied feature of the family in the past, represents only one aspect of life and change in the family. While household structure has changed only minimally, important transformations have taken place in family functions, and consequently in the relationships which they affect.

Over the past 200 years, the family has gradually shed many traditional functions. As John Demos has pointed out, the preindustrial family functioned as a workshop, a reformatory, an asylum, a school, and a church.[6] Under the impact of industrialization, economic activity moved away from the household and immediate kin group to the workplace. The family gradually changed from a production unit to a consumption one, particularly in the experience of the middle class. Specialized institutions of education, social welfare, and social control replaced the family through a process of differentiation in such fields as education and reform.[7] As a result, the functions of the middle-class family in particular shrank to a concentration on child-rearing, and the role of the wife was redefined and limited to domesticity and child-nurture. A large body of proscriptive literature idealized the nuclearity and privacy of the family and impressed upon its large middle-class reading public the importance of the family as a domestic retreat from the outside world of work.[8]

The separation of the workplace from the home caused a major shift in the functions of the household and the family. The first consequence was the transformation of the household from a busy workplace and social center to a private family abode. This involved the withdrawal of strangers, such as business associates, partners, journeymen, and apprentices from the household, as well as a more rigorous differentiation in the work responsibilities of family members. The new specialized work schedule led to the segregation of husbands from wives and fathers from children in the course of their workday. In middle-class families, housework lost its economic and productive value. Since it was not paid for, it had no place in the occupational hierarchy.

These transitions were gradual, and varied significantly from class to class. While historians have generalized upon the entire society on the basis of middle-class experience, it is now becoming clear that preindustrial family patterns persisted over longer time periods on the farm and in working-class families. Since the process of industrialization itself was gradual, domestic industries and a variety of small family enterprises carried over into the industrial system. For example, in New England, during the first half of the nineteenth century, rural families were sending their daughters to work in factories while the economic base of the family continued to be anchored on the farm. In most working-class families, work continued to be considered a family enterprise even if it did not take place in the home.

Research in progress has thus shown that modernization was not a linear and terminal process by which preindustrial peasants were transformed into "modern" urbanites. Individuals and families carried their cultural traditions into new social environments, and although they modified these traditions to some extent, they continued to adhere to them and to organize their lives along traditional patterns. Even under conditions of rapid social change, families held on to earlier traditions tenaciously. It is not surprising that "modern" attitudes transformed family behavior more slowly than other aspects of life such as work, consumption, and leisure patterns. Research in the next few years will have to analyze mechanisms of gradual change, and to delineate the ways in which families balanced their traditions with the demands dictated by the new industrial order, by urban living, and by different cultural standards. To attempt this, an index of "modern" characteristics of family behavior must be developed. Recognition of these complexities, particularly the gradual character of the process of modernization, is important for a realistic understanding of the impact of urbanization on family behavior.[9]

Since the publication in 1938 of Louis Wirth's "Urbanism as a Way of Life," students of the city have sought to identify the unique nature of the urban condition. Family behavior has been cited as a major illustration of urban-rural differences. However, historians have made little progress in articulating the differences between rural and urban society.[10] Through creative research, the "New Urban History" has illuminated major processes such as education, social and geographic mobility, and economic behavior, but, on the whole, the interaction of the family as a unit with these processes has been overlooked.[11] Nor have modern urban historians compared the phenomena they have discovered in cities with conditions in rural areas, failing to sharpen conceptualization of either rural-urban differences or different types of cities.[12] One problem has been the division of studies along chronological and territorial lines. Most investigations of the family in the seventeenth and eighteenth centuries concentrate on small villages or towns such as Plymouth, Andover, and Hingham, Massachusetts, while studies of nineteenth- and early-twentieth-century family patterns tend to focus on larger towns and cities. Studies of the family in preindustrial New England, modeled as they were on demographic analyses of preindustrial villages in England and France, succeeded in integrating the family into the ecological and cultural context of the community. However, studies of nineteenth-century families have generally analyzed population segments which happened to be living in cities, but without weaving the patterns into an "urban" context.[13]

The absence of a comparative rural-urban perspective has led historians to generalize about the nature of certain processes as uniquely "urban" without, in fact, their having been limited to the city. For example, the demographic transition of the eighteenth century, which was characterized by a decline of both fertility and mortality, occurred simultaneously in rural and urban areas, preceding the nineteenth-century burst of urban growth by several decades. Several scholars have suggested that although rural-urban differences in fertility and mortality persisted over the latter part of the eighteenth century and through the nineteenth, urban as well as rural populations responded simultaneously to demographic changes which occurred in the process of modernization. Subsequent declines in fertility and mortality in the nineteenth century were parallel in rural and urban areas, although a rural-urban gap as such persisted.[14]

Such findings are further reinforced by recognition that industrialization and urbanization were not simultaneous or interchangeable processes, as they have been frequently presented. Early stages of industrialization occurred first in the countryside, accelerating population changes which have been frequently attributed to the impact of urbanization. This is particularly true for New England, where the textile industry developed initially in the countryside. It is important to understand, therefore, what processes in rural areas facilitated industrialization and made rural populations responsive to new modes of production, and what changes in the New England countryside prompted or encouraged families to migrate to new industrial communities, or at least to send their daughters there. Historians have not been able yet to answer these questions, because most of the ongoing research has concentrated on industrial and urban communities, without any emphasis on their interaction with changes in rural society.

In this context, the essays by Rutman and Blumin in this volume are particularly valuable for an understanding of rural-urban differences because they discuss demographic change and household structure respectively in regional frameworks. Rutman examines the relationship between population growth, migration, and settlement patterns in New Hampshire towns, considers the role of the family as an agent of migration, and stresses the strong interrelationship between the development of new towns and migration in family units rather than as individuals. Blumin finds little difference in household size and family structure in rural and urban communities in the Hudson Valley during the first half of the nineteenth century, and concludes that whatever rural-urban differences may exist in family behavior are not reflected in household structure. These findings are reinforced by a comparative analysis of fertility patterns in select rural and urban communities in Essex County, Massachusetts, in the latter part of the nineteenth century carried out by Tamara Hareven and Maris Vinovskis. This study finds that the size of the community, its occupational structure (particularly whether women were employed outside the home), and the degree to which immigrant populations were concentrated within had a more profound impact on differences in fertility than a strictly "rural" and "urban" division.[15]

The diversity of the composition and ways of life of urban populations has also raised serious questions about the feasibility of a typology of "urban family." Since the middle of the nineteenth century, the composition of urban populations in the United States has become increasingly complex and diverse. The influx of rural migrants into expanding urban areas has tended to slow down the homogenization of social behavior into an "urban" way of life, even in settlements that qualified for the definition of "cities" according to the criterion of population density. Cultural and ethnic backgrounds, recency of migration, and adherence to previous traditions were contributing factors to differences in family and kinship organization, fertility ratios, and school attendance. As Herbert Gans has shown, the urban villagers in Boston's West End in the 1950's differed profoundly from their Yankee neighbors in the organization and ideology of their family life. Even members of the same ethnic group experienced different family patterns in different locations in the city.[16] In late nineteenth-century Boston, for example, Hareven has found that Irish immigrants living in the center city had different family patterns than Irish from the same occupational groups in South Boston. Irish women in the inner city had lower fertility and their nuclear families were smaller. Families in the center of the city took strangers into their households as boarders and lodgers much more frequently than the residents of South Boston, whose households were predominantly nuclear. Whether location influenced differences in behavior or whether individuals were attracted to those neighborhoods within a city because they were most suitable for their familial arrangements is still open to investigation.[17]

Historians have tended to focus on family and household structure almost exclusively as a measure of family behavior. Family and household structure in urban areas has shown little variation, however, when examined at one point in time rather than over the entire life cycle. Studies of nineteenth-century family and household structure have developed from the New Urban History, which has concentrated primarily on social and geographic mobility of urban populations and on their social structure. Such studies tend to be based upon household units in the nineteenth-century population census, with supplemental data from city directories, registers of vital records, and real estate or other property records. By contrast to the family and community reconstitution studies of the earlier period, most of these census analyses are limited to one point in time, or to several-decade intervals. They provide, therefore, only snapshots of family organization at one or several points in time.

Changes are far more visible in the context of the family life cycle from its formation through courtship and marriage to its dissolution through death, divorce, or migration. More recent studies have shown that family and household structure varied significantly over the life cycle. The essay by Glasco shows that men living in nuclear families at one stage of life often lived as boarders in other poeple's households at the next stage and headed nuclear or extended households as they moved through their middle years into old age. Particularly significant is his emphasis on the difference in the family arrangements of men and women at different stages of life. The transitions from one family type to another along the life course varied significantly among men and women and between different ethnic groups.[18]

This concentration on the household unit has also resulted in the study of the family in isolation from relatives not residing in the household. A case in point is Richard Sennett's study *Families Against the City,* which relies on household structure as an exclusive measure of family adaptability to urban life. The major weakness of Sennett's book is in its conclusion that "extended families," which it confuses with "households," were more adaptable to the urban environment than "isolated nuclear'' families. The difficulty with this conclusion is evident: since, on average, only 10% to 12% of all households in American cities were extended, one must conclude that the remaining 88% of families living in cities were not adjusted to urban life. Sennett fails to consider adequately the presence of kin residing outside the household. While they were not visible in the census, they performed significant functions nonetheless.[19]

More recent studies, some of which are exemplified in this volume, have begun to depart from these limited approaches. They have investigated those aspects of family development which change along the stages of the individual life cycle and the family cycle; they have attempted to relate urban residence to marriage patterns, to analyze fertility patterns on the household level, and to explore the role of family and kinship in migration, in business activities, and in industrial work.

All these studies share a view of the family as a process rather than a static unit. Instead of studying the family in isolation, they examine it as an institution interacting with other social institutions. The essay by May and Vinovskis shows the extent to which urban families interacted with the school system during the earliest stage of childhood—infancy; the ones by Hall, the Griffens, and Hareven document the significant role which the family had in economic activity. They provide new ways for assessing the family's adaptability to urban conditions or its impact on other aspects of urban economic life.

This exploration of family interaction with other social institutions significantly revises previous notions about family breakdown. The Chicago School of Sociology, in the 1930's, developed the prevailing theory of social disorganization, attributing it to the uprooting of individuals from traditional folk society, and to the severance of kinship ties as a result of migration. Recent studies suggest that the family did not break down as a result of migration and urbanization, and in fact that the family actually functioned as an *active* agent in facilitating migration and cushioned its members in their adjustment to new environments and unfamiliar living conditions. As Hareven's article points out, the pattern of chain migration was directed, organized, and assisted by relatives. Individuals and families migrating into cities or already living in them relied on kin or on former townsmen for support and sociability, and particularly for assistance in critical life situations such as illness, death, unemployment, or strikes.[20]

A variety of kin networks assisted the family in its daily work and living arrangements. Where relatives were not available, strangers residing with the family as boarders fulfilled similar functions. Modell and Hareven's study of boarding and lodging in nineteenth-century cities shows that the taking in of strangers in exchange for pay or services was more widespread than sharing household space with extended kin. Surrogate kin in the household served as important sources of support and adaptability to the new urban environments. Particularly significant is the fact that boarding and lodging not only served as temporary "emergency" measures in the family's adaptation to urban life, but were also life-cycle phenomena: they represented a normal stage in the transitional period between the departure of individuals from their parents' family to the setting up of their own family. Kin groups also performed important functions in the lives of middle- and upper-class families. In preindustrial society, kin functioned as intermediaries between the family and economic institutions. Entire business organizations were structured along kin lines. Hall's analysis of Boston Brahmin families suggests the extent to which family ties were inextricably enmeshed with business activities, and with the transfer or retention of property. Boston elites perpetuated their kin networks through cousin marriages in order to retain family control over economic enterprises and financial trusts. In their exploration of the business ties and credit activities of small merchants and shopkeepers in a mid-nineteenth-century small town, the Griffens illustrate the active role played by relatives in assisting each other and in transferring finances and credit from one relative to another.

The Hall and Griffen articles provide important evidence of the persistence of viable economic functions for kin in commercial urban society. While it has been traditionally argued that the economic importance of kin diminished once landholding ceased to be a major base for the family's economy and production left the home, this new evidence suggests that under new economic conditions, the kin group assumed viable new functions. These findings, combined with Hareven's conclusion on the important role of kin among working-class families in the industrial environment, considerably revise earlier assumptions that the majority of families in the nineteenth century were isolated from kin. This earlier misconception had been influenced primarily by Talcott Parsons, and a number of other sociologists who preceded him, who argued that the family most fit for the urban, industrial society is that of the nuclear, isolated type. Historians thought that this pattern existed in the nineteenth century due to a concentration on the household unit rather than the family. Many historical studies have used the terms "household" and "family" interchangeably and have ignored the presence of relatives residing outside the household but in close proximity to the nuclear family. *Households* were predominantly nuclear in the past, but *families* were extended, through important kin ties which transcended the household unit. This "discovery" of kinship ties in urban communities significantly shifts the central question of family history from taxonomies of household structure to the exploration of the broader meaning of family functions and of the role of different members within the family. Such new explorations must also be placed systematically in the context of the urban environment. Students of the city have long accepted the importance of the neighborhood as a social organization of critical importance in city life, yet equal attention has not been devoted to the social geography of kin. As current sociologists have shown, however, the kin group is deeply enmeshed with the urban environment and provides important linkages between the individual and the larger society.

Thus, recent studies in the history of urban families have contributed significantly to clearing the underbrush which had obscured the complexities of the family's interaction with urban life. But additional systematic work is needed to understand fully the family as an urban institution. Methods and approaches which have been tested in smaller communities should be applied to the study of major cities, where differences among neighborhoods, population groups, and socioeconomic groups must be pursued systematically. Particularly important is an understanding of the relationship between the occupational structures of the city and family behavior, in order to delineate the differences in family patterns between cities characterized by female-intensive or male-intensive industries. Systematic comparisons must also be carried out between urban and rural populations on a regional basis, particularly by differentiating family patterns of urban residents from those prevalent in their villages of origin; similarly, the family patterns of immigrants should be compared with premigration backgrounds. One of the most neglected aspects in this field is the study of the geography of family life.[21] The history of housing as it relates to the organization of the family's internal space and the journey to work are still among the great unknowns. Finally, still unexplored are the relationships between the family and other urban institutions—social welfare agencies, labor unions, educational institutions—all of which are critical for the understanding of the urban process.

What can the study of the family contribute to the understanding of urban society? What exactly urban history is and what it is the history of are still debatable subjects. Whether urban history deals with people and institutions in cities, analyzes the interaction of individuals and groups with the urban environment as ecological units, or concentrates on the study of an urban culture or "way of life" (and I hope it does all those), the family is a critical variable.[22] The study of the family sheds light on the migration process into cities, and on the demographic patterns which determine population change and which are critical for the process of urbanization. Such investigations provide an important understanding of the institution which prepares its members for urban life or which shelters them from it.

This checklist of family functions in urban society would be reduced to truisms unless they are explored in a dynamic way. Scholars must analyze the areas in which family behavior has an influence on the larger urban society, as well as those areas where family patterns are determined by external urban conditions. More than a decade ago Eric Lampard called for a "broadened view of urban history," namely, "the possibility of examining one of the most comprehensive, profound, and unprecedented manifestations of social change: *the urbanization of society*."[23] This integrated yet dynamic approach to the study of the urban process which combines the "demographic," the "structural," and the "behavioral" dimensions has not been pursued by historians. Urban historians have talked about population growth in cities, but have not analyzed the population dynamics in rural and urban areas, which would explain the population shifts involved in the process of urbanization. It is now becoming increasingly evident that major changes in demographic behavior occurred independently of industrialization and urbanization, as well as interrelatedly. Since changes in the family may have facilitated those larger processes, an understanding of family behavior becomes a critical aspect of the study of urban society.

The essays in this volume do not fulfill the agenda proposed above. They may bring us closer, however, to an understanding of the issues raised by pointing to the following areas of investigation: rural-urban comparisons in family and household structure and size, the role of kinship in urban family life, ethnic differences in stages of the individual and family cycles, and the relationships among the family and business activity and industrial work. All these represent new areas of research in the history of the family which go beyond the older classification of household types. They share a view of family organization and behavior as a *process* within certain historical periods and over time.

Ongoing and future research will carry the analysis of the family as an urban institution along more rigorous analytical lines which will map more explicitly the social geography of family behavior, and which will relate the "family process" to the "urban process."

NOTES

1. On the development of the history of the family see Tamara K. Hareven, "The History of the Family as an Interdisciplinary Field," *Journal of Interdisciplinary History*, II, No. 2 (Autumn, 1971) 399–414. Reports on ongoing research in the field, methodological discussions, book reviews, conference reports, and articles are published in *The Journal of Family History: Studies in Family, Kinship, and Demography*, which is edited by Tamara K. Hareven and published by the National Council on Family Relations.

2. See Hareven, "History of the Family as an Interdisciplinary Field." Several journals have published special issues in the history of the family: the *Journal of Marriage and the Family*, November, 1969, and again in August, 1973, under the editorship of Michael Gordon and Tamara K. Hareven; the *Journal of Interdisciplinary History* (Autumn, 1971); and the *Journal of Urban History* published a special issue on the urban family (May, 1975) under the editorship of Tamara K. Hareven. The study of sex roles and of women has not been explicitly connected with the history of the family. Useful material can be found, however, in Mary Hartman and Louis W. Banner, *Clio's Consciousness Raised* (New York, 1974), originally published as a special issue of *Feminist Studies*; Martha Vicinus, ed., *Suffer and Be Still: Women in the Victorian Age* (Bloomington, Indiana, 1972). Studies in the history of childhood, although focusing on the individual life cycle, have been an integral part of the development of the history of the family. See, for example: Lloyd DeMause, ed., *The History of Childhood* (New York, 1974) and Robert H. Bremner, John Barnard, Tamara K. Hareven, Robert M. Mennel, eds., *Children and Youth in America: A Documentary History*, 3 vols. (Cambridge, Mass., 1970–1974). The most seminal study, which has greatly influenced the development of the field, is Philippe Ariès, *Centuries of Childhood: A Social History of Family Life*, Robert Baldick, trans. (New York, 1962), originally published as *L'Enfant et la vie familiale sous l'Ancien Regime* (Paris, 1960). For major recent works on historical demography see E. A. Wrigley, *Population and History* (New York, 1969); E. A. Wrigley, ed., *An Introduction to English Historical Demography from the Sixteenth to the Nineteenth Century* (London, 1966); D. V. Glass and Roger Revelle, eds., *Population and Social Change* (New York, 1972); T. H. Hollingsworth, *Historical Demography* (Ithaca, N.Y., 1969); see also Pierre Goubert, "Historical Demography and the Reinterpretation of Early Modern French History: A Research Review," *Journal of Interdisciplinary History*, I (Autumn, 1970), 37–48; John Demos, "Notes on Life in Plymouth Colony," *William and Mary Quarterly*, 3rd series, XXII (April, 1965), 264–286; Philip Greven, Jr., "Family Structure in Seventeenth-Century Andover, Massachusetts," ibid., XXIII (April, 1966), 234–56; Daniel Scott Smith, "The Demographic History of Colonial New England," *Journal of Economic History*, XXXII (March, 1972), 165–183; Maris

Vinovskis, "The Field of Early American Family History: A Methodological Critique," *The Family in Historical Perspective: An International Newsletter,* No. 7 (Winter, 1974) 1–8; Maris Vinovskis, "American Historical Demography: A Review Essay," *Historical Methods Newsletter,* IV (September, 1971), 141–148; John M. Murrin, "A Review Essay," *History and Theory,* XI, No. 2 (1972), 226–275.

For studies of the family on the household level, see John Demos, *A Little Commonwealth: Family Life in Plymouth Colony* (New York, 1970); Philip Greven, Jr., *Four Generations: Population, Land, and Family in Colonial Andover, Massachusetts* (Ithaca, N.Y., 1970).

3. See Demos, *A Little Commonwealth;* Greven, *Four Generations.*

4. Laslett, *Household and Family in Past Time,* p. ix. Although Laslett uses the term "family" he is actually referring to the "household." It is important to emphasize here that the *household* was nuclear, while the family could, in fact, be extended through kinship networks not residing in the same household.

5. William Goode, *World Revolution and Family Patterns* (New York, 1963, 1972).

6. Demos, *A Little Commonwealth.*

7. Goode, *World Revolution;* Peter Laslett, *The World We Have Lost* (London, 1965); David J. Rothman, *The Discovery of the Asylum* (Boston, 1971); P. Willmott and M. Young, *The Symmetrical Family* (New York, 1974).

8. Bernard Wishy, *The Child and the Republic* (Philadelphia, 1968); Robert H. Bremner, ed., *Children and Youth in America* (Cambridge, Mass., 1970–1974); Barbara Welter, "The Cult of True Womanhood: 1820–1860," *American Quarterly,* 78 (1968) 151–174; Mary Ryan, "American Society and the Cult of Domesticity," unpublished Ph.D. thesis, University of California, Santa Barbara, 1972.

9. Richard D. Brown, "Modernization and the Modern Personality," *Journal of Interdisciplinary History,* II (1971); Herbert Gutman, "Work, Culture, and Society in Industrializing America, 1819–1918," *American Historical Review,* 78 (1973) 531–88; Tamara K. Hareven, "The Laborers of Manchester, New Hampshire, 1912–1922: The Role of Family and Ethnicity in Adjustment to Industrial Life," *Labor History* (May, 1975); Herbert Gans, *The Urban Villagers* (New York, 1962).

10. Louis Wirth, "Urbanism as a Way of Life," *American Journal of Sociology,* 44 (1938); Oscar Handlin, "The Modern City as a Field of Historical Study," in Oscar Handlin and John Burchard, eds., *The Historian and the City* (Cambridge, Mass., 1963); Robert E. Park, Ernest Burgess, et al., *The City* (Chicago, 1925); Adna F. Weber, *The Growth of Cities in the Nineteenth Century: A Study in Statistics* (New York, 1899) is still the best book on this subject. See also, Sam Bass Warner, Jr., *The Urban Wilderness: A History of the American City* (New York, 1973).

11. Stephan Thernstrom, "Reflections on the New Urban History," *Daedalus,* 100 (1971); Sam Bass Warner, Jr., "If All the World Were Philadelphia: A Scaffolding for Urban History, 1774–1930," *American Historical Review,* 74 (1968). For specific examples see: Stephan Thernstrom, *Poverty and Progress: Social Mobility in a Nineteenth-Century City* (Cambridge, Mass. 1964) and *The Other Bostonians: Poverty and Progress in the American Metropolis, 1880–1970* (Cambridge, Mass., 1973); Stephan Thernstrom and Richard Sennett, eds., *Nineteenth-Century Cities: Essays in the New Urban History* (New Haven, 1969); Howard Chudacoff, *Mobile Americans: Residential and Social Mobility in Omaha, 1880–1920* (New York, 1972); Sam Bass Warner, Jr., *The Private City: Philadelphia in Three Periods of its Growth* (Philadelphia, 1968); Michael Katz, *The Irony of Early School Reform* (Cambridge, Mass., 1968); Peter R. Knights, *The Plain People of Boston, 1830–1860: A Study in City Growth* (New York, 1971); Stephan

Thernstrom and Peter R. Knights, "Men in Motion: Some Data and Speculation About Urban Mobility in Nineteenth-Century America," in Tamara K. Hareven, ed., *Anonymous Americans* (New York, 1971).

12. Specifically on the question of rural-urban differences, see Tamara K. Hareven, "The Family as Process: The Historical Study of the Family Cycle," *Journal of Social History,* 7 (1974).

13. On studies of preindustrial families and communities, see Demos, *A Little Commonwealth;* Kenneth Lockridge, *A New England Town, The First Hundred Years: Dedham, Massachusetts, 1636–1736* (New York, 1970). For the nineteenth century, see Richard Sennett, *Families Against the City* (Cambridge, Mass., 1970); Elizabeth Pleck, "The Two-Parent Household: Black Family Structure in Late Nineteenth-Century Boston," *Journal of Social History,* 6 (1972); Barbara Laslett, "Household Structure on an American Frontier: Los Angeles, California, in 1850," *American Journal of Sociology,* 81 (1976). Ongoing studies on family structure in nineteenth-century cities are being carried out by: Theodore Hershberg and John Modell for Philadelphia; Michael Katz for Hamilton, Ontario; Tamara K. Hareven for Boston; Laurence Glasco for Buffalo; and Howard Chudacoff for Providence.

14. Maris Vinovskis, "American Historical Demography: A Review Essay," *Historical Methods Newsletter,* 4 (September, 1971); "Socio-Economic Determinants of Inter-State Fertility Differentials in the United States in 1850 and 1860," *Journal of Interdisciplinary History,* forthcoming; and "Mortality Rates and Trends in Massachusetts Before 1860," *Journal of Economic History,* 32 (1974); John Modell, "Family and Fertility on the Indiana Frontier, 1810," *American Quarterly,* 23 (1971). The demographic transition also preceded the industrial revolution in England. See Laslett, *The World We Have Lost,* and E. A. Wrigley, "Family Limitation in Pre-Industrial England," *Economic History Review,* 19 (1966); also Pierre Goubert, "Historical Demography and the Reinterpretation of Early Modern French History: A Research Review," *Journal of Interdisciplinary History,* 1 (1970).

15. Tamara K. Hareven and Maris A. Vinovskis, "Marital Fertility, Ethnicity and Occupation in Essex County, Mass., 1880," paper at the conference on "The Family in the Process of Urbanization," Williams College, July, 1974. An earlier attempt to compare rural-urban patterns in Michigan was limited because of the small sample size. See Susan E. Bloomberg, Mary Frank Fox, Robert M. Warner, Sam Bass Warner, Jr., "A Census Probe into Nineteenth-Century Family History: Southern Michigan, 1850–1880," *Journal of Social History,* 5 (1971).

16. Herbert Gans, *The Urban Villagers* (New York, 1962); Oscar Handlin, *Boston's Immigrants, 1790–1865* (Cambridge, Mass., 1941); David Ward, *Cities and Immigrants: A Geography of Change in Nineteenth-Century America* (New York, 1971) is magnificent in its mapping of ethnic neighborhoods, but does not pay attention to family patterns.

17. Tamara K. Hareven, "Urbanism and Ethnicity in Nineteenth-Century Boston," paper for the History of Urbanization Conference in North America, January, 1973; and Tamara K. Hareven and Maris A. Vinovskis, "Marital Fertility, Ethnicity and Occupation in Urban Families: An Analysis of South Boston and the South End in 1880," *Journal of Social History* (March, 1975).

18. For an elaboration of this approach see Hareven, "The Family as Process."

19. Sennett, *Families Against the City.* For a critique, see Hareven, "The Family as Process."

20. See, for example, Michael Anderson, *Family Structure in Nineteenth-Century*

Lancashire (Cambridge, 1971) and Howard P. Chudacoff, "Newlyweds and Family Extension: The First Stage of the Family Cycle in Providence, Rhode Island, 1864–1865 and 1879–1880," paper for the conference on "The Family in the Process of Urbanization," Williams College, July, 1974. On the role of kinship in the urban environment and the discussion of the literature, see the essay by the Griffens in this volume.

21. The imaginative approach of Sam Bass Warner, Jr., has not been followed up in other studies. See Warner, Jr., *Streetcar Suburbs: The Process of Growth in Boston, 1870–1900* (Cambridge, Mass., 1962). Warner's book does not focus on the family, but provides a model that could be used for the study of the relationships among family, housing, and patterns of suburbanization.

22. See Introduction by Raymond A. Mohl and Neil Betten, eds., *Urban America in Historical Perspective* (New York, 1970); Oscar Handlin, "The Modern City as a Field of Historical Study," in Handlin and Burchard, eds., *The Historian and the City;* Dwight W. Hoover, "The Diverging Patterns of American Urban History," *American Quarterly,* 20 (1968); Eric E. Lampard, "American Historians and the Study of Urbanization," *American Historical Review,* 67 (1961); Roy Lubove, "The Urbanization Process: An Approach to Historical Research," *Journal of the American Institute of Planners,* 33 (1967); Richard C. Wade, "An Agenda for Urban History," in Herbert J. Bass, ed., *The State of American History* (Chicago, 1970).

23. Eric E. Lampard, "Urbanization and Social Change: On Broadening the Scope and Relevance of Urban History," in Handlin and Burchard, eds., *The Historian and the City.*

2

People in Process: The New Hampshire Towns of the Eighteenth Century

DARRETT B. RUTMAN

The study of early New England society, from the beginning of settlement to the beginning of the mills, has in the last decade altered dramatically. From the vantage point largely of the study of specific locales, young scholars have been chorusing a suggestive if not always harmonious medley. The starring soloists are familiar: John Demos, Philip J. Greven, Kenneth A. Lockridge. But the chorus is larger than its soloists and significant parts are being sung by others. The major motif is familiar, too. Lockridge expressed it in 1968: "Clearly there were evolutionary patterns present within the society of early New England, patterns which reflect most significantly on the direction in which that society was heading. . . . A finite supply of land and a growing population, a population notably reluctant to emigrate, were combining to fragment and reduce landholdings, bringing marginal lands increasingly into cultivation and raising land prices. Ultimately, the collision of land

Author's Note: *Versions of this paper were delivered in April 1972. The author wishes to acknowledge the financial assistance of the Central University Research Fund of the University of New Hampshire and the almost unlimited time (both computer and counseling) afforded him by the university's computation center. Edward G. Fisher and, at a late stage, Fleurange Jacques undertook much of the programming.*

and population may have been polarizing the structure of society." More recently James A. Henretta has written of "a morphology of societal evolution" being played out in the New England towns, an "intricate interaction between land, population, technology, and culture;" "three distinct phases, corresponding roughly to the passage of generations, appear to characterize the social life of the towns." "The 'traditional' community of the first generations, with its emphasis on patriarchy, hierarchy, and stability" was "inexorably superseded by an 'expanding' society with very different social characteristics. And this, in turn, gave way to the 'static' town of the late eighteenth century."[1]

Compelling as this motif may sound, however, its weaknesses must be noted. First, it is unclear whether this evolutionary pattern, in whole or in part, was being played out only in towns laid down in the early and mid-seventeenth century and extending into the eighteenth— Lockridge's Dedham, Greven's Andover—or whether it was discernible in all New England towns, perhaps all Anglo-American communities, as a pattern initiated by the founding of a community, whenever that took place, and by extending three or four generations into the community's future. Certainly Henretta, in the passage quoted, implies the former, although he works the eighteenth-century town of Kent, Connecticut, into his analysis. Second—and a more important weakness—is the limited evidence on which the motif is constructed. In all of New England by the late eighteenth century there were some thousand-odd towns; a dozen odd have been or are being subjected to the type of analysis which initially suggested the morphology.

Commendably, all scholars involved have been quick to admit the inadequacy of building generalizations on too thin a base, their papers and prefaces abounding with calls for further town studies. But while it is true that each new study in which the course of events of a particular town is discerned as conforming to the morphology will add further credence to it, one can easily calculate the time and effort required to build a sample adequate to test the generalizations offered. What follows is an attempt to test and to refine the morphology, at least in part, in a less arduous and time-consuming way, using as a sample the towns, for the most part eighteenth century, of the single province of New Hampshire.

I

One hundred ninety-eight inhabited towns spanned New Hampshire in 1790, stretching from her narrow seaboard north and west into and beyond the White Mountains.[2] For each a variety of data have been gathered. The age of each has been established, defining age as the number of years elapsed since the first permanent settlement in the area which would become the town.[3] Early-nineteenth-century gazetteers and maps have provided a starting point for estimating time-specific areas for each town, a laborious process of addition and subtraction as boundaries were adjusted and readjusted, and as one town spawned another.[4] Modern soil and topographical materials have been used to establish a true profile of the agricultural potential of each,[5] while petitions from the towns, travelers' accounts, and gazetteers have been drawn on to estimate that potential as the eighteenth-century inhabitants might have envisioned it.[6] Key demographic indices have been compiled from occasional town inventories and from five successive censuses—the first in 1767, the last in 1790—and rates of change between censuses have been established.[7] And, finally, town histories and the papers of the province and state government have been searched for indications of economic opportunities other than agricultural, and of the cohesiveness of each town, or lack of cohesiveness.

At first glance this mass of data seems but a confused mélange. In 1790 the towns varied in age from 4 to 167 years old; in area from less than a quarter square mile—the island town of Gosport—to slightly over 127 square miles; in population from 6 to Portsmouth's 4,700 odd. Soils ranged from sand to rich alluvium to exposed bedrock; topographies ranged from plains and valley floors to rolling uplands and mountains; expressed potential, from a disgusted "very poor Baron Brooken and uneaven" to a delighted "beautiful interchange of small hills and valleys. . . . The scenery pleasant, and the soil rich." Densities ranged from less than 1 person per square mile to 372; sex ratios from 79 to 200 males per 100 females; widows, from none to over 16% of the female population; annual rates of population change over the years 1767 to 1790, from a population loss of almost 5% per year to a gain of just over 14%. Some towns seem shattered by dispute and confused associations and were towns in legal form only; indeed, one even disappeared as a town—its land and people divided almost as spoils of war by contiguous and contentious neighbors.[8] But other towns seem somnolent and undisturbed, the quintessence of M. Zuckerman's "peaceable kingdoms."

Can the mélange be made to give way to order? The morphology hypothesized—if it is to be applied to all towns regardless of founding date—depicts the towns as progressing through age-related stages much as schoolchildren progress through age-related grades; hence, just as the confusion of the playground, where all ages play together, gives way to the ordered ages of the classroom, the confusion of unordered data on the towns can be expected to give way when the towns are separated by age into what are already being conventionally referred to as "generations."[9]

Such indeed seems to be the case with regard to certain key demographic indices. Table 1 summarizes the data for density, white sex ratio, and population change as grouped in a generational schema. Generation by generation, density—the number of people per square mile—rises until, in the oldest towns in 1790, there are on the average but 37-odd acres of a town's land (good, bad, and indifferent) available for each household.[10] Generation by generation the sex ratio—the number of males per 100 females in the population—declines. And generation by generation the average annual rate of population change declines until, among the oldest towns, a percentage increase per year shifts to a percentage decrease and almost half the towns are in the losing column—steady exporters of people.[11] Specifically, the relationship between the rate of population change and age is curvilinear; at the earliest ages towns gain population at an extraordinary rate, but that feverish increase quickly subsides into a long, shallow, downward curve until it shifts imperceptibly from an annual gain to an annual loss. And approximately 55% of the variations among the towns in terms of their population change are accounted for by their differing ages.[12] Density and age are related in a more linear than curvilinear way with approximately 50% of the variations in densities accounted for by age. But correlating sex ratios and age reveals a break in the pattern of strong associations. The ratios plunge abruptly from extremes of several hundred males per 100 females in towns of 1 and 2 years old into what seems a near-random sprinkling about the value 100, with here and there an aberrant community. At most, 14% of the variations in the sex ratio are accounted for by the age of the town.

What can be demonstrated with three demographic variables can be demonstrated with others. Some show a fairly strong association with age—the percentage of males over 60, for example, and the percentage of females widowed, indicative of the interrelationship between the age of the population and the age of the town; others show surprisingly weak associations—age and percentage of the children in the population.[13]

But is age the most appropriate base on which to organize the demographic data of the towns? Demographic historians have suggested, in the context of European peasant societies, a cyclic, homeostatic adjust-

Table 1 | Density, White Sex Ratio, Population Change of New Hampshire Towns by Age Group 1767, 1790

Towns of Age	Number		Mean Density		Mean Sex Ratio		Population Change 1767–1790			
	1767	1790	1767	1790	1767	1790	No.	No. Losing	Percent Losing	Mean Annual Change (%)
3 and under	12	0	2.7	—	180.0	—	12	0	0	+9.56
4–33	37	103	11.8	14.8	113.9	106.8	36	3	8.3	+5.29
34–66	25	48	30.4	33.8	103.5	100.7	25	5	20.0	+1.63
67–99	1	11	—	37.1	—	96.8	1	0	—	—
100 and above	17	20	84.2	98.3	96.6	94.9	17	8	47.1	−.14
All towns	92	182	29.3	30.3	116.7	103.3	91	16	17.6	+3.78

SOURCE: See notes 2–7. Gosport (age 100+) is excluded from 1767 data and from the computation of the rate of population change.

ment of birth, death, and marriage rates as populations "sought"—and one realizes the anthropomorphism of the word—a rough equilibrium between the shifting levels of the economy and the size of the population to be supported. More to the point with regard to Anglo-American society, where economic conditions never brought on the crisis situations needed to trigger such adjustments, is the demographers' suggestion of a systematic link between the level of economic opportunity and migration.[14] The bare bones of that linkage in an Anglo-American context are charted in Figure 1.

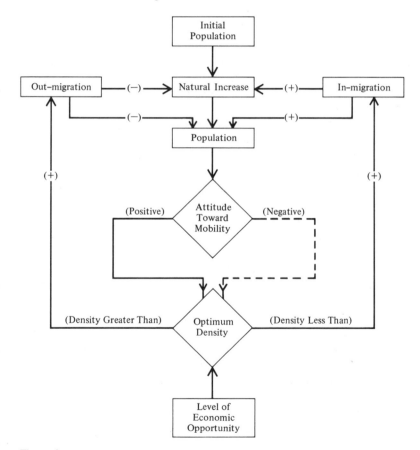

Figure 1

Obviously there can be no system in the absence of people, ergo we must initiate one by introducing a population through migration into the area of what will become a town. A simple identity basic to demography gives us a next step: that a population at a subsequent point in time is the product of the population at a previous point plus births, minus deaths (the net natural increase) plus in-migration minus out-migration (the net migration figure). Much effort has already been expended on the phenomenon of natural increase and all that has been said elsewhere of birth and death rates can be construed as implicit in the model. But what of in- and out-migration? What are the conditions governing these? The word "governing" is used with calculation for it immediately suggests the analogy of a governor—a servomechanism, if you will—with the task of controlling or governing the system.[15]

Two have been introduced into the model, diagramed as diamonds. The second is the operative device, continually reading the atmosphere of the system, specifically the population density, and testing density against an optimum established by the level of economic opportunity. When the governor senses that density is below optimum, it triggers in-migration much as a thermostat sensing a temperature below its setting triggers a heating device; when the governor senses density above the optimum, it calls for out-migration. Information is fed into our demographic thermostat through a prior governor, however, one set by communal and personal attitudes toward the very concepts of in- and out-migration. Given a low level of acceptance of the notion of mobility (in or out), either because of outright hostility to, or simple ignorance of, the possibility or benefits of movement, the operation of the primary governor is curtailed, while the higher the level of acceptance the more freely the primary can operate. But like all cultural switches, this screening switch seems faulty. No matter how low the level of acceptance of mobility may be, there is leakage through the switch and the primary operates to some extent.[16]

Neither governor is introduced here as a startling discovery. The stress of Lockridge, Greven, and others, for example, on the reluctance of the seventeenth-century son to leave the town of his birth and family even when economic conditions would seem to dictate a departure, is a recognition of the dampening effect of the cultural switch. The model, with its governors, is introduced only to shift attention from age—a measure of elapsed time from the initiation of the system and certainly important in that context—to the system itself.

II

In the New Hampshire material the initiative phase of the system is clear. Extreme sex ratios in the least dense and newest towns—towns of

Table 2 | Key Demographic Indices of New Hampshire Towns, 1767, Grouped by Density

Towns of Density	No.	Mean Age	Mean Density	Mean Percentage of all Males				Mean Percent Females			Mean White Sex Ratio	Mean % of Pop. Children
				16 & Under	17–60 Single	17–60 Married	Over 60	Single	Married	Widow		
2.0 and under	7	3.	1.3	35.5	36.2	28.0	.3	40.0	59.8	.1	246.5	46.3
2.01–5.0	14	8.2	3.6	48.4	17.5	33.1	1.0	58.6	40.5	.8	121.7	52.9
5.01–8.0	13	19.7	6.8	52.6	14.5	30.3	2.6	61.8	36.3	1.9	114.6	56.0
8.01–11.0	10	24.6	9.4	50.9	15.5	30.4	3.2	62.7	34.3	3.0	104.9	51.8
11.01–15.0	10	32.4	12.7	50.6	15.2	30.05	3.7	61.9	34.7	3.4	108.5	52.3
15.01–35.0	12	54.5	26.8	52.4	15.5	26.8	5.3	61.8	33.3	4.8	106.7	53.6
35.01–60.0	11	77.8	47.3	47.5	16.4	30.6	5.4	61.9	32.9	5.3	94.4	45.8
60.01 & above	17	102.5	91.7	48.0	18.4	27.9	5.7	61.8	31.0	7.1	97.3	46.4

SOURCE: See notes 2-7. Gosport (density=1,136) is excluded from the computation of the mean density. Mean age has been computed using only the 93 towns of 1767 for which age is established, i.e., the sample size for the second category is 13.

"the eastern frontier"—suggest the pattern by which town populations were first established in the mid- and late-eighteenth century: men journeying, frequently without women, to the site of the new town to begin the process of building and clearing. Yet new populations did not long exist in an imbalanced condition. One index after another suggests that these were largely young and middle-aged married men (possibly with a hired hand to help temporarily) and that their wives and children, if not present from the beginning, would follow within a year or so.[17]

Table 2 aggregates the towns of 1767 by density and displays group means for comparative purposes. The extreme sex ratio of the lowest density group drops radically toward the range of well-settled towns as density rises. The percentage of single males in the male population, which in the towns of least density is twice that of settled communities, halves as density rises to between 2 and 5 per square mile. The preponderance among females of those married over those single in low density towns is reversed (and normalized) as density rises; towns of densities 5 to 8 in this respect differ little from towns with densities 60 and above. That a large proportion of the married couples in the low-density towns were young marrieds either at or just beyond the beginning of their child-rearing activities is indicated by the near absence of elderly males and widows, and by the percentage of children in the total population—low as some men arrived in the town without their families, rising above the level of the more densely settled towns as the preponderantly young married couples brought children into the world, then dipping back into the range of the settled towns as the population aged, couples left the child-rearing years, and their children, spread in age, gradually entered married life and begot children of their own. Older couples were never entirely missing from the population, however, and density does not rise very high before one sees a significant percentage of the male population over 60 and of widows among women. In sum, halfway through the first "generation" and with density still well below 10 per square mile, the mean town among New Hampshire's eighteenth-century frontier towns had achieved a balanced population only slightly different—largely because of the relatively young age of its married couples—from the more settled towns. The population, in effect, had been initiated.

A surviving census, complete with enumeration, taken in the town of Orford in 1772 catches one town in the course of its rapid journey toward settled "normalcy."[18] Seven years after the first entrance of a population, the town contained 149 people (density equaling 3.4 per square mile). Fourteen of its people were indicated in the census as unattached single men, 6 of them as servants or transient laborers; 10 were characterized as married men making improvements on their land in the absence of families; the remaining 125 persons were subsumed in 26 family units, one of them "extended" in the sense that a 19-year-old son and his bride still resided in the father's household. Of the 27 couples, 11 were childless; 4 had 1 or 2 children living in the household; the remaining 12 had between 3 and 9 children, an average of just over 5. In all, children 16 years and under amounted to approximately 43% of the town's population.

From the standpoint of the model the most interesting index is the annual percentage change in the size of the populations. Table 3 summarizes the growth rates of the towns grouped by density for the period 1767–1773.[19] As is to be expected, extraordinarily high growth rates mark the initiation of populations, ranging in the 3 lowest density groups from means of 10% to 17% per year. (The percentage figure can

Table 3 | **Population Change 1767–1773, 1767–1790 among New Hampshire Towns of 1767, Grouped by Density**

Towns of Density	Mean Annual Population Change			
	1767–1773		1767–1790	
	N.	%	N.	%
2.0 and under	7	17.1	7	11.3
2.01– 5.0	13	11.2	13	7.5
5.01– 8.0	11	9.7	13	5.8
8.01– 11.0	9	7.5	9	4.6
11.01– 15.0	10	6.1	10	3.9
15.01– 35.0	11	2.7	12	1.4
35.01– 60.0	11	.8	11	−.05
60.01 & above	16	−.2	16	−.5

SOURCE: See notes 2-7. Gosport excluded.

be translated into people in Orford: with 75 persons and a density of less than 1 per square mile in 1767, Orford more than tripled in population over the succeeding 6 years, averaging an annual growth rate of just over 18%; at least 122 of the increase were newcomers to the town, the remainder a high estimate of the net natural increase.)[20] The population initiated, the feverish growth rates slackened. But these were still high opportunity towns in the sense of low densities and available agricultural land. The system's governors called for continuing growth through in-migration, but at steadily decreasing rates as in-migration combined with natural increase to raise densities and consequently limit opportunity.

The group means reflect the process as growth rates drop from 7.5% per year (for towns of densities of 8 and 10 per square mile) to 6, 3, and 1. And the figures gain significance when we realize that rates of 1% and 2% per year actually indicate that net in-migration has become a negligible factor in increasing the population: that what growth there is is being maintained by natural increase, and that, indeed, out-migration has quite possibly begun. A specific town makes the point: Wilton in the south central highlands, a town of just over 1,000 in 1786, grew at a rate of 2.1% per year in the period 1786–1790, but gained approximately 89 persons by natural increase, leaving only 7 to be accounted for as the difference of in- minus out-migration.[21]

One might anticipate that our mean population change should, in terms of the model, ultimately decline to zero and remain there, indicative of an optimum relationship between density and opportunity being maintained by a steady overflow of the excess population, departures from zero being indicative of a change in the level of economic opportunity either downward (forcing a greater part of the population out) or upward (drawing in population). But such anticipation assumes a precision perhaps uncharacteristic of social mechanisms in general and certainly uncharacteristic of our ability to perceive them. And it ignores a fundamental characteristic of both the mobile population and of the model, one which seems to make overcorrection—a population loss in excess of that demanded by the system—inevitable.

We have seen who, in the main, is attracted *into* a high opportunity agricultural town: preponderantly the young man with wife and children. Such is consequently the type attracted *from* an existent agricultural town. The economy being male- and adult-dominated, the system being governed by the relationship of density and economic opportunity, only the adult male is truly excess, and yet when he leaves he takes more than himself away. Indeed, the outflow of relatively few young, adult males can remove a significant proportion of a town's youth, leaving what remains relatively older and, as a group, incapable of sustaining the prevailing level of natural increase.

New Hampshire's Epping, a prosperous southeastern agricultural town, exemplifies the point. In 1767 the town contained just over 1,440 people in 20.5 square miles, density equaling roughly 69 per square mile. By 1773 density had risen to over 80, but in the succeeding years the population steadily declined, dipping to 1,255 by 1790 (density equaling 61). Between 1773 and 1790 an estimated 600 persons must have left in order to account for the net loss and the continuing natural increase of those being left behind. In terms of the system, the balance of density and opportunity seems to have been restored by the departure of roughly 100 adult males; the relationship of adult males to land in 1767 (40.4 acres per male) deteriorated in 1773 (34.8) and nearly recovered by 1790 (38.8 acres).[22] But a good portion of the young families of the town had gone, and where, in 1767, over 53% of the population had been children, in 1790 the children amounted to just under 41%. By the early nineteenth century, possibly reflecting a continued outflow, certainly reflecting the fact of fewer children maturing and procreating, the population dipped still further, to 1,100 odd.[23]

Mean rates of change in the 1767-1773 period—.8 and a minus .2 in our highest density groups in Table 3—seemingly reflect both attributes of the model: its tendency toward overcorrection and its imprecision. We can suggest that these towns are, as a group, roughly balanced at the crucial junction of density and economic opportunity. But the latter attributive—imprecision—makes negligible the chances of spotting minor yet meaningful changes in the rates, that is, those changes resulting from minor changes in the level of economic activity. We cannot make, for example, any comment on the advent of occupational specialization in essentially agricultural towns. That process, by which additional opportunities were incorporated into agricultural economies, thereby increasing the number of people capable of being supported and decreasing pressure for out-migration, was far too gradual to be silhouetted by the crude instrument we are using.[24]

Raw density figures, however, do reflect major differentiations in the level of economic activity. Very broadly, 60 acres of land can be considered the optimum farm for a single-family household in eighteenth-century New Hampshire. Below that figure the householder approaches and ultimately falls below subsistence; above, the land, if it is to be worked, requires more than the single family.[25] The optimum density in a purely agricultural town, consequently, lies around 60 per square mile.[26] Given the broadness of this estimate, however, a 20% margin seems in order, ergo the parameter falls between 48 and 72 persons per square mile. Among the New Hampshire towns of 1767, 9 had densities above this range; the census of 1773 adds 3 additional towns to the list. But 4 of the 12 drop back below the limit of 72 by 1790. Like Epping, noted above, they seem to have pressed beyond a limit, triggered out-migration as a corrective, and reflected the corrective by dipping below the critical value. Of the rest: 1 (Portsmouth) was the leading entrepôt of the province, another (Newcastle) an ancillary to Portsmouth; 2 (Exeter and Dover) were long-established secondary centers with substantial mercantile and artisan activities; 2 (Gosport and Rye) were fishing towns; 1 (Seabrook) combined fishing and the construction of small boats purchased and used by seamen all along the cost from mid-Maine to Boston. Only 1, Kensington, seems devoid of economic activity other than agriculture. The consistently high mean density of this subgroup (140 in 1767, 148 in 1790) reflects the high level of economic activity and consequent ability of these towns to maintain relatively large populations, while the removal of the 7 from the group of highest density towns in Table 3 reduces the mean of that group to 69.6, a value better reflective of the towns' essentially agricultural economies.

III

Categorizing the towns by density rather than age is clearly in order; age is a measure of elapsed time in a process governed in the main by density.[27] Indeed, categorization by age hazards confusion. Henretta's use of Kent, Connecticut, in a generational morphology is a case in point: Kent, below the midpoint of its second generation (40-odd years), is at a stage which Henretta associates with the third and fourth generations. Among the New Hampshire towns, a geographic cluster in the southeastern hinterland is placed, in a categorization by age, with a cluster along the middle-Merrimack, but the towns of the former were obviously at and beyond optimum densities and displayed rates of population change between 1767 and 1790 indicative of significant out-migration, while those of the latter seem well under optimum densities and still receive newcomers at a substantial rate.[28] One can speculate on the reasons for towns to pass through the demographic process at different speeds: the southeastern towns were easily, ergo more quickly, settled from old, contiguous towns, while the middle-Merrimack was more isolated and necessitated a longer trek for would-be settlers; the southeast was relatively protected during the Indian wars, which were not ended until the late 1750s, while the middle-Merrimack was an exposed salient; the southeastern towns were outside of a proprietary system which, it has been argued, tended to slow settlement elsewhere. Also, one can cogitate on the possibility that speed through the process varied distinctively between the seventeenth and eighteenth centuries, with the earliest agricultural towns (Andover, for example) consistently requiring a full three generations to move from the initiation of a population to excessive density and out-migration.

But the question here is: which variable gives the soundest base for generalizing on a broad process applicable to all the towns all the time? The extent to which anomalies disturb generalizations framed in terms of age is indicated by the strength of the explanatory power of age cited earlier. Consideration of the towns in terms of density is not without anomalies, certainly, but in the main density explains more of the demographic variation among the towns. With regard, for example, to settled agricultural towns—that is, removing from the sample towns in the process of initiating populations and towns known to have economic opportunities other than agricultural—density in 1767 can be said to explain 73% of the variations among the 1767–1790 rates of population change.[29]

The strong relationship between density and population change, as well as the clear contrast between what we can term low and high economic opportunity towns, is strong support for our bare bones model. And yet it cannot be stressed too much that it is bare bones, that there are secondary processes within it, and that these need and deserve extensive investigation. Density, for example, is not significantly related to the sex ratio, and yet the sex ratio appears to some extent a governor affecting the flow of single males and, surprisingly, females, among the settled towns.[30] Marriage potential, as well as economic opportunity, seems to have been an important determinant.

When the model does explain, however, it explains despite variations in soil (both real, in terms of modern soil data, and in the minds of eighteenth-century men) and in topography. No categorizations of the towns according to these variables, to date, have produced significant and distinctive groupings of the demographic data. The demographic process men and women were caught up in seems more determinative than the soil on which they lived.

What of other aspects of the morphology postulated? Lockridge has suggested overpopulation and the appearance of a rural proletariat. There is no support for this schema in the New Hampshire materials. The cultural governor seems wide open (a radical change from the seventeenth, perhaps even early eighteenth century) allowing the economic opportunity governor to operate freely. Towns surpassing an allowable density, moving toward the red zone which Lockridge describes so well, readily export their young and fall again into the safe green. With one exception (Kensington), New Hampshire towns remaining above the critical point are demonstrably towns with economic opportunities other than agricultural. One underscores that this is an expectable result in the Lockridgean scheme. In his initial essay, while contemplating the interrelationship of overpopulation and the Revolution, he nevertheless resuscitated Frederick Jackson Turner's "safety valve," albeit in a purely agricultural setting, suggesting its operation after 1790.[31] It was, however, operative in New Hampshire well before that date, indeed, through the last half of the century at least. At the same time, however, the New Hampshire materials underscore the most severe criticism of Lockridge: that he tended to ignore economic opportunities other than agricultural. When density rises and remains above the safety line, it is absolutely obligatory to look for a shift upward in the level of economic activity. Only where density exceeds that level can we speak of overpopulation.[32]

What of the changing social climate which, proceeding from Lockridge and Zuckerman, Henretta has built into the morphology and linked to a demographic process? The two can be conjoined only in a limited sense. We can conceive of the demographic process in the earliest seventeenth-century towns, when the cultural governor was set low and mobility restrained, ultimately contributing pressure which tended to change attitudes, to open the switch, and to allow density to affect migration. We can conceive of mobility, once a significant reality, affecting attitudes and opening the switch still farther. And we can conceive of changing attitudes toward community and an enlarged role for the family—both phenomena imbedded in Henretta's morphology—as concomitant with changing attitudes toward mobility. The linkage of the demographic process and changing attitudes can be phrased generationally in the sense that the early-seventeenth-century towns lived 2 or 3 generations with one set of attitudes which subsequently (in the third or fourth generation) shifted. But this is not a course to be rerun in each town—a point on which there must be no confusion. First-generation towns of the eighteenth century did not revert to the attitudes of the first-generation towns of the seventeenth century and did not reexperience an attitudinal change in response to an inexorable demographic process. The new towns were founded in the milieu of the new attitudes; "the history of . . . [eighteenth-century] settlements"—Henretta's words stressed here—"would not be completely congruent with that of . . . [seventeenth-century settlements] despite the existence of certain demographic similarities."[33] Orford exemplifies the new attitude toward mobility, for the town is not marked by a population gathering in the first years and settling in as a unit for a multigenerational stay; on the contrary, 63% of Orford's families, as listed in 1772, would be gone from the town of 1790.[34] Mobility was a continuing factor, as it was not in the settlement of the seventeenth-century towns. Orford suggests, too, the enlarged role of the family, for these were entire families disappearing from the early town and moving on—Ebenezer Baldwin, his wife and four children, Noah Dewey and wife, Shubel Cross, his wife and two children—and in the absence of strong community ties, as Henretta wrote, the family might well be taking on "more of the tasks of socialization and acculturalization . . . smoothing the passage from one generation and one community to the next."[35]

Clearly the attitudinal shift, however firmly linked to the demographic process, was time specific; only the demographic process itself was timeless. What of a shift in political attitudes, the "direct causal link between the growth of population and certain types of political change" which Henretta asserts?[36] Again, the linkage can be conceived of as time specific; the inexorable demographic process through which the earliest seventeenth-century towns passed might have something to do with the breakdown of a pattern of "patriarchy, hierarchy, and stability" *in those towns*. But it does not follow that there was a constant linkage. If shifting social attitudes were not timelessly linked to the demographic process—if first-generation eighteenth-century towns did not revert to the social attitudes of the seventeenth century's first-generation towns and reexperience a demographically inspired shift —is it logical to assume a timeless link between shifting political attitudes and the demographic process? But beyond logic, if the various "types of political change" are construed as reflected in (or reflective of) political disputes within the New Hampshire towns, there is little demonstrable relationship in the eighteenth century between the demographic process and the political climate. Disputes were related to topography as sections of towns separated by mountains, rivers, marsh, or simple distance argued and more often than not divided; to religion as churches of different persuasions sought support from limited resources; to the proprietary system as all parts of a town fought the tax-free status of unimproved proprietary lands. And disputes broke out as freely at any age and at any stage of the demographic process as at any other.[37]

IV

Succinctly put, what does this excursion into the granite hills of New Hampshire suggest?

Contextually, it would seem to demonstrate that there was indeed a demographic process at work in the towns of early New England, but one best generalized on in terms of population density and the level of economic opportunity rather than age qua "generations." Overpopulation and the appearance of an agricultural proletariat as general phenomena, however, are suspect, for the Turnerian safety valve opened soon enough in eighteenth-century New Hampshire to avoid that Lockridgean culmination of the process and to substitute another —mobility.

Methodologically, it underscores a cardinal distinction (for those historians with a bent toward a social science approach) between a timeless hypothesis of social behavior and a time-specific hypothesis. In the highly generalized "morphology of societal evolution" with which we opened, the two seem confused, while in the eighteenth-century excursion they have stood forth as separate—the process keyed to density and opportunity as timeless in that there seems little difference, except in terms of time in process, between the demographic course run in these towns and that described as running in seventeenth-century Massachusetts towns. The particular impact of the process on social and political attitudes was time specific in that attitudinal changes were cumulative, and the demographic process impacted on successive rather than repetitive sets of attitudes.

Finally, in terms of potential, the excursion seems to offer fruitful avenues for reflection. Our culmination—mobility—links to a broad spectrum of current scholarship. A relatively easy accommodation to sustained population growth, for example, links far easier than does Lockridge's portentious overcrowding and rural proletariat to James H. Hutson's recent suggestion of an interrelationship between a consciousness of demographic growth and Revolutionary optimism.[38] The link to studies of the family is clear in the proposition that changed attitudes toward mobility (ergo the acceptance both in new towns and in the older towns which spawned them of at least a partial disruption of family ties) were prerequisites to actual mobility, while a changed role for the family was a consequent. And the mobility of villagers links to the extensive work underway on American cities and on urban mobility. Two questions asked recently by Stephan Thernstrom and Peter Knights seem almost as applicable to the New Hampshire towns of the latter half of the eighteenth century as they are to the nineteenth-century city: "If American city-dwellers were as restless and footloose as our evidence suggests, how was any cultural continuity—or even the appearance of it—maintained? . . . American society in the period considered here was more like a procession than a stable social order. How did this social order cohere at all?"[39] Perhaps the changing role of the family suggested by the morphology for mobile villagers is a part of the answer with regard to both mobile villagers and mobile urbanites.

NOTES

1. Kenneth A. Lockridge, "Land, Population and the Evolution of New England Society, 1630–1790," Past and Present, XXXIX (1968), 74; James A. Henretta, "The Morphology of New England Society in the Colonial Period," Journal of Interdisciplinary History, II (1971), 380, 388, 391.

2. The word town is not used in a legal sense, but is to be construed as an inhabited location generally identified as a particular place at the time; legally, it might be a town, parish, precinct, or unincorporated but inhabited grant. This is the unit definition of the 1790 census. U.S., Department of Commerce and Labor, Bureau of the Census, *Heads of Families at the First Census of the United States Taken in the Year 1790: New Hampshire* (Washington, 1907) lists 205 localities in the state. Adjusting for double counting, unsettled towns, and the like reduces the number to 198. Note that not all localities have all values for all dates, ergo the size of the groups dealt with below will vary. Gosport—on an island 7 miles off the coast and marked by extreme values in 1767 because of the peculiarities of its situation—has been generally omitted from consideration.

3. Settlement dates have been established through particular town histories and from the documents and headnotes of Nathaniel Bouton, et al., eds., *Documents and Records Relating to the Province [Towns and State] of New Hampshire (1623–1800).* 40 vols. (Concord, N.H., 1867–1943)—hereinafter cited as *Provincial and State Papers* —particularly volumes IX, XI-XIII *(Town Papers),* XXIV–XXVI *(Town Charters),* and XXVII–XIX *(Masonian Papers).*

4. The process has been to establish a base area from Eliphalet and Phinchas Merrill, comps., *Gazetteer of the State of New Hampshire* (Exeter, N.H., 1817); John Farmer and Jacob B. Moore, comps., *A Gazetteer of the State of New Hampshire* (Concord, 1823);

the Philip Carrigain map of New Hampshire of 1816; and MS Town Plans, 1803–1808, in the Office of the Secretary of State, Concord; supplementing these with Alonzo J. Fogg, comp., *The Statistics and Gazetteer of New Hampshire* (Concord, 1874); *Town and City Atlas of the State of New Hampshire* (Boston, 1892); then work backward to establish age-specific areas on the basis of adjustments indicated in *Provincial and State Papers* and select early maps.

5. Categorization of modern soil data was done by John T. Engle of the University of New Hampshire, largely on the basis of U.S. Department of Agriculture county soil surveys (both published and unpublished) and USDA reports.

6. The best and most extensive of the travel accounts surveyed was Timothy Dwight, *Travels in New England and New York,* ed. by Barbara Miller Solomon and Patricia M. King. 4 vols. (Cambridge, Mass., 1969). Petitions were surveyed in *Provincial and State Papers,* key phrases were extracted from the Merrills' and Farmer and Moore's gazetteers cited in note 4.

7. The most valuable of the colonial censuses—for their completeness and because they can be combined with figures for rateable estates and polls—are those of 1767 and 1773. See "[Rateable Estates and Polls (1767), Census (1767)]," *Provincial and State Papers,* VIII, 166–170; "Census of 1773" and "[List of the Rateable Estates of the Several Towns]," ibid., X, 621–636,VII, 326–329. For the "Census of New Hampshire, 1775" see ibid., VII, 724–781; for the "Census of 1786," ibid., X, 637–689. All of these are aggregations by towns and counties; only the 1790 census (see note 2) contains an enumeration by name. Occasional town inventories are to be found in *Provincial and State Papers,* particularly in those volumes specifically cited in note 3, and in a manuscript volume of "Town Inventories" in the New Hampshire State Archives, Concord.

8. Monson, divided between Amherst and Hollis in 1770.

9. The basic generational scheme of Greven's *Four Generations: Population, Land, and Family in Colonial Andover, Massachusetts* (Ithaca, 1970) appropriately resulted in "generational" conclusions; others have adopted the generational terminology (e.g., Henretta, "Morphology of New England Society," and Lockridge in his "Afterthought" in Stanley N. Katz, ed., *Colonial America: Essays in Politics and Social Development* [Boston, 1971]) with only vague justification and at times even vaguer definition. In order to conform to the hypothesized morphology here and in Table 1, I have adopted a generational grouping, defining generation as 33 years—the sum of three such generations being the conventional three-life lease in England. To obtain a better fit of data to the grouping, however, I have had to separate from the first generation the first three years of settlement.

10. In contrast, towns aged 3 through 33 years offer a figure of just over 240 acres available per household. One stresses the crudeness of these figures, arrived at by dividing the average number of persons per household in 1790 in the towns as grouped (5.78 in the older towns, 5.62 in towns aged 3-33) into the average density of the group in 1790, and the results into 640, the number of acres per square mile.

11. The annual rate of population change has been computed as LOG $(P/100 + 1)/N$ where P equals the percentage change of population between two censuses and N equals the number of elapsed years.

12. Using eta as the most appropriate measure of a curvilinear relationship and eta squared to approximate the proportion of variance in the dependent variable accounted for by the independent variable.

13. The censuses do not give a figure for children per se; they do give, however, a figure for "boys"—ambiguously stated as males "under 16 years of age" and "16 years and under.'' The number of children has been arbitrarily constructed by doubling the number of boys; it is, consequently, a gross estimate and, when converted to a percentage of total population, can be quite erroneous in the youngest towns where adult men and boys tended to ''open'' the area in the absence of females (see below).

14. See E. A. Wrigley, *Population and History* (New York, 1969), 112–113; George W. Barclay, *Techniques of Population Analysis* (New York, 1958), 204–206.

15. See Walter Buckley, *Sociology and Modern Systems Theory* (Englewood Cliffs, N.J., 1967), particularly 36 ff., 52 ff.

16. For example, even while arguing for Dedham as a closed system in the mid-seventeenth century, Lockridge must acknowledge a trickle of movement in and out. See his ''The Population of Dedham, Massachusetts, 1636-1736,'' Economic History Review, Ser. 2, XIX (1966), 322.

17. The same conclusion, on the basis of literary evidence, is offered by Charles E. Clark, *The Eastern Frontier: The Settlement of Northern New England, 1610–1763* (New York, 1970), 221. The ''eastern frontier'' is, in this regard, similar to the later frontier investigated by Jack E. Eblan, ''An Analysis of Nineteenth-Century Frontier Populations,'' Demography, II (1965), 399–413.

18. In *Provinicial and State Papers*, IX, 645 ff. there are three lists: the first and third are censuses; the second is a memorandum of improvements. The second and third are dated 1772; the first is undated; comparison of the two censuses suggests that the undated first is some six to eight months earlier than the dated second. See also Alice Doan Hodgson, *Thanks to the Past: The Story of Orford, New Hampshire* (Orford, [1965]).

19. Figures for the annual percentage change of population 1767–1790 are included in the table for comparison purposes. Note, however, that the figures for the longer period will axiomatically show less increase inasmuch as the years of lowest density (and in the main highest annual rates of growth) for any given group are subsumed in the longer span of years.

20. The natural increase has been separated from the migration-related increase by a simulation operating on the basis of a transposition of the basic demographic identity $P_2 = P_1 + B - D + M$ (where P_2 equals the population in the year or period in question; P_1, the population in the preceding year or period; B. D, and M, the number of births, deaths, and net migration figure respectively), i.e., $M = P_2 - (P_1 + B - D)$, with values for succeeding populations, births, and deaths estimated by the use of given birth and death rates and the rate of population change. Birth and death rates have been adopted from Robert Higgs and H. Louis Stettler, ''Colonial New England Demography: A Sampling Approach,'' William and Mary Quarterly, Ser. 3, XXVII (1970), 283–294, and Lockridge, ''Population of Dedham.'' The procedure is crude and unrealistic, but the intent is to produce a *minimal* figure as an estimate of net migration.

21. Birth and death rates for Wilton were computed from Jeremy Belknap, *The History of New-Hampshire* (reprinted ed.; New York, 1970), II, 187.

22. Computed by dividing males 16 years and over (325 in 1767, 377 in 1773, 338 in 1790) into the area of the town. In terms of acres per household: 52.3 in 1767, 44.8 in 1773, 58.8 in 1790.

23. By 1820 the population had fallen to 1,158, 58 per square mile. Farmer and Moore, comps., *Gazetteer*, 120. No mills came to Epping to provide economic opportunities which might have reversed the trend.

24. The process has been argued as an alternative to Lockridge's overcrowding thesis; see his ''Afterthought,'' Katz, ed., *Colonial America*, 486 ff.

25. There are many estimates of the optimal size of the eighteenth-century ''family farm." See Charles S. Grant, *Democracy in the Connecticut Frontier Town of Kent* (New York, 1961), 36–38 where he arrives at between 40 and 89 acres. The figure offered in the text is a best, but still crude, estimate based on such factors as the agricultural techniques of the time (I suspect they had not changed radically from those described in Darrett B. Rutman, *Husbandmen of Plymouth: Farms and Villages in the Old Colony, 1620–1692* [Boston, 1967]) and the requisite size of the woodlot (itself an estimate, combining the needs of the household and the regrowth rate of woodlands—on the first see the high estimate in Ralph E. Brown, *Historical Geography of the United States* (New York, 1948), 108; on the second Dwight, *Travels,* I, 75). Given the uncertainty of the figure, however, the wide error margins in the text are an absolute necessity.

26. Using 5.7 persons per household. The figure for optimum density obviously would not apply to towns with extensive "waste" areas. But in the period in question all of the towns of high density were located in the southeastern part of New Hampshire where wastage was minimal.

27. Lockridge himself shifted to a density model in his "Social Change and the Meaning of the American Revolution," Journal of Social History, VII (1973), 406–407.

28. In the southeastern cluster (Brentwood, Kingston, East Kingston, South Hampton, Newton, Plaistow) a mean age in 1767 of 45 was matched with a mean annual population change in 1767–1790 of − .4 and a density in 1767 of 58; the middle-Merrimack cluster (Bow, Concord, Canterbury, Pembrook) had a mean age of 39, mean annual population change of +3.5, and a mean density of 13.3.

29. r (Pearsonian) = .856. For the same subset, age, and rates of population change compute an r of − .659. Within this particular subset the relationships proved linear rather than curvilinear.

30. A stepwise regression with population change (1767–1790) as the dependent variable and the 1767 census variables as the set from which to select independent variables selected density 1767 as the primary in step 1 and white sex ratios in step 2. A simulation varying the values of the percent single males among total males and the white sex ratio to establish the direction of the single female population (increasing or decreasing) in particular towns gave correct prediction in 75% of the cases; the errors, moreover, were almost entirely in towns with opportunities additional to agriculture, indicating that the simulation did not take into account a relevant factor and that with that factor entered success of prediction would be in the 90% range.

31. Lockridge, "Land, Population and the Evolution of New England Society," 481–482.

32. Lockridge's Dedham, for example, from which he drew so much of his thesis, is ranked in the highest "commercial-cosmopolitan" group in the most sophisticated classification of eighteenth-century towns to date, that of Van Beck Hall in *Politics Without Parties: Massachusetts, 1780–1791* (Pittsburgh, 1972), chap. I. Hall's classification, being constructed for a period later than Lockridge's, cannot be applied to the earlier period of course, but it is suggestive.

33. Henretta, "Morphology of New England Society," 393.

34. Figures generated by a name analysis of the Orford censuses cited in note 18 and the entry for Orford in *Heads of Families at the First Census.*

35. Henretta, "Morphology of New England Society," 397.

36. Ibid., 391.

37. While there is some slight indication in the figures for population growth and disputes of a link between the rate of change and disputes (defined as intra-town disputes 1765–1778 reaching the New Hampshire province or state government via petitions from

one or more parties to the dispute) the trend is simply not significant enough to support a hypothesized relationship between disputes and a particular position in a growth model.

38. Hutson in Jesse Lemisch et al., "The White Oaks, Jack Tar, and the Concept of the 'Inarticulate'," William and Mary Quarterly, Ser. 3, XXIX (1972), 140 ff.

39. Thernstrom and Knights, "Men in Motion: Some Data and Speculations about Urban Population Mobility in Nineteenth-Century America," in Tamara K. Hareven, ed., *Anonymous Americans: Explorations in Nineteenth-Century Social History* (Englewood Cliffs, N.J., 1971), 40.

3

Family Structure and Economic Organization: Massachusetts Merchants, 1700–1850

PETER DOBKIN HALL

The study of the colonial family promises to yield significant insights into the origins and nature of modern social and economic organization in the United States. Early American society, like that of preindustrial Europe, was one in which there was little separation between household and productive enterprise. Thus, as Peter Laslett states in *The World We Have Lost*, "economic organization was domestic organization."[1] That is, the economy of a preindustrial nation consists of the sum of productive and consumptive activities taking place in its households. And if one seeks to understand modernization—the transformation of traditional, household-centered societies into innovative, corporate ones— one must look to the family both as a source and a sensitive indicator of change.[2]

American historians have in recent years moved steadily toward a

Author's Note: *Earlier versions of this paper were presented to the annual meeting of the American Sociological Association, Panel on Family Structure, Montreal, Canada, August, 1974, to the Conference on Marxian Approaches to History sponsored by the New School for Social Research Chapter of the Union for Radical Political Economy, New York, April, 1975, and the Faculty Seminar of the Department of History, Wesleyan University, April, 1975.*

recognition of the central role of the family in the society and economy of early New England. In the mid-fifties, Bernard Bailyn's *New England Merchants of the Seventeenth Century* showed the importance of the family in determining patterns of commercial and political alliances, in creating access to capital, and as an armature for the development of merchant group solidarity.[3] In the late sixties, Edmund S. Morgan and Philip Greven, writing from very different viewpoints, showed the family to be the central institution in early New England society—the mediator of socialization, welfare, religion, politics, and production.[4] Finally, Bernard Farber, writing in 1972, attempted a thorough analysis of the relation between family patterns and the distribution of wealth and power in a colonial community.[5] These recognitions of the family as the central institution in the economy, polity, and culture of early America open a promising line of enquiry for social and economic historians. For the wealth of data on large populations—in vital records, genealogies, censuses, city directories, and manuscript materials—plus the tremendous improvement in techniques for handling such information make possible a broad quantitative and qualitative examination of the dynamics of a great modern revolution.

This essay will attempt, through a case study of Boston merchant families who stand at the forefront of the capitalist revolution, to indicate some of the specific alterations in the structure of the family and its social and economic functions which enabled them to move from traditional family firms toward modern incorporated enterprises.[6] This urban commercial group will be contrasted with the rural population described by Philip Greven in his study of Andover in an attempt to sketch out the structural basis for differential responses to the new economic world of the last eighteenth century and the ultimate dominance of urban-based corporate enterprises in the commerce and culture of Massachusetts.

It is hardly an exaggeration to say that until the late eighteenth century the major social and economic organization in Massachusetts was the family. It was the organization that carried out virtually all major governance, socialization, social welfare, and economic activities. While there was a formal state, consisting of the colonial legislature and the town meetings, its duties were almost exclusively concerned with making policy. Lacking a state bureaucracy, standing army, or police force, implementation of state policy depended on the family. The church was also dependent on the family for daily supervision of morality and behavior, for it was nonhierarchical and lacked any direct means of enforcing its mandates. Both the state and the church looked to "family government" as the basis of social action. There were no individuals in early New England society, for all persons were required to be members of households and under the authority of its head.[7]

The family was also the center of economic activity, for there were no banks, insurance companies, corporations, or other formal economic organizations. Thus, whatever capital a merchant might require for his enterpreneurial activities was personal capital, contributed from his own estate, by his family, or from other individuals. This created a host of problems. First, it meant that business losses resulting from poor judgment or accidents had to be paid out of the merchant's personal estate—and if the loss was serious enough, it could mean his complete impoverishment. Secondly, it meant that he was duty-bound to pay his creditors, for they were his kinsmen and neighbors. Finally, it meant that he was necessarily restricted to a narrow capital base and to a fairly small scale of operations.

A merchant could broaden his capital base through partnership. But this created hazards as well. Such a relationship made each partner wholly responsible for the acts of the other and, as a result, necessarily required a degree of "mutual respect, confidence, and belief" which could seldom be found outside the family.[8] Because of the intimacy of the relationship of partners, the personal nature of capital, and the fact that the survival of the individual merchant and his family was at stake in all business transactions, it is hardly surprising that primary commercial ties were concentrated within a small circle of kin. As Table 1 shows, partners tended to be members of the merchant's own family —sons, brothers, uncles, cousins, or persons whose relation to the merchant was cemented through marriage.

The use of family members in business firms was more than a convenience: it was both a necessity and an obligation. It was a necessity, not only because kin were assumed to be the most trustworthy employees, but also because of the chronic labor shortage in the colonies. It was an obligation because "family government," the sole means of positive social action, included within it responsibilities toward destitute or unfortunate persons in the larger community and for basic vocational and professional training. Ideally under this system all would be cared for or trained if each family looked after its own kin. In fact, those who were able to do so did carry out these responsibilities. And those who were without families or who desired training which their own circle of kin could not offer were boarded out in established families. A family's first obligation was to care for its own members, training them and

Table 1 | **Partnerships among sons in the Cabot, Higginson, Jackson, Lee, and Lowell families by birth cohort of fathers and type of kin partnership, 1680–1779.**

| | *Types of Partnership among Sons* | | | | |
Birth Cohorts of Fathers	*With Father*	*With Brothers*	*With In-Laws*	*With Uncles or Cousins*	*Alone or with Non-Kin*
1680–1699	2	2	—	—	2
1700–1719	3	7	4	5	—
1720–1739	2	—	2	2	2
1740–1759	7	8	10	16	7
1760–1779	14	17	20	27	19
Totals by Type	28	34	36	50	30
N=178					

employing them in the family enterprise in positions commensurate with their abilities. It could also take in non-kin apprentices and cases assigned to it by the town authorities. In either case, the family acted as the primary means for the delivery of social services, not only for its own members, but also for the whole society.[9]

The method of wealth transmission in Massachusetts was consonant with the ideals of family government. The founders of the colony had rejected primogeniture in favor of a system of partible inheritance in which the paternal estate was divided between the widow and all children regardless of sex or birth-order position.[10] While this system did not explicitly preclude an individual making out a will which passed over one or all of his children, the courts were empowered to make adjustments in estate division if it was felt that the family or any of its members had been left an insufficient competence.[11]

Although in accord with the ideology of the Massachusetts Puritans and their English heritage of manorial communalism, the system of partible inheritance was incompatible with mercantile goals.[12] Its effect was to make capital accumulation—a commercial necessity—extremely difficult. Since business capital was identical with personal capital, partible inheritance prevented the settling of entire estates on those children who were in business with their fathers. Instead, it was divided among all children. This rendered it impossible for merchant firms to become cumulatively more wealthy and powerful over the years and across generations. For, on the death of a partner, his share of the firm's capital would have to be withdrawn and partibly divided among his survivors.[13] Even if some or all of his sons had succeeded him in business, their shares would be less than their father's undivided capital—since the widow and daughters, who were not in business, would have subtracted their shares from the total.

There were a number of ways of counteracting the capital-vitiating effect of partible inheritance. The first involved *inter-vivos* transfers of capital from fathers to sons who were their business partners. The second involved a system of preferential marital selection. The former had major limitations. It was inherently unfair to the testator's other children, reducing their shares in the ultimate divisions of the paternal estate. Further, the merchant father could not transfer too much of his property without threatening his own authority as head of the family and senior partner in the family firm. Given the importance placed on the family and on paternal authority, this method of wealth transmission was only a partial solution to the problem of accumulating commercial capital.[14] The system of marital selection offered a solution which was not only more capital efficient, but which was more consonant with the dominant ideologies of patriarchal authority and family welfare. Further, it made it possible for the merchant family to actively alter its own structure in order to achieve economic ends which lay outside —and were in a significant sense contrary to—the social and ethical mandates of the Puritan Commonwealth.[15]

There were two basic forms of marital selection that favored capital concentration. The first involved first-cousin marriage; the second, sibling exchange. In their ideal forms they worked the following way. For the first-cousin mode, visualize three generations of a family: a set of parents who have four children, with each of those children having two children of his or her own. Thus, the estate of the parents would be divided four ways in the generation of their children and eight ways in the generation of their grandchildren. First-cousin marriage would necessarily reduce the number of divisions. If one took place (i.e., if two grandchildren married), the number of estate divisions would be reduced from eight to seven—for the shares of the marrying cousins would be combined into one share representing 25% of the grandparental estate. If two first-cousin marriages occurred, the number of divisions would be reduced from 8 to 6, thus recombining 50% of the grandparental estate.

The sibling-exchange model was more efficient as a means of capital consolidation. It worked this way. Visualize two families consisting of two sets of parents, each set with four children. By the generation of the children, the number of possible divisions of the two sets of parents' estates would be eight. If one sibling exchange took place—the marriage of two children in one family to two children in the other—the number of possible estate divisions would be reduced from eight to six. If two sibling exchanges took place—three children in one family marrying three children from the other—the number of estate divisions would be reduced from eight to five. This pattern of kin-marriage was clearly more capital efficient than first-cousin marriage. Not only did it bring about capital concentration in a far shorter time—within one generation of the testator rather than two—it also combined the fortunes of two families rather than merely reconcentrating the estates of a single set of grandparents. It also had more immediate advantages from a commercial standpoint. Sibling exchanges could be used to cement partnership alliances with non-kin merchants. Persons from outside the circle of kin could be taken into partnership without violating any of the mandates of kin-support while, at the same time, adding considerably to the capital of an enterprise.

In practice the two patterns of kin-marriage were followed in an overlapping fashion. They were in no sense contradictory—for both forms furthered capital accumulation, not only in a short-term commercial sense, but also in a longer-term testamentary one. That the motivation underlying the adoption of these patterns of marital selection was primarily economic is indicated by the fact that the higher up the socioeconomic scale one goes, the more exogamous the favored forms of kin-marriage. This fact is shown in Table 2, which compares the kin-marriages occurring in the general population of Salem during the

Table 2 | **Comparison of types of first-cousin marriages in the general population of Salem by SES during the period 1770–1820, with marriages in the Amory, Cabot, Codman, Higginson, Jackson, Lawrence, Lee, Lowell, and Peabody families.**

Wife's Relation to Husband	Boston Brahmins	Salem High SES	Salem Low SES
FaBroDa	0 (0%)	7 (28%)	9 (53%)
MoBroDa or FaSiDa	5 (71%)	8 (32%)	7 (41%)
MoSiDa	2 (29%)	10 (40%)	1 (6%)
Totals:	7 (100%)	25 (100%)	17 (100%)

period 1770–1820 with those occurring among the merchant families who came to Boston at the end of the eighteenth century to become the nucleus of the "Brahmin" group.[16]

Those in the low SES column—farmers, mechanics, artisans, and laborers—had more need for manpower than for financial capital. Therefore, first-cousin marriages of the father's brother's daughter type were preferred since they tied sons back into the paternal enterprise, conserving the manpower represented by the son. For merchants, on the other hand, less endogamous forms of kin-marriage were preferred —ones that were capital- rather than labor-intensive. Thus the more exogamous forms of cousin-marriage and sibling exchanges were more prevalent.[17] And the most successful merchants, those who would leave provincial ports like Salem and Newburyport after the Revolution to seek their fortunes in Boston, were those who preferred forms of kin-marriage that were the least labor-intensive and the most capital-intensive. These forms tended to tie together previously unrelated males, bringing their capital and their skills into family firms, enlarging their capital, and, as a result, increasing their potential for success.

By the middle of the eighteenth century, the merchants of eastern Massachusetts seem to have developed a remarkably stable system of activity in which family and business concerns were highly integrated. Families supplied merchant firms with manpower and capital. Business relationships and capital combinations were cemented by marriages. And businesses provided basic career training and livelihoods for family members. In addition, because of the dependence of the state on the family for the implementation of social policy, the family continued to provide basic social services for the society as a whole. An ironic outcome of the mercantile use of family economic and marital resources was the development of the merchants as the dominant social and economic group in the colony. While this development was to some degree a product of the increasingly economic emphasis in British colonial policy which, as the eighteenth century progressed, was steadily more interested in the colonies as sources of raw materials and as markets for British manufactures, it was just as much a product of the merchants having strategically adopted familial patterns which encouraged capital accumulation and economic achievement. For the merchants, in shaping their family structure in ways which both fulfilled the ideological mandates of patriarchal family government and which furthered their own economic goals, had developed into a group which, while fairly small in numbers, was politically and economically dominant and socially cohesive.

It is important to note, however, that even before the Revolution the merchant families were adopting a structure which would be conducive to a flexible response to new economic and political conditions. Although it is clear that as late as 1800 families were still highly patriarchal and that sons married and chose careers under paternal direction and control, it is also clear that, among the more successful merchants at least, marriages were being made along increasingly universalistic lines. That is, rather than occurring for reasons of family solidarity and mutual support within a fairly small circle of kin, marriages were being made for the achievement of economic ends—for purposes having no direct connection to the family except insofar as it benefited from the increased profitability of the family firm. The increased flexibility lies in the relation between the structure of authority and the family structure. Each type of kin-marriage gives rise to a distinctive authority structure. A system of preferred marriage of the son to his father's brother's daughter reaffirms the connection between the two fathers (who are also brothers) and, in a system where the major authority figure is the eldest male, extends the authority of the paternal grandfather through three generations. There is no ambiguity in this authority structure: both husband and wife share the same paternal grandfather, who is the dominant authority figure for both. Situations in which the son marries his father's sister's daughter or his mother's brother's daughter are ambiguous. Husband and wife have different paternal grandfathers. Lines of authority are parallel rather than converging. However, there is still a direct line of male authority for both husband and wife: the son to his father to his paternal grandfather; the daughter to her father to her paternal grandfather. Although authority is less concentrated than in the FaBoDa pattern, the FaSiDa and MoBroDa types still possess considerable temporal depth and are not structurally inconsistent with a patriarchy.

When sons marry their mother's sister's daughter or when sibling exchanges take place, a radically different authority structure results: the nuclear family is freed from temporally deep patriarchal patterns. In the MoSiDa marriage, the only link to a potential patriarch is through women. The fathers of the son and his bride are unrelated and owe deference to fathers who are unrelated. In the sibling exchange there is no direct line of authority at all. The dominant male for each set of siblings is the father of each set of siblings—and the dominant relationship in such a situation is between the unrelated fathers. In both these patterns authority loses its generational depth. Since primary relationships are between unrelated males, the paternal grandfather ceases to be an important element. In such a situation the nuclear family and the authority of the father as its head becomes far more important than the authority of the kin-group and the grandfather. Clearly such structures are more suitable to rational modes of economic activity than patriarchal ones. Freed from temporally deep structures of authority and kinship, males, as heads of their own nuclear families, are able to make commercial and marital arrangements in a far more autonomous fashion. At the same time, they benefit from the capital consolidating features of kin-marriage. With the loss of generational depth in the authority structure, attachment of the nuclear family to the kin-group becomes voluntary and opportunistic.

The differences in types of kin-marriage and authority are of little importance until major changes occur in the social, political, and economic context in which the merchant families functioned. This kind of change did not occur until after the Revolution. When it did, the families most able to adapt themselves to new conditions were those families that had practiced the most exogamous forms of kin-marriage. Families that were mired in endogamy were too bound in their kinship and authority structures to respond with any great flexibility. No major decisions could be made without reference to the authority of others. Families that had not practiced kin-marriage at all were disadvantaged too. While they might have possessed great flexibility—being free from the demands of kin—they lacked supportive kin-structures to fall back on. The families in the best possible position for facing the brave new world were those that could possess the advantages of traditional structures without being encumbered by them.

The American Revolution placed enormous strains on the traditional system of family and business integration. Freed from the restrictive trade policies of British mercantilism, the merchants found themselves able to engage in large-scale global trade and domestic manufacturing. It quickly became apparent, however, that such enterprises required far more capital and better means of reducing risk than the majority of merchant families could supply on their own. The decade following the war was replete with business failures resulting from attempts by merchants to engage in large-scale trade using organizational forms that were more suited to marginal operations.[18]

The solution of the problem was obvious. Merchants would have to specialize their operations, reducing the amount of capital in each component of trading activity. Rather than the traditional firm of the sedentary merchant which combined shipping, wholesale and retail sales, manufacturing, credit, insurance, warehousing, wharfage, and other operations, separate firms would have to handle particular activities. Thus risk could be broken down and shared among a number of entrepreneurs. Secondly, they would have to create credit and insurance operations, combining their capital to create pools which could be allocated into the economy as loans and which could be used to insure ventures against accidental losses. Finally, they would have to begin to create joint stock enterprises—corporations—which combined funds from many sources into organizations with large capital bases. All these solutions required a disengagement of capital from family firms. This could not be done without disrupting the familial and social activities which were carried on through the integrated family business.

The disengagement of capital from family firms was achieved through two fundamental innovations in the means of wealth transmission: the testamentary trust and the charitable endowment. Under testamentary trusts it became possible for testators to entirely avoid the partible division of their estates. The principal of the estate could be left in the hands of a trustee who could invest it in commercial enterprises.[19] At the same time, the traditional mandates of family welfare and kin-support could be fulfilled through dividing the earned income of the estate among the survivors of the testator.

The charitable endowment was also a kind of trust. Through it moneys could be left in perpetuity to trustees or to a corporate body for the accomplishment of a variety of social welfare purposes—most of which had, in Massachusetts, been traditionally carried out through families.[20] Once the merchants began to search for means of disengaging capital from familial concerns, they quickly recognized the usefulness of charitable endowments both for the accumulation of capital and for relieving their families of the burdens of welfare activity. After taking over governance positions at Harvard in 1780, they moved steadily in establishing a range of social welfare institutions—the Harvard Medical School (1782), the Boston Dispensary (1795), the Boston Atheneum (1807), the Massachusetts General Hospital, the McLean Asylum (1811), and a multitude of endowment funds for scholarships, for the care of the poor, and for other public purposes. By creating these institutions, the merchants were able to shift responsibilities for social services from the family onto corporate bodies. At the same time, the endowments of these institutions acted as blocks of capital of major significance for the underwriting of new corporations for profit.[21] Finally, the creation and endowment of these institutions served as means of freeing capital from familial demands. By supporting these endowed colleges, hospitals, and other cultural and social welfare organizations, the merchants could continue to fulfill traditional mandates of child training and child support while, at the same time, freeing their capital from the demands which would have been made on it had all sons continued to enter business.

While the creation of testamentary and endowment trusts was crucial to the freeing of capital from familial demands, even the adoption of these devices required fundamental alterations in the family itself. For without a decrease in the family's need for capital, the trusts would be ineffective. The most direct means of reducing this demand was to encourage vocational diversity among merchant sons. If some sons were encouraged to become professionals, demands on family capital would be reduced. Mercantile activity is dependent on control of capital—and as long as all sons became merchants it was difficult to take capital out of family firms for investment in nonfamily enterprises. But a professional's stock in trade is his education and his skill—which involve a far smaller and shorter-term capital outlay. Such vocational diversification required involvement of professionally trained sons in endowed welfare institutions. For these institutions not only became the locus of merchant-group socialization and professional training, but also provided livelihoods and status for sons who were not in commerce. Thus they both counteracted the centrifugal force inherent in vocational diversity, preserving group solidarity, and they served as means of broadening merchant group influence from commerce and politics into control of the culture itself.[22]

The consequence of the reorganization of business, trust-making, and vocational diversity was an effective separation of economic activity from the family. This created interesting new configurations of family structure and authority. Under the old system, personal autonomy was limited. A man remained under his father's authority until he was able to accumulate enough capital to marry and become head of his own household. Usually, his ability to do this was determined by the father—for he controlled the family business and made decisions about whether or not a son should remain with the family concern or could apprentice himself to another man. In sum, up to the end of the eighteenth century, family structure was genuinely patriarchal, organized around the father, who, as head of the household, head of the family business, and agent of the state and church for the implementation of social policy, controlled the actions of those under him and could extend or deny autonomy for his sons at will.

Table 3 | **Occupational choices of sons of fathers born in birth cohorts 1680–1839, in the Amory, Cabot, Codman, Higginson, Jackson, Lawrence, Lee, Lowell, and Peabody families**

Birth Cohorts of Fathers	N	1680–99	1700–19	1720–39	1740–59	1760–79	1780–99	1800–19	1820–39
Business	221	91.7%	85.6%	83.3%	73.2%	54.9%	51.6%	40.5%	29.5%
Law	55	—	14.4%	8.3%	11.5%	9.8%	11.9%	12.8%	18.2%
Medicine	34	8.3%	—	—	1.4%	11.6%	6.3%	11.9%	8.0%
Clergy	10	—	—	—	3.8%	2.0%	1.1%	1.8%	4.5%
Arts	12	—	—	—	—	2.0%	4.3%	1.8%	6.8%
Engineering	6	—	—	—	—	3.9%	—	1.8%	2.3%
Education	10	—	—	—	—	—	—	1.8%	9.1%
Nothing	46	—	—	—	10.1%	7.8%	21.5%	22.9%	13.7%
Misc.	13	—	—	4.2%	—	—	1.1%	4.6%	6.8%
Unknown	8	—	—	4.2%	—	7.8%	2.2%	—	1.1%
Total %		100.0	100.0	100.0	100.0	100.0	100.0	100.0	100.0
N	436	12	7	24	52	51	93	109	88

The creation of corporate organizations by the merchants led to a very different kind of configuration. While the nuclear unit remained with the father as its nominal head, it was supplemented by two new factors. Above it was erected a network of organizations which, while presided over by members of merchant families, operated according to criteria of competence and specialized function. The other new factor lay within the family: the autonomous individual whose subjection to paternal authority was very limited. While the father could exercise his arbitrary will in enforcing day-to-day behavior, he could do little else. The child could determine his own career preferences, make his own marital choices, and seek employment wherever he wished. Paternal authority became more oriented to shaping the behavior of children in order to make them conform to norms of behavior which were institutionally determined. Paradoxically, as the children were shaped to these norms, they became more autonomous in relation to their families, but less autonomous in relation to the institutions in which they would be schooled and employed. Thus the family, both in its form and its content, became steadily more dependent on decisions made by commercial and cultural corporations.[23]

In discussing this great change in family structure, it is necessary to distinguish between the families who actively initiated it and those who were merely affected by it. The merchant families of Boston who created family trusts, corporations, and endowed institutions did so in an essentially private fashion. While the institutions they created did serve the public, their private functions in facilitating the separation of family and business and in capital formation seem to have been at least as important as their public benevolent purposes.[24] The institutionalization of economic and social activities by the merchants seems, however, to have affected everyone. Institutions were clearly more able than families and family enterprises to care for the sick and destitute, to educate and train, to produce goods and services, and to provide incomes. Because of their inherent efficiency and because of the desire of the merchant group to expand its influence, families at all levels of society became increasingly involved in corporate institutions—the most crucial of which appear to have remained in the hands of those who created them.

It is this public feature of privately owned commercial and cultural corporations that appears to have created the basis for class organization in New England and the remarkable continuity of power enjoyed by the merchant group. It is crucial to recognize, however, that ''privately owned" does not, in this context, mean "individually owned." It means collectively owned and managed by the merchant group, who, by transferring central functions which had been carried out within the family, were able to collectivize their capital accumulation, socialization, and productive activities. It was through this collectivization that the merchants were able to move from individualistic family-based merchant capitalism toward corporate organization of the productive and cultural activities of the whole society.

It is clear that by the middle of the nineteenth century Boston's capitalist class had organized a coherent network of institutions of commerce and culture that had an intrinsic advantage over traditional forms of organization for the production of goods and services. Clearly a factory could produce items more cheaply than independent craftsmen. Clearly a physician or lawyer trained at Harvard and in the hospitals and law offices of Boston had greater mastery over his subject and was a more effective practitioner than a doctor or lawyer trained by traditional apprenticeship or taught by his own efforts. Yet the relation between the merchant group with its institutions and the rest of society was more than a simply competitive one. It involved the internal structure and dynamics of rural and artisan groups and their inability to resist or provide alternatives to merchant group organizations.

The analysis of the rural population of Massachusetts presented by Philip Greven in his study of Andover suggests that some of the reasons for this failure to create alternative organizations lie in the family structure of agrarian groups.[25] Like the merchants, the farmers were subject to the erosion of their property due to the system of partible inheritance. As long as town lands remained for distribution, this was not a serious problem—children could be provided for out of increases in paternal property resulting from successive distributions of town lands held in reserve. But as soon as all lands had been distributed, farmers were faced with a serious problem. They could either subdivide their farms among their children—with a resulting decline in productivity and diffusion of control. Or they could, like the merchants, adopt a system of kin-marriage which would recombine landholdings through the testamentary process. They appear to have done this—although Greven does not provide a detailed analysis of the types of favored kin-marriage.[26] But it did not have the desired effect. For even a rigid system of prescribed first-cousin marriage could not have absorbed the increase in population relative to the finite quantity of land in any given town. Some children would have to become mobile—either occupationally (by being apprenticed to a craftsman or professional) or geographically (by being staked to a farm in another place). Either way, the continuity of rural culture would be eroded—capital and manpower would be dispersed rather than concentrated.

Unlike financial capital—which is theoretically infinite—land capital in a particular town is finite. There is only so much of it. And when it is gone, there is no more to distribute. Where the merchants could expand their operations in order to absorb the increase in the number of their children, the farmers could not without engaging in activities which would lead to a weakening of family cohesion and their ability as a group to concentrate capital and manpower. Farmers were forced away from traditional patriarchalism and subsistence operations by the dynamic of their own social organizations. In order to fulfill traditional mandates of kin-support they were forced toward farming for profit to earn the money necessary for apprenticeship bonds and to buy more land for their expanding families. And even when they did so, the result was not cohesion and capital consolidation. It was a dispersion of families across the landscape and across the occupational spectrum.

This disunity was aggravated by the forms of kin-marriage that they may have chosen for the purpose of consolidating their landholdings in the paternal line. Since their need was for forms of kin-marriage that promoted the retention of land and the labor of the sons, they may have favored the FaBroDa marriage—a type which is also particularly consistent with the maintainance of temporally deep patriarchal authority. The problem with this form of marriage is that its ultimate social consequence is isolation of the family from the rest of the community. Males, with their labor, skill, and shares in their paternal estates, are not exchanged with other families—but are concentrated in the male line. In a community in which this form of kin-marriage was preferred (as Bernard Farber suggests it was for the Salem low-SES groups), one would expect to see the formation of relatively exclusive kinship groups. It is difficult to form bonds of common interest and collective action among families practicing endogamous forms of kin-marriage. For property is too concentrated and there are too few points of social and economic reciprocity between family groups.

While the merchants were following patterns of kin-marriage conducive to universalistic alliances and to the sharing, consolidation, and collectivization of resources in new ways, the rural population appears to have been trapped in a structure of kinship which, while recombining and consolidating old holdings, cut it off from common intercourse, from the development of common interests and values, and which —because of its basis in finite land capital—introduced a constant element of disorganization and discontinuity in the midst of a narrow patriarchal concentration of wealth and authority. Hence the paradox of the New England village: stability, kin-cohesion, and social order coexisting with a high degree of out-mobility and discontinuity.[27]

It is clear that while farmers might have in common the activity of cultivating the soil, a common religion, and common participation in village cultures of mutual aid and support, their social structure was not conducive to the formation of coherent alliances among villages. Even if farmers could intellectually recognize where their common interests lay, their social structure, with its paradoxical mixture of narrow patriarchal solidarity and disorganizing out-mobility, did not provide a structural basis for organizing themselves as a class with consciousness of its situation. And the dynamic of their social and economic arrangements led them increasingly toward a common dependence on Boston merchants for credit, for markets, for manufactured goods, and, for farm children who wished to become professionals, for training and accreditation.

For the merchants, on the other hand, there were abundant pressures both for the development of class organization and for the growth of class consciousness. Their social and economic activities were collective endeavors in which the capital and manpower of a group of families had been pooled in corporate organizations. Such pooling and institutionalization required the adoption of universalistic criteria of competence and talent for employment—initially as a means of mediating among the various families, subsequently as a means of ensuring that funds invested in collective endeavors would be directed to functionally specific purposes of the enterprises, not diverted to private ends. But universalistic criteria for employment and for participation in institutions of commerce and culture contained a paradoxical element. It required that the most talented and competent persons in the whole society be advanced to positions of responsibility in their corporate enterprises—thereby compromising the integrity of the merchant group itself. For, given standards for employment and participation that were based on competence rather than consanguinity, there would of necessity be a steady inflow of "obscure persons" into merchant-controlled institutions.

This does not appear to have unduly troubled the Boston merchants until the middle of the nineteenth century. In 1800 their own identity as a group was only vaguely formed. They were, after all, only a group of families from different parts of Massachusetts who were in the process of pooling their resources in pursuit of certain economic goals. Because of their diverse backgrounds a coherent group identity could not be formed without impeding the formation of alliances and the collectivization of resources. Two factors, however, impel the formation of class consciousness. The first involved the collective socialization of merchant-group children: they went to the same schools, lived in the same neighborhoods, played together, married one another, did business together, and participated in common institutions. Such common upbringing and direction toward common goals of achievement and life-style naturally led, as the first cohorts of merchant children emerged into the world of productive adulthood and into positions of responsibility in corporate organizations created by their fathers, to a recognition of a commonality of experiences and values that differentiated them from the rest of society.[28] Secondly, as the first generation of merchant-family founders died off in the 1820s and 30s, there appears to have been an increasingly explicit interest in using corporate institutions as normative means of leadership selection. Although anyone was, in theory, eligible for leadership if he possessed the necessary qualities of character and competence, merchant-group children were more eligible because of their common background and because they, more than any other group in society, had been intentionally socialized to the norms of major institutions.

Nonetheless, it was necessary to articulate those norms for leadership selection and to tie them to the specific characteristics of the merchant group itself. Such an articulation would have the dual effect of clarifying and reinforcing the identity of the merchant group while, at the same time, making explicit the personal and educational qualities for those desirous of mobility into positions of power. This is what Oliver Wendell Holmes, the writer who coined the term ''Boston Brahmin,'' was attempting to do in his discussion of the characteristics of ''a man of family'' in *The Autocrat of the Breakfast Table:*

—Self-made men?—Well, yes. Of course everybody likes and respects self-made men. It is a great deal better to be made that way than not to be made at all. Are any of you younger people old enough to remember that Irishman's house on the marsh near Cambridgeport, which house he built from drain to chimney-top with his own hands? It took him a good many years to build it, and one could see that it was a little out of plumb, and a little wavy in outline, and a little queer and uncertain in general aspect. A regular hand could certainly have built a better house; but it was a very good house for a self-made carpenter's house, and people praised it, and said how remarkably well the Irishman had succeeded. . . .

Your self-made man, whittled into shape with his own jack-knife, deserves more credit, if that is all, than the regular engine-turned article, shaped by the approved pattern, and French-polished by society and travel. But as to saying that one is in every way the equal of the other, that is another matter. The right of strict social discrimination of all things and persons, according to their merits, native or acquired, is one of the most precious republican privileges. I take the liberty to exercise it, when I say, that, *other things being equal*, in most relations of life I prefer a man of family. . . .

No, my friends, I go (always, other things being equal) for the man who inherits family traditions and the cumulative humanities of at least four or five generations. . . . One may, it is true, have all the antecedents I have spoken of and yet be a boor and a shabby fellow. One may have none of them, and yet be fit for councils and courts. Then let them change places. Our social arrangement has this great beauty: that its strata shift up and down as they change specific gravity, without being clogged by layers of prescription. But I still insist on my democratic liberty of choice, and I go for the man with the gallery of family portraits against the one with the twenty-five daguerreotypes, unless I find out that the last is the better of the two.[29]

What Holmes is saying is that common socialization and the possession of inherited wealth, while not guaranteeing that an individual will embody the qualities necessary for leadership, greatly increase the probability that he will. The persons most in possession of these qualities are the members of the merchant group. At the same time, however, he makes clear that the ascriptive characteristics of the "man of family" are not the central issue. They are simply indicators of character and competence. Even though the odds are against it, one can "be fit for councils and courts" without being a man of family. And, as Holmes knew from his own family's experience, inherited traditions could be acquired for a talented upwardly mobile person's children through marriage into an old and established family.[30] Holmes, in sum, is articulating standards of a universalistic type which are based on behavior rather than on bloodlines or place of birth. In so doing, he is both opening and closing the door to power—simultaneously delineating the boundaries of the merchant class while pointing out that entrance into it is not impossible.

What was the effect of this mercantile hegemony on the institutions of commerce and culture in other societal groups? It was very great. The pressure of increasing economic centralization and the internal dynamics of their own social and economic patterns made it increasingly difficult to sustain traditional modes of productive activity. Individuals were faced with the choice of maintaining traditional patterns by moving west (as thousands of New England farmers did during the first half of the nineteenth century) or of becoming occupationally mobile. If they chose the latter, it was distinctly to their advantage to move toward the cultural forms of the mercantile hegemony, entering business or the professions and affecting the manners and morals of the dominant group. This movement led ultimately to the development of the "new middle class" of bureaucratically minded specialists that has preoccupied Robert Weibe. Those who went west only postponed the ultimate showdown between cultures that would occur between the Civil War and the turn of the century—the competition between the small-scale organic cultural forms and roles of the village and the farm, which socialized individuals only to their own localities; and the cosmopolitan universalistic cultural forms of institutions that fitted individuals for participation in the great world of commercial and cultural organizations that were national in scope.

There is of necessity an element of indeterminacy in the study of the family. For, as this essay suggests, the family varies in structure, function, and organization at different points in time and, as modernization occurs, with the social and economic position of various groups in society.[31] One cannot, therefore, simply study "the family" without an awareness of its relation to the whole society and to the broad range of activities that compose social action.

Because the nature of the family varies with the nature of society, the study of kinship becomes particularly useful. Through it one can examine the relative importance of secondary institutions such as schools, corporations, and welfare agencies to society as a whole and to particular groups in society. For there appears to be a significant relation between kinship and the effectiveness of secondary institutions: strong kin ties exist to the extent that families are dependent on their own resources for the satisfaction of basic needs; kin ties grow weaker and less significant as socialization, production, and cultural activities are shifted into secondary institutions.[32] Moreover, the position of particular groups in society can be examined through kinship studies. For variations in the importance of kinship appear to be linked with the extent to which groups participate in powerful secondary institutions. It thus becomes possible to use kin studies to shed light on the distribution of wealth and power in society as a normative process rather than simply as a static arrangement of income and education levels.[33] Finally, because kinship is one of the basic common denominators in human societies, there already exists an extensive body of theory and field work on which historians can draw and to which they can contribute in the course of their inquiries into the family and its role in the origins and consequences of modernization.

NOTES

1. Peter Laslett, *The World We Have Lost* (New York, 1965), 3–4.

2. The remarkable advances in our understanding of modernization over the past two decades are eloquently attested to by Thomas Cochran's despairing evaluation of the problems facing historians of economic growth in the early fifties:

> On the basis of present historical materials, it is impossible to treat statistically the historical effect of entrepreneurs on capital formation in the United States. The most that the historian can do is to indicate some of the general outlines of entrepreneurial development, call attention to additional material that might be investigated more carefully, and suggest some relevant factors that have not in the past been much considered by theoretical economists. . . .
>
> Problems regarding the entrepreneur in capital formation do not differ greatly from those in general economic growth. . . .
>
> . . . [a] general theory of society—specifically, some sort of sociology of change—is necessary to account for economic development. The role of the entrepreneur in capital formation and other activities is shaped by a combination of factors involving personality types, cultural attitudes, technological knowledge, and available physical resources. Merely to list these factors calls attention to the intangible character of all but one of them. The personality-culture complex may someday be segmented into measurable factors, but that achievement appears to be far in the future.

These remarks reflect the influence of psychoanalysis, with its emphasis on the role of the individual personality. Current work recognizes that the individual does not interact directly on society—but does so only through intermediaries: other individuals, the family, and institutions. The major contribution of historians of the family to understanding economic development is probably their addition of a sociological dimension to the problem. This in turn has made it possible to segment the "personality-culture complex" into measurable factors. Cochran's essay, "The Role of the Entrepreneur in American Capital Formation," appeared in a National Bureau of Economic Research publication, *Capital Formation and Economic Growth* (New York, 1955).

3. Bernard Bailyn, *The New England Merchants of the Seventeenth Century* (Cambridge, 1955).

4. Edmund S. Morgan, *The Puritan Family* (New York, 1966) is an excellent account of the place of the family in Puritan ideology. Philip Greven's *Four Generations: Population, Land, and Family in Colonial Andover, Massachusetts* (Ithaca, 1970) adds sociological flesh to Morgan's account of the Puritan word.

5. Bernard Farber's *Guardians of Virtue: Salem Families in 1800* (New York, 1972) is a provocative and much underrated book. Its major problems lie in two areas. First, intellectual materials, Puritan theology in particular, are approached in a somewhat naïve fashion. Second, it is based on a community which, by 1800, was no longer a typical colonial town—its major entrepreneurs having left for Boston after the Revolution and the town itself well on the way to becoming a commercial and political satellite of Boston. Nonetheless, it is an ambitious and exciting attempt to apply the techniques of kin network analysis to the social and economic structure of colonial New England.

6. The research population and the analysis on which this paper is based are contained in a dissertation by the author entitled *Family Structure and Class Consolidation among the Boston Brahmins* (1973). It is available from University Microfilms.

The research population consists of all descendants of certain individuals born between 1680 and 1720. Because almost all their descendants remained in eastern Massachusetts during the period under study, and because they participated in the same processes and activities, it is meaningful to deal with them as a collectivity. Since the term ''family'' as used here includes all descendants, both male and female, any given family name includes persons bearing other names. Thus the Amorys include the Dexters, Sohiers, Paynes, Austins, and others. The Cabots include the Lodges, the Higginsons include the Storrows, and so on.

The families studied were chosen on the basis of their success—on the fact that they were and continue to be Boston families of consequence. They appear, however, to be structurally differentiated from other, less successful, Massachusetts merchant families. See Peter Dobkin Hall, ''Marital Selection and Business in Massachusetts Merchant Families, 1700–1900'' in Rose Laub Coser, *The Family: Its Structure and Functions, Second Edition* (New York, 1974), 226-239.

7. The most persuasive discussions of family government in New England are contained in the works of Morgan, Greven, and Farber mentioned above.

8. For the legal nature of the relation of partners, see Joseph Story, *Commentaries on the Law of Partnership* (Boston, 1836). For discussions of the relation between early New England business practice and family life, see K. W. Porter, *The Jacksons and the Lees* (Cambridge, 1937); W. T. Baxter, *The House of Hancock: Business in Boston, 1724-1775* (Cambridge, 1945); S. E. Morison, *The Maritime History of Massachusetts* (Cambridge, 1921); and Carl Seaburg and Stanley Paterson, *Merchant Prince of Boston, Thomas Handasyde Perkins* (Cambridge, 1971). Although there are few general works on early business and family life, vast amounts of useful information can be found in family histories and genealogies. Particularly useful are Lloyd Vernon Briggs, *The Cabot Family: History and Genealogy* (Boston, 1927); Frances R. Morse, *Henry and Mary Lee, Letters and Journals* (Boston, 1924); and G. E. Meredith, *The Descendants of Hugh Amory, 1605-1805* (London, 1901).

9. For the family's responsibilities in social welfare, see Morgan, *op. cit.,* 133–160; Farber, *op. cit.;* and the early chapters of David J. Rothman, *The Discovery of the Asylum* (Boston and Toronto, 1971).

10. George L. Haskins, ''The Beginnings of Partible Inheritance in the American Colonies,'' *Yale Law Journal*, 51: 1280–83. Partible inheritance does not, in the New England context, mean equal division of the paternal estate. Often the eldest son received a double portion. Sometimes the widow received either outright ownership or a life interest in a third of her husband's estate. Although the practice might vary from place to place and from time to time, the effect remained the same—i.e., the continual erosion of accumulated property as it was transferred from generation to generation.

11. Ibid., 1,285.

12. For a discussion of the survival of medieval village communalism in New England, see Sumner Chilton Powell, *Puritan Village* (Middletown, Conn., 1963).

13. A description of this practice and its disruptive effect on trading activities and capital accumulation can be found in Edward Brooks, *A Correspondence between Edward Brooks and John Amory Lowell* (Boston, 1847) and John Amory Lowell, *A Reply to the Pamphlet Recently Circulated by Mr. Edward Brooks* (Boston, 1848).

14. On *inter-vivos* transfers of property, see Greven, *op. cit.,* 79.

15. For the conflict between Puritan ideology and mercantile goals, see Bernard Bailyn, *The New England Merchants of the Seventeenth Century* (Cambridge, 1955) and *The Apologia of Robert Keayne* (New York, 1964).

16. The figures for first-cousin marriage for the Salem general population in Table 2 are taken from Bernard Farber, *op. cit.,* 128. The apparent frequency of cross-cousin marriage in the Brahmin group during this period is misleading. By this point sibling exchanges had largely replaced first-cousin marriage in the Brahmin group.

17. For the 1760–1820 period, of 26 kin-marriages, 19 (73%) were sibling exchanges or marriages to cousins beyond the first degree of consanguinity. Of the 7 first-cousin marriages, 3 were of the most exogamous type—with the son marrying his mother's sister's daughter. See Hall, "Marital Selection and Business," in Coser, *op. cit.,* 236.

18. Before the Revolution, New England merchants conducted most of their dealings with British correspondents. This eliminated the need for traveling partners and a great deal of the risk and uncertainty of trading in a free market. After the war, however, partners had to be sent out to deal as free agents in international markets. Even if they behaved responsibly, there was constant danger of ruin. The traveling partner might contract to purchase a shipment of goods at a certain price in Germany, France, or the Orient. On returning to Boston with his cargo he might find that a dozen other ships had come in with similar cargoes, glutting the market and forcing him to sell at a loss. This kind of instability was virtually unknown before the war. For descriptions of commercial problems stemming from traveling partners and the overall problem of post-Revolutionary instability, see Porter, *op. cit.,* 1–124; James Jackson, *Reminiscences of the Hon. Jonathan Jackson* (Boston, 1866); and John, Charles, and Francis Codman, *An Exposition of the Pretended Claims of William Vans on the Estate of John Codman* (Boston, 1837).

19. On the role of trustees as investors, see Hall, *Family Structure and Class Consolidation* (1973), 206–323; Donald Holbrook, *The Boston Trustee* (Boston, 1937); A. W. Scott, *The Law of Trusts* (Boston, 1939); and Geralt T. White, *A History of the Massachusetts Hospital Life Insurance Company* (Cambridge, 1955).

20. For the kinds of activities for which charitable endowment trusts could be created, see A. W. Scott, *op. cit.* Samual Atkins Eliot's articles on charity in Boston published in 1845 and 1860 are excellent summaries of ante-bellum charitable activities and their objects.

21. For the role of endowments as sources of investment capital in England, see Wilbur K. Jordan, *Philanthropy in England, 1480–1660* (London, 1959), 38–39. For their capital function in Boston, see Hall, "The Model of Boston Charity" *Science and Society* (1974) and S. E. Harris, *The Economics of Harvard* (New York, 1969).

22. The endowed institutions of culture and social welfare counteracted the centrifugal force of vocational diversity in two major ways. First, because they were privately funded, they were necessarily dependent on the good will of the merchants who were the primary source of donations. Secondly, they institutionalized roles in which professionals and merchants would have to work together in a co-operative fashion. Students of private institutions are familiar with the inevitable dominance of businessmen and lawyers on boards of trustees. This phenomenon functioned as a unifying force for the merchant group when, as was the case until almost the turn of the century, both staff and officers of governance were members of the same families.

23. The increasing dependence of merchant families on institutional norms can be seen in the relation between paternal occupations and career choices by sons. One would expect a differential following of the father's occupation depending on the birth order of sons—i.e., that the first-born would be most likely to enter his father's occupation, with freedom of choice for the later-borns. What actually happens is that differential effects disappear entirely for the sons of fathers born after 1780—with less than half of sons in any birth-order position following the father's career and with no significant differences in this pattern in any birth-order position. This suggests a radical change in parental expectations. See Hall, *Family Structure and Class Consolidation,* 116–168.

24. See Hall, ''The Model of Boston Charity,'' *op. cit.*

25. P. J. Greven, *op. cit.*

26. Although Greven does not provide a detailed analysis of kin-marriage in Andover, his description of the Abbot family and its pattern of marital selection suggests that cousin marriages served to concentrate property in the paternal line—i.e., he states that of 51 marriages before 1755, 15 were marriages of Abbots to other Abbots. This high proportion of FaBroDa or other paternal-line alliances suggests that the Andover families follow patterns of mate selection similar to those analyzed by Farber for the Salem low SES group. Greven, *op. cit.*

27. Ibid., 261–289.

28. Perhaps the most concise description of this recognition of common experience and upbringing is contained in Henry Adams' description of the effects of Harvard College:

> For generation after generation, Adamses and Brookses and Boylstons and Gorhams had gone to Harvard College. . . .
>
> . . . [C]ustom, social ties, convenience, and, above all, economy, kept each generation in the track. . . . All went there because their friends went there, and the College was their ideal of social self-respect.
>
> Harvard College, as far as it educated at all, was a mild and liberal school, which sent young men into the world with all that they needed to make respectable citizens, and something of what they needed to make useful ones. . . . In effect, the school created a type, not a will. Four years of Harvard College, if successful, resulted in an autobiographical blank, a mind on which only a watermark had been stamped.

The Education of Henry Adams (New York, 1931), 54–55. In fact, Harvard was for the Adamses, as it was for most of the merchant group, only relatively new as an experience shared by most male members of the merchant group. Henry was only the fourth generation to attend Harvard. Over half of the sons in the merchant group did not attend the college until the cohort of fathers born 1760–1779. By the cohort of fathers born 1800–1819, 76% of sons attended the college. The falsification of history inherent in Adams' characterization of Harvard attendance as a common and traditional experience of his social group testifies to the impact of group socialization and the degree to which it facilitated the creation of group identity through the creation of group history.

29. Oliver Wendell Holmes, *The Autocrat of the Breakfast Table* (New York, 1957), 21–26. See also, O. W. Holmes, *Elsie Venner* (New York, 1962), 15–19.

30. Holmes's father, Rev. Abiel Holmes, was an impecunious but talented parson from western Massachusetts. His marriage to Sarah Wendell, daughter of Boston merchant

Oliver Wendell, made it possible for Oliver to lay claim to the attributes of "the man of the family." This was a common pattern—as the Adamses, Holmes, and numerous other merchant-group families moved from commercial success to social legitimization through marriage into older, more distinguished families.

31. Excellent general accounts of kinship are Bernard Farber, *Kinship and Class; A Midwestern Study* (New York, 1971); Nelson Graburn, ed., *Readings in Kinship and Social Structure* (New York, 1971); Rodney Needham, *Structure and Sentiment: A Test Case in Social Anthropology* (Chicago, 1962); and certain essays in Coser, *op. cit.*

32. Farber, *Kinship and Class.*

33. The major problem with most studies of class structure in the United States is their circularity. Ruling-class membership is defined by the participation of individuals in certain institutions; those institutions are designated as "ruling-class institutions" by the participation of certain individuals therein. Standard measures of socioeconomic status (SES) are equally circular and static, defining class position by the amount of income, education, and occupational prestige an individual has. It is necessary for scholars of class to return to the first principles of their discipline—to see class position, not as a thing, but as a relation (to the means of production), and as a process by which some groups and individuals are more likely to occupy positions of power than others.

4

A Ray of Millennial Light: Early Education and Social Reform in the Infant School Movement in Massachusetts, 1826–1840

DEAN MAY AND MARIS A. VINOVSKIS

But a ray of millennial light has shone on us, and reveals a way in which poverty, with all its attendant evils—moral, physical, and intellectual, may be banished from the world.

—5th Annual Report
Infant School Society of the City of Boston, 1834

The editors of the Boston *Recorder and Religious Transcript* showed little restraint in the enthusiasm with which they reported an 1829 demonstration by children of a Boston infant school:

> Infants, taken from the most unfavorable situations in which they are ever placed, from the abodes of poverty and vice, are capable of learning at least a hundred times as much, a hundred times as well, and of being a hundred times as happy, by the system adopted in infant schools, as by that which prevails in the common schools throughout the country. The conclusion most interesting to every friend of education is, that the infant school system can be extended through every department of the *popular education*. And that in any school district where there is interest and liberality enough to raise Ten Dollars to procure apparatus, a *beginning* can be made the present season.[1]

The objects of this enthusiasm, the infant schools, were religious and educational institutions intended to provide instruction for children of the poor from the ages of about 18 months to the earliest age when public institutions would accept them. They were founded and under-

Authors' Note: *The authors would like to gratefully acknowledge financial support for this study from the U.S. Office of Education Research Grant No. OEG–1–72–006 (509).*

written by civic-minded persons in Europe and America during the third and fourth decades of the nineteenth century.

Robert Owen began the movement in 1816 with the opening of an infant school at New Lanark, Scotland.[2] The schools rapidly spread throughout England, Scotland, and Ireland. Americans, always sensitive to reform movements in England, quickly picked up the idea. In February, 1827, plans were made in Hartford, Connecticut, to establish the first infant school in America. In May of that same year an infant school society was founded in New York City and the organization of such societies in Philadelphia and other American cities quickly followed.[3]

The infant school movement spread to Massachusetts in 1828. In June of that year, infant schools were opened on Pleasant Street and Salem Street by two different infant school societies. Shortly thereafter, schools were begun in a number of other towns in the Commonwealth including Salem, Worcester, Concord, Haverhill, and Charlestown.[4]

The peak of public enthusiasm for the new institutions occurred in the early 1830's. However, the middle of that decade saw a drastic decline in enthusiasm. By the end of 1835, almost all public comment on the infant schools in Massachusetts had ceased and the activities of the once flourishing infant school societies quickly ended. In fact, infant schools seem in subsequent years to have faded, not only from public memory, but even from the recollections of some of those who had actively participated in the movement. When kindergartens became popular in Massachusetts in the 1860's and 1870's, they were greeted by the public as a new and unique European contribution to the cause of public education in America with almost no association to the infant education movement some three decades earlier.[5]

The infant school movement provides an ideal opportunity to study the dynamics of an educational reform effort. The interaction of theorists of educational reform, social reformers, civic-minded social elites, public school officials, and the general public buffeted the movement in directions which none of the groups alone would have planned. Their attitudes toward infant schools and their differing expectations of what the schools would accomplish for society also influenced the early successes and the abrupt decline of that movement.

Though public enthusiasm for the infant education movement lasted only a few years, the short duration does not diminish its significance to the social historian. The discussion of infant schools focused public attention upon the importance of infancy, and stimulated a vigorous re-examination of the social institutions which related most directly to infants. The role of the family and the school in an infant's life received particular attention. These considerations gave rise to questions concerning the role of women in society as mothers, students, and teachers. Thus, the infant school movement provides a rare opportunity to explore these issues at the family level and in different social institutions.

Clearly, it is impossible to discuss all of the issues raised by the infant education movement in a short paper. We plan to examine the major ideas and considerations which led to the founding of the infant schools; to trace the attitudes and interactions of the local groups involved in the establishment of these schools; and to show how confusion as to objectives and lack of unanimity within and among the groups led to the decline of the schools at the very time when changing social conditions made the needs they were designed to meet more pressing than ever. We will tentatively suggest that infant education might have been a major factor in encouraging parents to send their children at a very young age to public schools even after the movement itself had faded from the scene.

Educators in England, attempting to fuse two major European traditions of educational theory and practice, developed the infant school system. Much of the difficulty in making infant schools viable in America arose from the fact that the two traditions led the sponsoring groups to work at cross purposes in their promotion of the schools.

The first of these traditions developed on the Continent from foundations laid by Jean-Jacques Rousseau with the publication of *Emile* in 1762. Rousseau proposed two major innovations in *Emile*. Viewing human society as essentially corrupt, he stressed that the role of education should be primarily that of encouraging the young mind to shake off the impositions of the old society and arrive at its own conclusions as to what was worthy of its study and attentions. Education is not the transmission of a body of knowledge from master to pupil, but rather a process of freeing the pupil's mind to explore the world on its own.

Rousseau's second major innovation concerned his division of youth into three periods and his contention that specific aspects of the child's total educational experience were appropriate to each period in the child's development. Before the age of five—a period when the senses are most important—education should consist of exposing the senses to as great a variety of concrete experiences as possible. The key idea was that children are not young adults but rather are developing individuals whose education must be appropriately attuned to their stages of development.

Aspects of these two fundamental ideas were further developed in a long series of educational experiments carried out by various proponents of educational reform during the next hundred years. Most continental reformers had visited the schools of at least one other member of this group and, though each had distinctive ideas which he sought to emphasize and develop, they agreed on some general principles. All shared an implicit rejection of the old society and had a desire to isolate the children from the harmful influences of that society. This desire found expression in the fact that the schools were physically isolated from centers of population and were run as boarding schools where the master could hope to control the whole environment.[6]

These continental reformers shared a revulsion against force of any kind and a general feeling that if the children's senses were sufficiently exposed to a natural world about them the children themselves would begin to ask questions and explore the world in their own way. Overall, there was an emphasis upon the necessity of a balance between physical, moral, and intellectual development. And each reformer stressed that certain teaching methods were appropriate to certain stages of development and that it was unnatural and hence wrong to try to thwart nature by attempting teachings that were not properly keyed to the stage of development of a child.

It should be emphasized that none of these educators advocated institutions specifically for children under the age of four or five as the proponents of infant education were to do. Given the common effort to remove the children from environments which might contaminate them, one might have expected some of these continental reformers to advocate the removal of children to a more rational environment as early as possible. But here their distrust of old society and their love of nature came into conflict. It seemed obvious to them that, early in a child's life, parents are the most important conveyors of the values and the norms and that their teachings will most likely be those of the old society. But to remove infants from their home, from the loving care of the mother and the family, would have violated their rule of strict adherence to nature.[7]

Johann Heinrich Pestalozzi, the great Swiss educator, was the major student of the perceptual and learning faculties of infants. He concluded that children could begin to learn at a very early age, but that all such learning should take place in the home under the mother's influence. Pestalozzi's work suggested that girls and mothers should be given every opportunity to learn the new and progressive educational techniques so that they might apply them to their own children. And, in fact, the emphasis on "female education," "maternal education," and "fireside education," so common in the first half of the nineteenth century in America as well as in Europe, derived in part from Pestalozzi's ideas.[8]

But what if some parents were not sufficiently enlightened to be fit teachers of their infant offspring, as advocates of the infant schools contended? The fact that the European educational reformers of this period provided no answer to such a question suggests either that they felt that the infant was not sufficiently impressionable to have irreversible harm done to him in an unenlightened home or that the development of qualities of natural affection and love was the most significant part of the education process at this age, and that even an unenlightened mother could do better than the most enlightened schoolmaster at that.

In England quite a different tradition dominated educational reform. The English produced almost no educators of the renown of Pestalozzi until the effects of industrialization and urbanization began to be felt late in the eighteenth century—a striking fact. The only educational innovations in England in the eighteenth century and early decades of the nineteenth century were the Sunday school movement, which began in 1780, and the Lancastrian/Bell system of monitorial instruction, which began in the first decade of the nineteenth century. Both of these movements were practical reforms designed to extend at least a modicum of education to the lower classes at the least possible cost. They did not involve new concepts as to the *content* of education.[9] Nor did the English reformers advocate special teaching methods based upon novel conceptions of the infant mind, as did the continental reformers.

The first major educational innovation in England in the early nineteenth century was Robert Owen's infant school at New Lanark in 1816. The principles underlying the school, which formed part of his New Institution, were expressed by Owen in his *New View of Society*, where he recommended that

the governing powers of all countries should establish rational plans for the education and general formation of the characters of their subjects. . . . These plans must be devised to train children from their earliest infancy in good habits of every description (which will of course prevent them from acquiring those of falsehood and deception). They must afterwards be rationally educated, and their labour be usefully directed. Such habits and education will impress them with an active and ardent desire to promote the happiness of every individual, and that without the shadow of exception for sect, or party, or country, or climate.[10]

Owen's establishment of an infant school was followed up in 1818 when an eminent group of English reformers founded a school on Brewer's Green, Westminster. Another infant school was organized in the Spitalfields section of London shortly thereafter, and in July, 1824, these same reformers founded the Infant School Society and began to solicit public subscriptions to support the institutions. Within a year, at least 55 infant schools were in operation in various parts of England, Scotland, and Ireland.[11]

The discussions at Freemason's Hall in London, which led to the founding of the Infant School Society in 1824, underline the fact that in England the infant schools were perceived as a means of dealing with pressing social problems. Whatever the designs of Robert Owen at New Lanark, it is strikingly obvious that the schools were a perfect answer to problems created by the factory system of production. With children safely in school, mothers and older children were freed to work in the factories. This consideration was not lost upon those who spoke at the meeting at Freemason's Hall, though they emphasized, in this context, the positive advantage to the family of the incremental income of working mothers rather than the value to factory owners of the increased labor supply. But it is clear from their discussions that the growth of an urban pauper class was the major problem which occupied the minds of the London reformers. Participants in the meeting told tales of Fagin-like criminals who kept large numbers of impoverished vagrant children in their employ as thieves and pickpockets.[12]

The sequence of events which led to the founding of the London Infant School Society is significant. The London reformers saw in Owen's fundamental idea of sending infants to school a possible means of ameliorating social problems caused by urbanization and industrialization. The instructors they hired soon found the management of several dozen infants no easy task. These teachers, in their search for ideas and techniques which might prove useful in an infant school, turned to the European tradition we have described, especially the work of Pestalozzi. They were the first to apply Pestalozzian principles for the teaching of infants in an institutional setting—even though Pestalozzi himself had never intended the establishment of such institutions. In the process of working out a practical combination of Owen's idea of infant schools and Pestalozzi's principles of teaching infants, they created what they were commonly to call the infant school system.

The early advocacy of infant schools in the United States coincided with the emergence of a group of educators and public-minded citizens sufficiently large to sustain publications specializing in discussions of the theory and practice of public education. Before 1826 only three journals exclusively concerned with education had been published in this country. During the next two and one-half decades over 60 magazines and papers devoted exclusively to education were established.[13]

The first journal to contribute significantly to this flowering of interest in educational theories and reforms was William Russell's *American Journal of Education*, published in Boston from 1826 through 1830 under his editorship. Russell's position on infant education was made abundantly clear when he commented on the subject in his opening editorial in 1826:

> There seems to us to be no danger of beginning instruction too soon, if it is begun in the right way, and with expectations sufficiently moderate. . . . Within a few years public sentiment has undergone a favorable change on the subject of early education. . . . The establishment of infant schools we look upon as one of the most important epochs in the history of education. We shall use every endeavor to render this subject familiar to the minds of our readers by communicating all the information we can procure regarding the details of the system and its progress abroad and at home.[14]

Through the rest of his editorship William Russell did not fail to make good on his promise. Nearly every issue of the journal for the rest of the decade contained articles advocating or reporting the progress of infant schools in Boston and in other parts of the country.

Russell was the chief figure among the American theorists of educational reform. There can be little doubt that his popular journal was a major influence in building the sentiments which led to the founding of the first infant school societies two years after the first issue of his journal appeared. Born in Scotland and trained at Glasgow under Professor George Jardine, Russell was one of the first to begin teaching in America the new European doctrines which had begun to influence educators in England.[15]

In Boston the sequence of events leading to the establishment of infant schools was almost precisely the reverse of the process in England. William Russell's attentions were drawn early to the infant school system by the publications of Samuel Wilderspin, William Wilson, and other teachers of infant schools in Britain. The system thus came to America more or less intact, where theorists of educational reform such as Russell were quick to notice its novelty and its possible applications in the American setting. Boston already had over 50 primary schools in operation—schools which accepted children as young as four years old. As a result of the relative availability of educational opportunity for even the very young of all classes of society, Russell's enthusiasm for the infant school system was understandably placed more upon the pedagogical theories than upon the idea of creating new institutions. Certainly he advocated the establishment of infant schools, but he saw them primarily as pilot schools for proving the value to the public school system of the exciting new principles. His major problem was to find a group in Boston with the interest, the expertise, and the financial resources to found the first infant schools and to sustain them long enough to prove the efficacy of their principles.[16]

Russell's efforts to encourage Bostonians to found an infant school were successful in 1828. By that time such schools had been in operation in Philadelphia and New York for nearly a year and favorable reports on their progress had appeared in Boston newspapers as well as in the *American Journal of Education*. In that year two separate infant school societies were founded, one opening a school on Salem Street and the other a school on Pleasant Street.[17] As there is only sketchy information available on the Salem Street society we will concentrate on the much more solidly documented activities of the Infant School Society of the City of Boston, which favored the Pleasant Street School. Due to the lack of evidence, our analysis also excludes the private infant schools in Boston which catered to middle- and upper-class pupils.

In the June, 1828 issue of the *American Journal of Education*, Russell announced with obvious satisfaction a meeting of some 90 Boston ladies at the home of Mrs. William Thurston. After a prayer from Reverend Thomas H. Skinner, they proceeded to organize the Infant School Society of the City of Boston. The details of this announcement said a good deal about the new society. Mr. Thurston, a lawyer of considerable wealth, was a leading figure in the orthodox Trinitarian reaction to the Unitarian establishment. Similarly, Reverend Skinner had been recently called from Philadelphia to serve in one of Boston's newly organized Trinitarian churches. It appears that the women who formed the new society were a part of a remarkable group of Bostonians who set out with evangelical fervor in the second decade of the nineteenth century to rescue the city from the moral and spiritual lassitude of Unitarian complacency. Though well-to-do middle-class citizens, the Trinitarian commitment of the group kept them apart from the Unitarian-dominated elites of Boston.[18]

In a certain sense, the membership of this group was ideally suited to carry out William Russell's hope for the establishment of an infant school. The husbands of these ladies had pursued a large variety of reform efforts during the decade since they had organized the Society for the Religious and Moral Instruction of the Poor in 1816. The credo of these men had been set forth clearly in the third annual report of that society where they emphasized the relationship between poverty, vice, and ignorance and proposed that moral and religious instruction were much more effective deterrents to crime than ''the mere dread of legal punishment.''[19]

The society had been a major influence in the establishment of the primary schools in Boston, had pursued a program of bringing religious instruction to the city's seafaring population, and had founded and maintained an ambitious Sabbath-school program for the children of the poor. The Sabbath schools accepted children as young as five, instructing them during most of the day on Sunday. The curriculum was not entirely the learning of scriptures and catechisms, as a serious effort was made to instruct the children in rudimentary reading, writing, and ciphering.

The infant schools in Boston were thus initially underwritten by social reformers who saw in them a means of combating the ills of urban society. The first infant schools in London had drawn their support from a similar group. But there is a significant difference in the role played by the groups which founded and sustained the two movements. Whereas in London the social reformers first established infant schools and then called upon the educational theorists for guidance in teaching young children, the process was exactly the reverse in Boston. Educational theorists such as Russell advocated the establishment of infant schools because they were attracted to the progressive pedagogical theories applied to infant education in Europe. The Boston social reformers responded to Russell's pleas willingly though with very different goals in mind.

Most of the discussion of the social reformers about the value of infant schools concentrated on their usefulness in dealing with urban problems. This was of particular relevance in a state such as Massachusetts, which was much more urbanized than the rest of the nation during the entire ante-bellum period.[20] Nonetheless, though the Commonwealth, particularly the eastern counties, was relatively quite urban by the 1820's, the great increase in the percentage of people living in large urban areas over 8,000 persons did not occur until the late 1830's—after the decline of the infant education movement in the state.

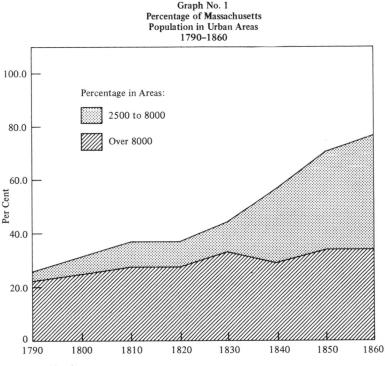

Graph No. 1
Percentage of Massachusetts
Population in Urban Areas
1790–1860

Percentage in Areas:

2500 to 8000

Over 8000

Graph No. 1

Boston was the largest urban area in Massachusetts throughout this period. Though it had a smaller population than cities such as New York and Philadelphia, it experienced many of the social problems due to urban crowding and rapid population growth.[21] But just as in the state as a whole, the period of the most rapid population growth occurred after the peak of enthusiasm for the infant schools.

It is difficult to obtain accurate estimates of levels and trends in

SOURCE: Maris A. Vinovskis, ''Demographic Changes in America from the Revolution to the Civil War: An Analysis of the Socio-Economic Determinants of Fertility Differentials and Trends in Massachusetts from 1765 to 1860,'' unpublished Ph.D. thesis, Harvard University, 1975, pp. 310, 324.

poverty and crime for nineteenth-century Boston. One very crude approximation of the level of concern about these problems is indicated by the per capita expenditures of the city on these issues.

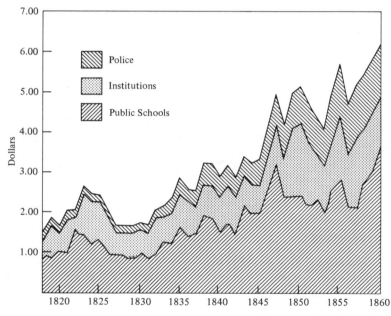

Graph No. 2
Boston's Per Capita Expenditures on Public Schools, Institutions
and Police, 1818–1860

Graph No. 2

It is interesting to note that the per capita expenditures for institutions for the poor and the mentally ill as well as for the police were considerably less than the expenses of educating the children in the public schools. Furthermore, these expenditures did not increase drastically during the period when infant schools were being advocated.[22]

SOURCE: Calculated from Charles Phillips Huse, *The Financial History of Boston from May 1, 1822, to January 31, 1909* ("Harvard Economic Studies," Vol. XV; Cambridge, Mass., Harvard University Press, 1916), pp. 348–351.

CHART No. 1

KNOWN INFANT SCHOOLS IN THE CITY OF BOSTON 1828-1835*

Location (See Map)	Founded	Closed	Instructor	Enrollment+	Note
Schools of the Infant School Society of the City of Boston					
1A Pleasant St.	June 1828	August 1828	Miss Blood	0	Moved to Bedford St.
1B Bedford St.	August 1828	1833	Miss Blood	129	Closed by competition of 2 neighboring schools.
4A Stillman St.	1829	1835	0	73.8	Reported moved to Charlestown St.
4B Charlestown St.	1835	0	0	0	Planned, but no evidence that school was opened.
7 Garden St.	Oct. 1833	0	Miss Mary Jones	65.3	In the Mission House.
Schools of the "Other Infant School Society" of Boston					
2A Salem St.	June 1828	Before July 1829	B. Alcott	50	Alcott left in Sept. 1828 to found own school.
2B Atkinson St.	By July 1829	Before April 1832.	Mrs. Brush	0	
2C Theatre Alley	By April 1832	0	Mrs. Brush	0	New building built for the school.
8 Broad St.	By Oct. 1835	0	0	0	Assumed to be supported by this society, though this is uncertain.
Private Schools					
3A Common St.	Oct. 1828	April 1829	B. Alcott	20	Name of Common St. changed to Tremont St. in 1830, but Alcott's 2nd school in new location, near St. Paul's.
3B Tremont St.	April 1829	May 1830	B. Alcott	30	
5 Belknap St.—African	Summer 1830	0	0	0	Established by Miss E.O. Lane
6 Near Bedford St.	By 1833	0	0	0	

*Numbers indicate order of founding. Letters indicate new location of same school—i.e. same instructor.
+ Annual average of all known figures.
0 No information available.

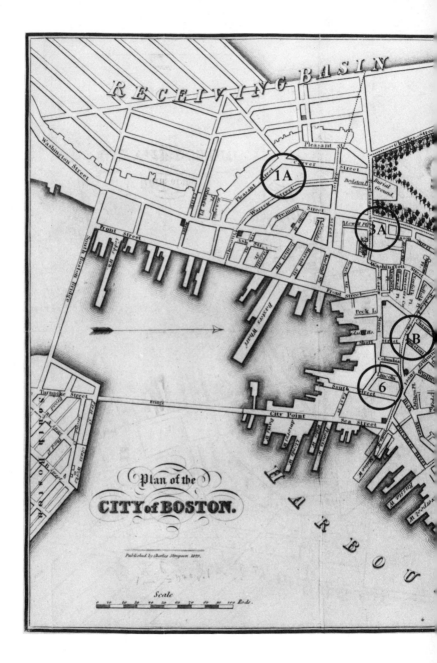

Plan of the
CITY of BOSTON.

Published by Charles Simpson 1829.

Scale

0 10 20 30 40 50 60 70 80 90 100 Rods.

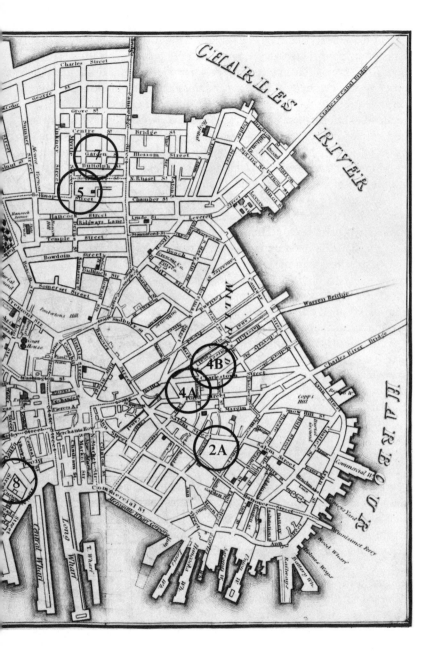

But the interest and focus of social reformers in Boston on the problems of the poor is missed by examining only public expenditures on the poor. The crucial changes during this period were not in the financial costs to society but rather in the attitudes of the reformers. Social reformers began to distinguish among different types of poor and attempted to reform them morally as well as to provide them with a means of livelihood. More attention was now given to breaking the vicious cycle of poverty by reaching the young children within the homes and providing them with the social norms and necessary skills to escape from a life of continued dependence on society.[23]

The issue of poverty was the major factor motivating the founders of the two infant school societies in Boston. They saw in the infant schools a means of permanently eliminating poverty by educating and "properly" socializing children from poor families.

Crime rather than poverty had been uppermost in the minds of the founders of the Infant School Society in London. But it appears that the incidence and severity of crimes in Boston were much lower than in Europe. Though crime was often mentioned by the American advocates of infant education, they usually used the term "vice" rather than "crime" in describing the evils the schools were intended to prevent. There are few indications of concern for immediate public safety in the arguments on behalf of infant schools or references to gangs of young hoodlums terrorizing whole districts of the city as there were in England.[24]

Since 1816, when Owen had founded his infant school at New Lanark, the infant school movement in England had been viewed as an ideal means of dealing with the harmful effects of industrialization. It offered the advantage of providing an institution for the moral and literary instruction of the urban poor at the earliest possible age while their mothers were freed to work. As Massachusetts was a leader in industrial development in America during the 1820's and 1830's, one might have expected that the social reformers in this state would have reiterated the arguments of their English counterparts. Yet the nature of the manufacturing system in Massachusetts minimized the usefulness and need of relieving working mothers from caring for their children. Most Massachusetts manufacturing firms using female labor tried to hire young, single women rather than married women with young children. In Boston itself manufacturing was not of major economic importance during the 1820's and 1830's.[25] As a result, even when the advocates of infant education did use the argument that the schools freed the mothers to work, the nature of the employment opportunities for those women was not specified.

A sizable immigrant community existed in Boston by the 1830's, especially Catholic Irish. During the first three decades of the nineteenth century, native Bostonians and the immigrants lived in relative harmony. Hostility increased against the Catholic immigrants in the 1830's, but it seems unlikely that fear of immigrants was the major motivating factor in the establishment of infant schools. The Boston infant school societies had closed their doors before the large waves of Catholic immigrants and the increasing hostility between the Catholics and Protestants in the 1840's occurred.[26]

Our review of social conditions in Massachusetts and Boston in 1828 suggests that population growth, the level of poverty, crime rates, industrialization, and immigration were not yet causing problems sufficiently grave to account for the early support given the infant education movement. Rather, the importation of instruments of reform caused educational reformers to seek out objects for the use of their new techniques. Social problems in Boston were not so severe at this time as to encourage social reformers to see their crusade as an Armageddon. The reformers' arguments placed more emphasis on the need to avoid the excesses of English urbanization and industrialization than on combatting the same type and degree of problems in Boston. Ironically, just as the infant education movement began its sudden decline, most of the social problems mentioned above became increasingly serious. The gradual intensification of social problems, however, did not save the already faltering infant schools because the causes of their demise were not based on their relevance or lack of relevance to the social conditions of the city.

What, then, were the circumstances which led to the decline of the infant schools, just at the time when the need for them was becoming most acute? The first circumstance arose from the hopes and expectations of the ladies who had accepted part of William Russell's arguments and determined to support the schools. The ladies who founded the Infant School Society of the City of Boston were less concerned about educational reform than they were about moral reform. They saw infant schools as an extension of the work their husbands had been so long engaged in with their Sabbath schools. Believing the infant mind to be especially susceptible to influence of its environment, whether good or bad, and having used this argument to garner support for Sabbath schools, it was a natural step to extend the beneficient influence of such schools to still younger children.

The officers and managers of the society throughout its known existence were a small, closely knit group. Nearly 20% of the entire number were wives or relatives of men who were officers or patrons of the Society for the Religious and Moral Instruction of the Poor. The group was composed entirely of ladies and the only official relationship of men to the society was a group of five men chosen each year to serve as a board of advisors, which included an auditor of accounts and a physician. Management of the schools seems to have been entirely under the guidance of the women. This is in marked contrast to the Sabbath school movement, and a careful reading of the infant school movement's discussions seems to reveal a modest degree of militancy in the insistence that the schools provided one educational cause which fell squarely and exclusively within women's provenance. Characteristic is the 1830 assertion in the *Ladies' Magazine* that " . . . it is well observed that *'females* have many natural qualifications for instructors of infants,' which men have not—it is also true that females are competent, and might be advantageously employed in the business of education to a far greater extent than has ever yet been practiced."[27]

The relatively small group of women who were the officers and managers of the Infant School Society are those whom we have singled out and designated the "social reform" group. They were those whose devotion to the cause sustained their activity and commitment whatever vicissitudes were to befall them. Their financial resources were not sufficient in themselves to be able to support the society. In their effort to raise funds they were able to mobilize the support of a much larger body of Boston women—mostly of the orthodox congregations. These women we have chosen to call the "civic-minded social elites"—women who read their *Ladies' Magazine*, kept up on current fashions, and were quick to respond to causes which the core of social reformers would bring to their attention. It was these women who formed the larger body of patrons of the society in its early years and who supported the annual fund-raising fairs conducted by the society during its first three years of operation.

By February, 1829, the *Ladies' Magazine* was reporting that

> The interesting subject of Infant Schools is becoming more and more fashionable. . . . We have been told that it is now in contemplation, to open a school for the infants of others besides the poor. If such course be not soon

adopted, at the age for entering primary schools those *poor* children will assuredly be the *richest* scholars. And why should a plan which promises so many advantages, independent of merely relieving the mother from her charge, be confined to children of the indigent?

The editor of the magazine then added a long list of arguments for the founding of the infant schools for the well-to-do, including the evocation of the charming image of the father, after coming home from a hard day at "counting-room or shop," being pleased to hear his son "with his yet scarcely formed accents . . . singing our national air . . . to the words, 'Five times five are twenty-five, and five times six are thirty, and five times seven are thirty-five, and five times eight are forty.' "[28]

This enthusiasm mounted when the infant schools began to give public demonstrations early in 1829. The founding of infant schools for the children of the well-to-do had already begun and extension to the outlying villages was under way. More public demonstrations were to follow in short order. Infant schools had clearly become a favorite charity of the Boston orthodox community.

Public demonstrations were to contribute to exaggerated public expectations and misunderstandings of the nature of the schools. The ladies in the infant school movement were primarily interested in the potential of the institutions as instruments of moral reform in the community. And yet, how does one demonstrate the progress made in reforming the morals of infants? The very name chosen for the institutions, "infant *schools*;" the fact that those who taught were called "instructresses;" and the whole experience of the public with the concept "school" determined what the standard of success would be. A public trained over decades to think of schools as institutions where children were taught order and discipline so that they might master the fundamental skills of reading, writing, and ciphering found itself captivated by the idea that two- or three-year-olds were capable of learning what it had been previously thought only older children could learn.

The public assumption that infant schools were the same as primary schools, except that they taught younger children, was subversive to the intentions of William Russell as well as to those of the ladies of the Infant School Society. The reformers were unsuccessful in convincing the public that infant schools embodied new principles, the efficacy of which could not be judged by the old standards and assumptions. The institutions had been tagged by their founders with the name "schools." The public demonstrations necessitated the display of their accomplishments as "schools." Once the image had been firmly set there was no other basis upon which the institutions could demonstrate their worthiness of public support and emulation. Initial tactical errors denied Russell his hope of seeing the pedagogical techniques of infant schools spread into the public school system.

In an 1829 address Russell stressed his desire that infant school methods be adopted by public schools.

An Important subject in immediate connection with the present subject, is the good effected by infant schools, through their influence on elementary instruction generally and the useful hints which they offer for the management of primary schools, and even of arrangements of the nursery.[29]

Yet given the negative attitude of the Boston School Committee, and especially the Primary School Board, with regard to innovations in the schools, there was little chance of the infant schools or their principles being adopted into the public schools in any major way. The persistent hints by Russell and others that the infant schools offered great benefits to the public school system were specifically taken up by the Primary School Board in 1830. After gathering information from teachers of primary schools who had accepted children from infant schools, they cited the observations of John P. Bigelow as typical of the reports they had received:

With regard to children from "Infant Schools," it is the decided opinion of every instructress in the district, who has had any experience on the subject, that it is better to receive children into the Primary Schools who have had no instruction whatever, than those who have graduated with the highest honors of the Infant Seminaries. It is stated that these children are peculiarly restless in their habits, and are thereby the cause of restlessness and disorder among the other children; and it does not appear that their previous instruction renders them, in any respect, peculiarly proficient or forward in the studies of the Primary Schools.

Other teachers reported the infant school children as "intractable and troublesome, restless from want of constant excitement, and their attention fixed with difficulty upon their studies." The Primary School Board, in condemning occasional introductions of "Exercises in geometry, geography, and natural philosophy" into some primary schools, had already made it clear that it saw its mandate to be that of training the children in "correct reading and thorough spelling" only.[30]

It is no wonder that the Boston Primary School Board objected to the deportment of pupils from the infant schools. For the issue was fundamentally between two different conceptions of the infant mind and its capabilities and nature. Derived from these differing conceptions were opposite theories on the purposes and techniques of teaching children. The theory which lay behind the infant school movement was in essence an early challenge to the Enlightenment establishment by Romantic reformers. In the Boston of the 1830's there could be little doubt as to the immediate victor.[31]

The Primary School Board had no fundamental objection to teaching children of tender years. The fact that the primary schools accepted children as young as four years by law was evidence of that fact. But they could not imagine that the infant mind, blank and open as it was, should be approached in any other manner than through the strict discipline and the rote memorization which had always been a part of their experience. Nor could they imagine that education could serve any other purpose than to prepare children to read and write—to make them more efficient recipients of the knowledge which society had to offer them. This, to them, was the meaning of schools and schooling.

Added to the conflict of opposing ideas of proper teaching principles was the simple problem of expense. As we have already seen in Graph No. 2, the period of retrenchment in public expenditures of all kinds which followed Mayor Quincy's expensive reforms continued until about 1831.[32] And when the expenditures began to rise again, the proportion spent on schools did not grow as rapidly as other city services. The Boston public officials simply were unwilling to expend much money on primary school education. While there are dramatic increases in the amounts spent on the higher level schools beginning in 1831, the expenditures on primary schools show only a moderate increase. Since the cost of educating a child in the infant schools was quite high, it was unlikely that the political leadership in Boston during these years would be willing to incur that additional expense even if they had approved of the institutions in principle.

There were also major obstacles which prevented the infant schools from continuing as private philanthropies. It has been noted that Pestalozzian principles made their dramatic entry into this country as part and parcel of the infant school idea. But by the late 1820's Pestalozzi's ideas were flowing to America through other channels as well— channels which gave American educators an opportunity to see them in a context other than that of infant schools.

The early literature of the infant school movement reveals a belief that, under normal circumstances, the home was the most desirable place to begin infant instruction. Both the theorists and the sponsors of the infant schools belied their uneasiness in perpetuating the unnatural act of taking children of the poor from their own homes when they defended the infant schools as homes themselves—homes likely to promote the happiness of both children and society in ways that their natural homes would never do.

The enthusiasm shared by those in the movement for the reform potential of the schools, however, overcame whatever qualms may have existed about taking children from their parents:

> Such is the power of bad example—especially that of parents—that it will probably do much to counteract the good influence of the infant school. Indeed there would be every thing to fear, were not its good influences brought to bear on the mind so early. Making every allowance for this evil, will not these children, trained up under the same system, be better than they; and perhaps, in the third generation, the work of moral renovation will be complete. Then ignorance and vice will be gone and poverty must go too.[33]

But the later stream of Pestalozzian teachings concerning infant education—a stream which came to America free of the association with infant schools—reinforced a growing attitude among Boston's elites that the infant is better off at home whenever possible. An interesting expression of the direction of this evolution was made by the editors of the *Ladies' Magazine*, who in their early enthusiasm had suggested as a part of their 1829 argument favoring infant schools for children of all classes that "it is nearly, if not quite impossible to teach such little ones at home, with the facility they are taught at an infant school. And if a convenient room is prepared, and faithful and discreet agents employed, parents may feel secure that their darlings are not only safe but improving."[34] Still enthusiastic about the schools a year later, in May of 1830, they nonetheless had changed their emphasis to the importance of the schools in their effects upon the common schools and especially upon the home: "In the nursery—that retired and scarce heeded place of instruction, but which nevertheless shapes more minds than all the public schools on earth—these experiments on the infant mind will operate with a power that must cause a great and rapid change."[35] By 1832, though still urging support for the schools, the editors displayed a revealing lapse of memory when they maintained, "We have never urged their adoption, by those who have the means to provide for their infants, and the time to take care of them. These poor mothers have neither."[36]

Such a change in views suggests to us that the civic-minded social elites of Boston were imbibing through their *Ladies' Magazine* and the

Annals of American Education the aspect of Pestalozzi's teaching which the advocates of infant schools had obscured—that the home was the proper institutional setting for the education of infants and that the informed mother was the best instructress. Pestalozzian principles, as embodied in the infant school system, had captured the public imagination by offering the promise that children could be taught at a very early age. This novel conception of making use of "what has hitherto been considered the waste years of human life" gave infant schools their early impetus.[37] But shortly the fuller exposition of Pestalozzi's thought began to work *against* the institutions, as his stress upon the home and family as the ideal "infant school" permeated the attitudes of Boston's elites.

Still another strand of current European educational theory tended to diminish enthusiasm for the infant schools as it came to be better understood in Boston by the early 1830's. This was the concept of the necessity for a *balance* in a child's early education—not only training the intellect but also developing the body and the spiritual faculties. The Boston infant schools, at least throughout most of their history, appear to have been shining exemplars of this "balance" principle. Every effort was made to provide a play ground and recess period for the children and there was much emphasis upon marching and clapping exercises and moral lessons. It is also clear that in the short run, physical and moral development is much more difficult to demonstrate than intellectual (or academic) achievement; and the leaders of the movement felt impelled to show quick, dramatic results in order to garner the public financial support needed to continue the schools. Thus, the infant school became associated in the public mind with the type of demonstration of intellectual precocity so glowingly referred to in early remarks about the infant schools in the news media, such as opens this essay. While these displays of the infant school children's intellectual advancement were very helpful in gaining initial financial support for the infant schools, they also created an image of those schools that made them very vulnerable to the charge that they were promoting premature intellectual precocity at the expense of more balanced development.

In 1829 William Russell gave up his editorship of the *American Journal of Education* in order to assist Bronson Alcott in founding his own infant school for a wealthy patron in Pennsylvania. His successor, William C. Woodbridge, had just returned from a long stay at Hofwyl, the estate of European educational reformer Philipp de Fellenberg. Fellenberg maintained the mind could not properly be instructed unless adequate attention was given to the development of the body. Physical exercise occupied nearly half the daily routine of pupils in his school.[38] The "manual training schools" which began to be popular about this time were undoubtedly influenced by his theories. William Woodbridge began immediately to stress in his journal the importance of physical development and of timing intellectual training with the proper stage of physical growth. While continuing to encourage early education, Woodbridge was hedging the idea with qualifications which were certain to diminish the shallowly rooted public enthusiasm for infant schools.[39]

Woodbridge pushed the point in his August, 1830 number when he compared the training of children with that of plants, animals, or athletes. He said that training should begin early, but with great attention to the changing capacities of the child at each stage:

> It is too little considered . . . *when the infant begins* to be a proper subject of training, and at what age he may become in one respect or another, *insensible to its influence*. . . .
>
> All the efforts of misjudging teachers and parents who wish to see their children early prodigies, only sacrifice the fruit in order to produce an earlier expansion of the flower, and resemble the hot-bed in their influence in 'forcing' a plant to maturity, whose feebleness or early decay must be proportional to the unnatural rapidity of its growth, and a consequent want of symmetry in its parts.[40]

Such expressions became increasingly common in the *American Journal of Education* after Woodbridge assumed editorship in 1830. The dire hints of "feebleness" and "early decay" can hardly have escaped the notice of the civic-minded social elites whose donations were the major source of support for the infant schools. The increasing emphasis upon a balance between physical and intellectual cultivation, itself a part of Pestalozzi's principles of education, was eroding public support for the idea of infant schools which the public had once found so much to its liking.

The final blow may well have been the Boston publication in 1833 of Amariah Brigham's *Remarks on the Influence of Mental Cultivation and Mental Excitement upon Health*. The preface to the first edition, which had appeared the year before in Hartford, made the author's intentions clear:

> The object of this work is to awaken public attention to the importance of making some modification in the method of educating children, which now

prevails in this country. It is intended to show the necessity of giving more attention to the health and growth of the body, and less to the cultivation of the mind, especially in early life, than is now given.[41]

The influence of Brigham's book was nothing short of sensational. There is every indication that his intentions, as expressed in the preface, were quickly and dramatically realized. Favorable reviews were published in the *Annals of American Education,* the *Christian Examiner and General Reviewer*, and in the *Ladies' Magazine*. Especially significant is the fact that the *Ladies' Magazine*, which had made the schools objects of special attention almost since their founding, made no mention whatsoever of them in its 1834 editions. But their February number *did* include excerpts from Brigham on the causes of insanity, which listed "the predominance given to the nervous system, by too early cultivating the mind and exciting the feelings of children" as the second most important cause.[42] That same year, our own tabulation of articles opposing infant schools in Boston journals went from a previous high set in 1828, when there were two such articles, to seven. And all of those seven related early instruction to the danger of either mental or physical debilitation in children.

It is important to note that Brigham's book did not cause the parents of the infant poor to withdraw their children from the schools. The enrollment in those schools for which we have records are higher than in any year since 1831. Attendance figures are closer to enrollment figures in both the Stillman Street School and the Garden Street School than they had ever been—both the attendance and enrollment being between 60 and 65 pupils for each school. Even more impressive is the fact that the token weekly payment which the ladies of the society asked of the pupils' families had risen from its lowest figure of $.75 per pupil per year to $1.35 per pupil per year in 1835 (see Graph No. 3). Apparently the parents of the children who attended the society's infant schools were sufficiently convinced of the value of the schools that they were sending their children in greater numbers and willing to pay more for the privilege in spite of the dire warnings of Amariah Brigham.

Nor did the ladies of the society seem to lose faith in their reform movement. They did all within their power to correct the "hothouse" image which they had been trapped into cultivating. They explained their position in the last annual report we have been able to find:

In commending Infant Schools to the attention of the Christian community, we wish their nature and design to be distinctly understood, and kept in mind. They are not *schools* in the common acceptation of the word. The use of this appelation has probably done much to excite a prejudice against them. They may with more propriety be termed neighborhood nurseries, or infant asylums.[43]

The ladies went on to urge financial backing, not only for the existing schools, but also for sufficient funds to found several more to meet the needs of a growing number of children in various parts of the city.

If Amariah Brigham's book did not deter the parents of the infant poor from sending their children to the schools, nor the social reformers who made up the Infant School Society from continuing their support, how does one account for the collapse of the society? We would suggest that the key group involved in both the rise and the decline of the movement was that large body of civic-minded women who were initially willing but later reluctant to support the society. Their donations and contributions at annual fund-raising fairs helped keep the society solvent during the years when infant schools were a fashionable cause. Priding themselves on keeping in touch with the latest intellectual currents, literate and well-informed, they were a most sensitive barometer of the rise and fall of intellectual fashions.

The ladies of the smaller reform group were more constant because they had invested much more in time and thought to sustaining the movement. Moreover, they were convinced that as instruments of reform the infant schools were as badly needed as ever. The parents of the infant poor probably were not aware of Amariah Brigham or the implications of his writings until they found one day that the infant schools had closed their doors for want of funds.

The surviving annual budgets of the Infant School Society of the City of Boston, as portrayed in Graph No. 3, would seem to substantiate our hypothesis. The most striking aspect is that the society's annual records show a decline from a positive balance of $380 in 1832, the year before Amariah Brigham's book was published in Boston, to a negative balance of $372, the year that the book was published. It should also be noticed that the greatest volume of that decline by far was in donations—exactly the category where we expect to find the large group of civic-minded social elites. A solid core of subscribers remained and even grew in the subsequent year. The church collections which brought the budget nearly into balance in fiscal 1834 were the result of a special campaign promoted by the pastors of the Park Street, Essex Street, Bowdoin Street, and Federal Street Baptist churches. Our judgment would be that they represent an expression of loyalty to their pastors and their churches rather than any special enthusiasm to the cause of infant education.

It is also interesting to observe that the deficits occurred in spite of a continuing decrease in operating expenses gained through cutting back the costs of both housing and teachers' salaries from the peak of fiscal 1830. Note also the contribution of the pupils rising from 1832 in volume and even more dramatically in proportion to the total income of the society. There can be no doubt that the society continued to enjoy the solid support of those for whose benefit it was intended.

What, then, was the ultimate cause of the demise of the Infant School Society of the City of Boston? The trend in social conditions would seem to argue that the need for the schools as envisioned by the ladies of the society was never greater than in the late 1830's. One can only conclude that in this instance the underlying social conditions were not as important to those in Boston who might have sustained the society as were the tides of intellectual fashion. Convinced by ideas expounded in Amariah Brigham's book and in a number of current intellectual journals, the ladies recoiled from the thought that their benevolence, far from ensuring the eradication of poverty and vice, might be contributing to the insanity of future generations. There is a heavy irony in the fact that their reaction was against a misleading image of infant schools which their advocates had felt forced to assume in order to gain these ladies' support.

The demise of the Infant School Society of the City of Boston symbolized the end of efforts to create educational institutions designed specifically for infants in the Boston area until Elizabeth Palmer Peabody began the kindergarten movement in the 1860's.[44] It will be remembered, however, that an early hope of William Russell, among others, was that the principles and spirit of the infant schools would be taken into the public schools and that if this were achieved the survival of infant schools as separate institutions was not important. There is some evidence that in the 1830's and 1840's the Boston Primary School Board did adopt some of the progressive techniques that had been earlier advocated by educational theorists such as William Russell. But it would be impossible to say with confidence that such proposals came from the infant school movement, since, as we have indicated, not all of the innovations in educational techniques for children of the period came directly from the infant schools themselves.

One distinctive feature of the infant school system was its advocacy

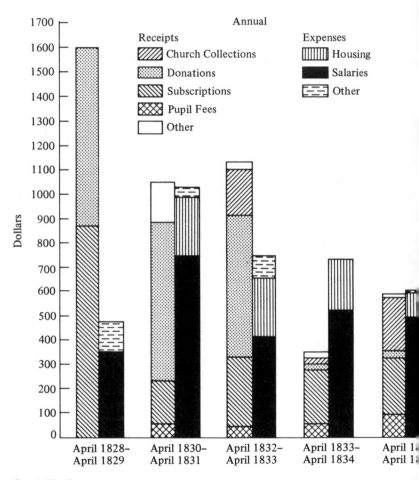

Graph No. 3
Annual Budgets for the Infant School Society of the
City of Boston, 1828–1835

Graph No. 3

NOTE: The budget of fiscal 1828 is misleading because of difficulty in interpreting their bookkeeping procedures. It probably does not account for all of the expenses of setting up the first schools. The four remaining budgets are divided into two bars, that on the left representing the receipts in any one fiscal year (exclusive of balances brought forward) and that in the right representing the expenses for that year. Receipts are further divided into subscriptions, which we regard as the firmest expression of support for the infant school movement; donations, which we would regard as a less firm commitment of of the practice of sending children to school at much earlier ages than had hitherto been the practice. In studying the practices of parents in the ages at which they send their children to school, there is hope of finding evidence for the possible influence of the infant school movement upon the general public. In Boston such an influence is impossible to detect because it was one of the few towns in the Commonwealth that specifically excluded children under four from attending the public schools. But in some of the outlying towns where infant schools are known to have existed, the public school systems did not specify a lower age of admissions to the public schools. In those areas we can get a glimpse of public behavior on the issue of educating young children.

In this regard, it might first be useful to describe how we were initially brought to this study of the infant school movement in Boston. Our attention was called to the movement by a recent discussion of the influence of Horace Mann upon public education in nineteenth-century Massachusetts. Data collected and analyzed independently by Albert Fishlow and Maris Vinovskis suggested that the enrollment rate in the public and private schools was stable or even declining in Massachusetts during the period of Mann's tenure as the secretary of the Board of Education. This appeared to be a startling reversal of traditional interpretations of Mann's impact on the school system in the state. Upon closer examination of the data, Vinovskis noted that most of the decline in the rate of attendance came in the group of children under four and that the attendance record of children between four and sixteen, the category on which Mann had focused his efforts, actually increased. The reputation of Mann on this point seemed safe.[45] But the observation had raised interesting questions about public attitudes toward the rearing and training of young children in the first half of the nineteenth century.

Vinovskis' data revealed that for the earliest period when relatively reliable school attendance data is available, a surprisingly large percentage of children under age four were attending schools. In 1840 at least 10% of the children under four were in school statewide, and many localities had a much higher percentage attending.[46]

Not only was there a high percentage of young children attending

---

support in that they do not involve being enrolled in the society; church collections, which we regard as the least firm expression of support for the society in that they are solicited by the pastors of the churches and represented a more direct loyalty to the pastor and the cause of religious charity than to the infant schools themselves. The pupils' fees are self-explanatory and the "other" category consists primarily of interest earned on the society's bank accounts.

schools in the 1840's and 1850's statewide, but there was a steady decrease of children under the age of five attending school during those decades. The dramatic change in the ages at which parents chose to send children to school in the decade between 1840 and 1850 suggested to us that attitudinal changes toward young children, their place in society, and their aptitudes might lie behind the statistical record. Accordingly, we began to search the earliest possible Massachusetts educational journals to see if there was explicit discussion of infancy and the role of infants in public education.

In general there was very little mention of the public education of very young children outside the context of infant schools. But there were some hints that in the 1820's there might have been a major shift in the attitudes toward sending young children to schools. William Russell mentioned in 1826 that "within a few years public sentiment has undergone a favorable change on the subject of early education."[47] We also noticed occasional references to the Boston practice of accepting children in primary school as early as four years as being quite unusual. The Sabbath school movement practice of accepting children no younger than age five was further evidence for the supposition that the sending of children to schools at ages younger than four was not a common practice. It was then that we began to consider the possibility that the flurry of intense devotion to the cause of educating children as early as possible generated by the infant school movement might bear a relationship to the large numbers of children under four attending public schools in the 1840's and that some of the causes which led to the abrupt decline in enthusiasm for infant education among reformers in the mid-1830's might be related to the later gradual decline in public practice of sending infants to school in the late 1840's and 1850's.

Our hypothesis suggested, in fact, that the reformers who pushed the cause of infant education in the 1820's and 1830's might have been more effective than the abrupt and early end of the institutions they created would suggest. Unfortunately, there is very little data currently available to test this hypothesis. We were successful in obtaining data from one Concord primary school that leads us to suggest very tentatively that the practice of sending infants into public schools may have been influenced by the infant school movement in areas where this practice was not banned outright by law.

Teachers in the East Centre District School for the Concord school system kept a record of the names, dates of admission and withdrawal, parentage, ages, days attended, and days absent of all of their pupils

over a twelve-year period extended from 1830 to 1842.[48] It is possible
to analyze this data for a full decade in order to get at least one small
glimpse into the public practices in sending children to school before
reliable school reports on the attendance of young children are available
for the state.

Graph No. 4 shows an age distribution of the children attending the
East Centre District School from 1830–1842.

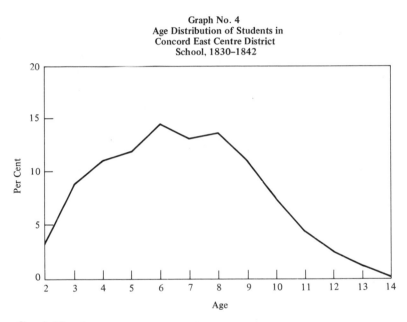

Graph No. 4
Age Distribution of Students in
Concord East Centre District
School, 1830–1842

Graph No. 4

As we can see from the above graph, a sizable percentage of the children enrolled were under the age of four. We would like to examine
changes over time in the percentage of children under four in the East
Centre District School but we are handicapped by the lack of information on the number of children under four who were expected to be
served by this particular school. One way of getting an estimate of
changes over time would be to calculate the percentage of children
under four in that school during this period. There is some danger,
however, that the total population of the school might be a misleading
base figure since there was no set age at which one entered the next

higher school—the Concord grammar school. As a result, if there were any changing pattern in the ages at which children entered the grammar school, it would distort our results. Consequently, we decided to use the percentage of children attending the East Centre under age four compared to all students under nine since this age cutoff would minimize our chances of making a miscalculation due to changes in the age when children left primary schools.

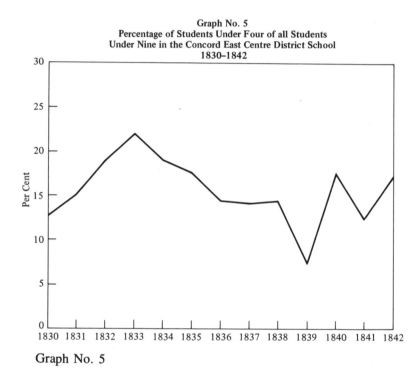

Graph No. 5
Percentage of Students Under Four of all Students
Under Nine in the Concord East Centre District School
1830–1842

Graph No. 5

Graph No. 5 shows that the percentage of students under four of all students under nine in the Concord East Centre District School was following an upward trend in 1830 at the time the data is first available. A steady rise in the percentage of students under four continued to a peak in 1833 of nearly 22%. It is interesting to note that this peak year is the same in which Amariah Brigham's book was published in Boston; and that thereafter an erratic, though obvious, decline occurred until we lose the data in 1842. We have no satisfactory explanation for the erratic changes in the percentage of students under four between 1838 and 1841 and we are well aware of the dangers of overgeneralizing from one case, especially when the total number of pupils in any given year was usually under 100. The data we have presented on Concord, however, is the only information currently available on enrollment practices of young children before 1840. On the basis of this limited statistical information and the few literary references we have on this issue, we would like to offer a tentative hypothesis of the effect of infant schools on the school enrollment of the general public.

The infant school idea of sending children to school at ages younger than had been previously the practice *did* gradually influence the general public throughout the state. This was particularly true in towns like Concord that had infant schools established within them though we suspect that the general attitude penetrated into areas which had not set up such schools. The impact of the arguments against sending young children to school, which was felt so sharply in Boston, was less pronounced in outlying areas. The common people were not as responsive to new intellectual currents as were the well-to-do citizens of Boston. A decline in the practice of sending young children to school *did* occur, but as a secular trend it was very slow to return to the level of such practice in 1830. It lingered through the 1840's and gradually died out in response to the formalization of public school system regulations which eventually set lower limits on ages of admission. This probably resulted from a disinclination upon the part of teachers to tolerate the extra attention and special techniques required to keep the youngest children from disrupting the work of older children. But the almost total absence of discussion of what the lowest ages of admission to schools should be makes such hypotheses little more than guesses. The absence of such discussion is itself evidence that the attentions of the Horace Mann generation of educational reformers were focused upon upgrading the upper levels of the school system. They were simply not as concerned about the problems of the young child first entering the school system.

The 1860's and 1870's saw a resurgence of interest in early education. This interest drew its impetus from the writings of Friedrich Froebel, a student of Pestalozzi's, who had visited the famous school at Yverdun while the great master was still alive and who in 1840 began his own infant school, which he christened with the felicitous name *"Kindergarten."* The kindergarten movement spread rapidly in America, achieving a degree of establishment which the infant school movement had not even approached.

It cannot be said with confidence, at this stage in our knowledge, why the kindergarten movement flourished while the infant school movement declined. There was little difference in the principles or techniques of the two systems. In fact, David Salmon treats the kindergarten as part of the movement which had begun at New Lanark. In America the connection seems to have been completely forgotten.[49] One immediately thinks of the great influx of immigration which had taken place since the 1830's and the possibility that educators felt a more pressing need to find a means of acculturating the children of immigrants into American society than they felt in the 1830's. One also suspects that the magnitude of the problems due to poverty, urbanization, and industrialization were much more severe than in the 1830's. Also, by 1870 the cause of public education had a wide following and a strong professional bureaucracy to support it. There was not the ambiguity over responsibility for public education and objectives of educational innovation which had characterized the Boston infant movement of the 1830's. In addition, it is significant that the kindergartens took children no younger than three years of age, thus mitigating the threat to the home and family implicit in the infant education movement. But ultimately, one suspects, the leaven of the continental tradition of educational reform had by 1870 time to do its work. The theories and techniques recommended by kindergarten advocates and the conceptions of infancy from which they came were not as alien to the American mind in 1870 as they were in 1830. And perhaps there was much to Froebel's fortunate choice of a name for his institution. A garden seems an entirely appropriate place for even the youngest of children. A school does not.

NOTES

1. Boston *Recorder and Scriptual Transcript*, July 9, 1829.

2. David Salmon and Winifred Hindshaw, *Infant Schools: Their History and Theory* (London, Longmans, Green, and Co., 1904), pp. 8, 17. Salmon and others refer to Jean Frederic Oberlin (1767–1826), who founded several schools for the children of Alsatian peasants in the last quarter of the eighteenth century. Oberlin's work was not continued, however, and Owen's infant school was the model for later infant schools on the Continent as well as in England and America. For Owen's account of the founding of the infant

school at New Lanark, see his autobiography (first published in 1858), *The Life of Robert Owen by Himself* (New York, Alfred A. Knopf, 1920), pp. 191–212.

3. An account of plans for an infant school in Hartford, Connecticut, is reprinted from the Hartford *Observer* in the Boston *Recorder and Scriptual Transcript*, February 22, 1827. The *Recorder* enthusiastically reported the founding of infant schools in Philadelphia on February 1 and 8, 1828. The *American Journal of Education*, III (June, 1828), 346–356, reported the founding of the Infant School Society of the City of New York.

4. The most complete account of the founding of the Infant School Society of the City of Boston is in the Boston *Recorder and Religious Telegraph,* April 18, 1828. The opening of an infant school by the Infant School Society of the City of Boston is reported in the *First Annual Report* of that society (Boston, T. R. Marvin, 1829), pp. 7–8. The Salem Street infant school, opened the same month under Amos Bronson Alcott (1799–1888), was sponsored by another infant school society. We have been able to unearth little concerning this latter society. Alcott left the Salem Street school to found a private infant school of his own in October, 1828, as described in Dorothy McCuskey, *Bronson Alcott, Teacher* (New York, Macmillan Company, 1940), pp. 51–54. Reference to the opening of other infant schools in Boston and in Massachusetts is made in the Infant School Society of the City of Boston, *Third Annual Report* (Boston, 1831), p. 9. Further references to reports of this society will be designated Infant School Society, *Nth Annual Report,* 18. Scattered references to infant schools in other Massachusetts towns have been found in several sources, especially the *American Journal of Education* and in occasional surviving annual reports of the societies which sponsored the schools. *Ladies' Magazine,* published in Boston under the editorship of Sarah J. Hale from January, 1828 to December, 1836 was unusually attentive to the progress of infant schools. This publication reported on the African infant school in vol. 3 (May, 1830), p. 239 and (October, 1830), p. 485. See Chart No. 1 and the accompanying map for further information on the founding and location of Boston's known infant schools.

5. The most striking example is Elizabeth Palmer Peabody. Through her association with Alcott she was actively involved in the infant school movement in the 1830's. Yet, when she became a leader in the kindergarten movement in the 1860's she made few explicit references to her earlier experiences and did not stress the obvious similarities and common antecedents of the two movements. For a study of her career, see Ruth M. Baylor, *Elizabeth Palmer Peabody: Kindergarten Pioneer* (Philadephia, University of Philadelphia Press, 1965).

6. Hugh M. Pollard, *Pioneers of Popular Education, 1760–1850* (Cambridge, Mass., Harvard University Press, 1957), provides a good summary of the contribution of these figures to modern educational theory.

7. A most competent and useful study of the early nineteenth-century emphasis upon the mother in education is found in Ann L. Kuhn, *The Mother's Role in Childhood Education: New England Concepts, 1830–1860* ("Yale University Studies in Religious Education," Vol. XIX; New Haven, Connecticut, Yale University Press, 1947). On the role of women in education during these years, see Richard Bernard and Maris A. Vinovskis, "Women and Education in Ante-Bellum America," paper presented at the Berkshire Conference on Women's History, Cambridge, Massachusetts, November, 1974.

8. Pestalozzi's ideas played a major role in influencing American education. For analyses of his career and impact, see Gerald Lee Gutek, *Pestalozzi and Education* (New

York, Random House, 1968); Will Seymour Monroes, *History of the Pestalozzian Movement in the United States* (Syracuse, Bardeen, 1907).

9. Pollard, in *Pioneers of Popular Education,* pp. 133–145, reviews the state of popular education in Britain in the early decades of the nineteenth century. For a very useful discussion of the Lancastrian/Bell system of monitorial instruction in Britain, see Carl F. Kaestle, ed., *Joseph Lancaster and the Monitorial School Movement: A Documentary History* ("Classics in Education," No. 47, New York, Teachers College Press, 1973), pp. 1–49.

10. From the "First Essay" of Robert Owen's *A New View of Society,* first published in 1813. Quoted from *Robert Owen on Education,* ed., Harold Silber (Cambridge, The University Press, 1969), p. 76.

11. Samuel Wilderspin (1792–1866) gave an extensive account of the founding of the first infant schools in London in his *Infant Education; or Remarks on the Importance of Educating the Infant Poor, from the Age of Eighteen Months to Seven Years* (3rd edition, London, J. S. Hodson, 1825), pp. 8–40. A list of infant schools functioning in 1825 is found on page 284. Wilderspin was instructor of the second infant school founded in London and became self-appointed apostle of the movement, traveling extensively throughout England, Scotland, and Ireland promoting the establishment of infant schools. His *Infant Education* was probably the most widely read of all infant school manuals.

12. Wilderspin, *Infant Education,* pp. 17–40.

13. Frank Luther Mott, *A History of American Magazines, 1741–1850* (Cambridge, Mass., Harvard University Press, 1957), p. 490.

14. "Prospectus," *American Journal of Education,* I (January, 1826), 4–6.

15. Russell's close friend and colleague, Amos Bronson Alcott, contributed to the infant education movement as instructor of infant schools and as author of an important tract, *Observations on the Principles and Methods of Infant Education* (Boston, Carter and Hendee, 1830). His primary activity was as instructor rather than publicist, however, and his opinions as to the objectives of instruction quickly became so idiosyncratic as to limit his influence upon the broader movement. The purpose of educating young children became for Alcott to elicit the spiritual nature of those who in point of time he thought to be closest of all men to undefiled spirit. In encouraging the free expression of the infant mind he was a practioner and advocate of continental theory. But while he promoted the methods of the continental theorists his objectives were almost wholly theological—to better understand the nature of spiritual existence. His schools were founded not so much as institutions to better instruct children as to better instruct himself in eternal truths. Thus his contribution to the infant education movement was not so significant as that of William Russell and we have not treated him as a major figure in this study. For a discussion of Alcott's relationship to the infant education movement, see Odell Shepherd, *Pedlar's Progress: The Life of Bronson Alcott* (Boston, Little, Brown and Company, 1937), pp. 120–135.

16. For a statement of his position on infant schools, see William Russell, *The Introductory Discourse and Lectures Delivered in Boston before the Convention of Teachers, and Other Friends of Education to Form the American Institute of Instruction, August 1830* (Boston, Hilliard, Gray, Little and Wilkins, 1831), p. 101.

17. See notes 3 and 4.

18. Russell's announcement is in the *American Journal of Education,* III (June, 1828), 383. A profile of the Trinitarian community of the Boston of this period emerges from J. Leslie Dunstan's useful *A Light to the City: 150 Years of the City Missionary Society of Boston, 1816–1966* (Boston, Beacon Press, 1966).

19. Boston Society for the Religious and Moral Instruction of the Poor, *3rd Annual Report*, p. 22.

20. For a discussion of urban development during this period, see Jeffrey G. Williamson, "Ante-bellum Urbanization in the American Northeast," *The Journal of Economic History*, XXV (December, 1965), 592–608. On the growth of Boston in particular, see Peter R. Knights, *The Plain People of Boston, 1830–1860: A Study in City Growth* (New York, Oxford University Press, 1971) and for a critique of some of that book's statistical analysis, see Maris A. Vinovskis's review of it in the *Journal of Interdisciplinary History*, III, No. 4 (1973), 781–786.

21. For a general introduction to the problems of Boston during this period, see Oscar Handlin, *Boston's Immigrants: A Study in Acculturation* (rev. edition; New York, Atheneum, 1968), pp. 1–24. Though Boston experienced many of the same social problems as New York and Philadelphia, living conditions in Boston were probably significantly better than in the other two cities before 1860. Maris A. Vinovskis, "Mortality Trends in Massachusetts Before 1860," *Journal of Economic History*, XXXII, No. 1 (1972), 184–213.

22. Most scholars agree that poverty was less prevalent in America than in England in the first half of the nineteenth century. There is considerable debate, however, on whether there was an increase or decrease in the amount of poverty in America during this period. For instance, Raymond Mohl argues that there was an intensification of poverty in northern cities at the beginning of the nineteenth century. Raymond Mohl, *Poverty in New York, 1783–1825* (New York, Oxford University Press, 1971), pp. 3-34. Unfortunately, we do not have adequate quantitative studies of the level or the extent of poverty in nineteenth-century America to arrive at any definitive judgment at this time. It is unlikely that the increases in the levels or the extent of poverty in American cities before 1840 was of such a large magnitude that they by themselves account for the sudden increased interest in this subject by social reformers. Rather, we suspect that the growing belief in the early nineteenth century that poverty was not inevitable in all societies led social reformers as well as the general public to become more aware of and interested in solving the problems of urban poverty.

23. Carroll Rosenberg dates this shift in attitudes toward the poor in the 1820's and 1830's in New York City. Carroll Smith Rosenberg, *Religion and the Rise of the American City: The New York City Mission Movement, 1812–1870* (Ithaca, N.Y., Cornell University Press, 1971). Redmond Barnett's analysis of the poor in Massachusetts locates this shift between 1812 and 1820. Redmond Barnett, "From Philanthropy to Reform: Poverty, Drunkenness, and the Social Order in Massachusetts, 1780–1825" (unpublished Ph.D. dissertation, Harvard University, 1973).

24. Roger Lane's investigation of the development of the Boston police found little evidence of a high level of crime in Boston during this period. In fact, before the 1830's Bostonians were content to rely upon constables and watchmen for their safety and it was only after the inability of the police to handle the anti-Catholic mob violence that a new and more professional police force was recruited. Roger Lane, *Policing the City: Boston, 1822–1885* (New York, Atheneum, 1971), pp. 3–58.

25. Caroline F. Ware, *Early New England Cotton Manufacture: A Study in Industrial Beginnings* (New York, Russell & Russell, 1966); Norman Ware, *The Industrial Worker, 1840–1860: The Reaction of American Industrial Society to the Advance of the Industrial Revolution* (Boston, Houghton Mifflin, 1924); Handlin, *Boston's Immigrants*, pp. 9–11.

26. Handlin, *Boston's Immigrants*, pp. 25–177.

27. *Ladies' Magazine*, III (April, 1830), 189.

28. *Ladies' Magazine,* II (February, 1829), 89–90.

29. William Russell, *Address on Infant Schools* (Boston, Tupper, 1829), p. 13.

30. Joseph M. Wightman, *Annals of the Boston Primary School Committee* (Boston, G. C. Rand and Avery, 1860), pp. 123, 125. For a very useful, comprehensive discussion of Boston public schools during this period, see Stanley K. Schultz, *The Culture Factory: Boston Public Schools, 1789–1860* (New York, Oxford University Press, 1973).

31. See John L. Thomas, "Romantic Reform in America, 1815–1865," *American Quarterly,* XVII (1965), 656–681, for an insightful overview of pre-war reform. Thomas' emphasis upon the tendency of the Romantic reformers to place their hopes for reform in moral regeneration of the individual rather than in established institutions is supported by our study. Though the social reform group we have studied, in fostering infant schools was creating a new institution, these schools were expected to be the institution to end all institutions. The infant schools, by giving proper moral instruction to the children of unregenerate parents at the earliest possible age and by insulating the children as much as possible from the harmful influences of improper homes and corrupting street life, were expected eventually to eliminate the need for all other reform institutions.

32. For an analysis of Josiah Quincy's policies during his period, see Robert A. McCaughey, "Josiah Quincy, 1772–1864: The Last of the Boston Federalists" (Ph.D. dissertation, Harvard University, 1970).

33. Infant School Society, *5th Annual Report,* 1833, pp. 5–6.

34. *Ladies' Magazine,* II (1829), 89–90.

35. *Ladies' Magazine,* III (May, 1830), 224.

36. *Ladies' Magazine,* V (April, 1832), 180.

37. Infant School Society, *3rd Annual Report,* 1831, p. 12.

38. A detailed discussion of the regimen at Hofwyl can be found in Pollard, *Pioneers of Popular Education,* pp. 42–52.

39. "Education of Infants," *American Annals of Education,* I (May, 1830), 204.

40. "Infant Education," *American Annals of Education,* I (August, 1830), 355–356.

41. Amariah Brigham, *Remarks on the Influence of Mental Cultivation and Mental Excitement upon Health* (Hartford, F. J. Huntington, 1832), p. iii. The preface of this first edition was reprinted without change in Boston by Marsh, Capen & Lyon, 1833, 2nd edition, p. vii.

42. *Ladies' Magazine,* VII (February, 1834), 79.

43. Infant School Society, *7th Annual Report,* 1835, p. 79.

44. One infant school founded in Charlestown in 1833 did survive into the 1870's though in a form significantly altered from that of the early infant schools. By 1870 its primary activities were the care of orphaned children though it apparently continued, with little success in attracting a clientele, to serve as a day-care center. It is significant that by 1870 its director was not called an instructress but a matron. This school had apparently survived by successfully achieving the transition in character from school to home, a transition which was made official in 1870 when the name was changed to the Infant School and Children's Home Association. It had become by 1870 a very modest enterprise with fewer than ten children in residence. Infant School and Children's Home Association, *First Annual Report* (Boston, Arthur W. Locke & Co., 1870).

It is possible that private infant schools or infant schools in other Massachusetts towns survived the decade of the 1830's though we have as yet been unable to find evidence of such survival.

45. Albert Fishlow, "The American Common School Revival: Fact or Fancy?" in

Industrialization in Two Systems: Essays in Honor of Alexander Gershenkron, ed., Henry Rosovsky (New York, John Wiley and Sons, 1968), pp. 40–67; Maris A. Vinovskis, "Trends in Massachusetts Education, 1826–1860," *History of Education Quarterly,* XII (Winter, 1972), 501–529.

46. When Mann first inaugurated the procedure of requiring school committees to report the number of children under four in school in 1840, many of the school committees were unable to give information on this question because they had not required their teachers to keep sufficiently detailed records. Unfortunately, when Mann reported the number of children under four in his annual report, he did not make the distinction between towns which were able to provide information on this question and those that were unable to because of inadequate records. Therefore, calculating the percentage of children under four in 1840 who were attending school from Mann's annual report underestimates that figure. An examination of the local manuscript returns for 1840 indicates that the actual percentage of children under four in school in 1840 would be about 13% rather than the 10% figure derived from Mann's published annual report for that year. Most local school committees immediately remedied their lack of information on this question by 1841 so that the number of children under four reported by Mann is a very good estimate of the actual number of children in that age group in school after 1840. For a further discussion of the problems of Massachusetts school data, see Vinovskis, "Trends in Massachusetts Education."

47. "Prospectus," *American Journal of Education,* I (January, 1826), p. 6.

48. We would like to thank the Concord Free Public Library for permission to use the manuscript records of the East Centre District School and we are indebted to Mrs. William Henry Moss, reference librarian of the Concord Free Public Library, for her invaluable help and guidance.

49. Marvin Lazerson's *Origin of the Urban School* provides important insights into public education in Massachusetts between 1870 and 1915. In dealing with the kindergarten movement, however, he has apparently followed the lead of its nineteenth-century promoters and failed to notice that four decades earlier the founders of infant schools had sought to employ early education as an instrument of urban social reform. Especially puzzling, in view of the widespread attention to early education in the 1830's (of which infant schools were only one expression) is Lazerson's assertion that "not until the end of the nineteenth century did American educators generally acknowledge the importance of the early years in shaping adult behavior." Marvin Lazerson, *Origins of the Urban School: Public Education in Massachusetts, 1870–1915* (Cambridge, Mass., Harvard University Press, 1971), p. 41. For a fuller discussion of this issue, see Dean May's review of Lazerson's book in *The Family in Historical Perspective,* No. 5 (Fall, 1973), pp. 4–7.

5

Rip Van Winkle's Grandchildren: Family and Household in the Hudson Valley, 1800–1860

STUART M. BLUMIN

In recent years, several wide-ranging and systematic studies have demonstrated that rural development, as opposed to urban growth, contributed most heavily to a 30% decline in fertility in the United States in the period 1800–1860.[1] Those who have advanced this point, of course, do not doubt that fertility declined rapidly in American cities during this period, but correctly point out that in 1800, and even in 1860, the urban population was too small to have had any profound effect on the national fertility rate. This fact alone suffices to tell us that the pronounced decline in American fertility occurred on farms and in country towns, where, as late as 1860, more than four-fifths of the American population resided. Still, it is curious that those who have so meticulously analyzed the rural contribution to fertility decline have given so little effort to comparing fertility rates in particular localities of differing size and character.[2] It is regrettable that they have not considered the influence of cities on the formation of rural families. Both of these tasks, as well as others relating to the precise structure of rural and urban households, are best accomplished in the context of the developing economic region.

The purpose of this paper is to investigate the basic structures of family and household within the localities of a single, developing region of ante-bellum America—the Hudson Valley of New York State. How did these structures change during the first sixty years or so of the nineteenth century? Did fertility decline at even rates throughout the valley, or did it follow different patterns in the cities and in the countryside? Did households change significantly in composition: that is, in the numbers of persons and the types of family and nonfamily relationships contained within them? Again, are there important differences to be noted between town and country? These are a limited set of questions to be sure, but they relate to the basic structural interactions between economic development and family life, and to equally interesting questions concerning the impact of regional development on rural and urban social organization. Regional economic development ordinarily produced a landscape clearly differentiated into cities, towns, and rural townships of varying size and character. At the same time, it increased the interdependence and the tempo of exchange between those who lived on commercial farms and those who lived in nearby entrepôts and manufacturing centers. Did farmers (and their wives and children) grow more like the city people with whom they exchanged increasing amounts of farm produce, retail goods, credit, and information? Or did the physical differentiation of the region simply create wide gaps in the life styles and values of its rural and urban people? Rural-urban differentials in fertility and household structure provide one answer, and probably a very important one, to the general question of whether economic development increased or decreased the differences between the city and country.

At first glance the Hudson Valley might appear to be a surprising locale for this analysis. Following Diedrich Knickerbocker, American historians have tended to regard the region lying between the cities of New York and Albany as something of a picturesque curiosity. Colonized by a nation which made no other significant contribution to the American population, encumbered with "feudal" land tenures and a "landed aristocracy" unknown north of Maryland, and, partly for this reason, lying largely undeveloped until the nineteenth century, the Hudson Valley was indeed a rather curious exception to the general structure of colonial society from Pennsylvania to New Hampshire.[3] During the course of the nineteenth century, however, the valley lost much of this social and cultural distinctiveness. The semi-feudal land system did remain intact in many places until quite late in the century, and the special beauty of the river and the highlands survives even today. But by mid-century the Hudson Valley was no longer simply a region of patroons, Dutch farmers, and beautiful "prospects." The Hudson River

Railroad now supplemented steamboats and innumerable other craft in transporting freight and passengers between the eastern terminus of the Erie Canal and New York City. The latter had become America's first great metropolis. Between the canal and the metropolis, scattered villages and partly developed farmland gave way to industrial cities, large commercial villages, and fully developed agricultural towns. Immigrants from Ireland, Germany, and Canada worked the mills, shops, docks, and decks owned by Yankees as well as Yorkers. The land of Wouter Van Twiller and Rip Van Winkle, in short, had become part of the urbanizing, industrializing world of nineteenth-century America.

This configuration of rapid development from a long-standing rural base line actually makes the Hudson Valley a highly useful locale for the study of the interactions between family structure and urban-industrial growth. Unlike those areas to the west which developed rapidly out of frontier conditions, the eighteenth-century valley contained a relatively "normal" distribution of age groups and sexes, and a stable core of long-settled families. Yet, compared to other Eastern regions, its nineteenth-century growth was a more dramatic departure from a more static, or at least more undeveloped, past. The peculiarities of the region, moreover, have been overemphasized. There were, in fact, large numbers of fee simple farms and independent yeomen in the Hudson Valley, and the Dutch farmers there did not *all* sit around smoking their pipes while Hendrik Hudson's men played ninepins in the "Kaatskills."

Comparing the domestic arrangements of all Hudson Valley towns, of course, would be an enormous and cumbersome undertaking. Instead, I have selected three localities, each representing a significant variant of the region's economic development, and have collected sufficient information to permit a close analysis of their families and households. The first, the city of Troy, was a young, rapidly growing industrial center, founded and settled late in the eighteenth century, mainly by business-minded New Englanders who quickly put the stamp of commerce and industry on what a few years earlier had been a nondescript portion of the Manor of Rensselaerswyck. By 1860, Troy, with a population of just under 40,000, was the Hudson Valley's third largest city (behind New York and Albany) and an important center for the processing of metals and the manufacture of machinery.[4] The second town, Kingston, was quite different from Troy. Settled in the mid-seventeenth century by farmers from Rensselaerswyck, Kingston retained its agricultural character until shortly after it became the terminus of the Delaware and Hudson Canal in 1828. Its growth after that date was steady but not dramatic—from a population of about 3,000 just before the canal was built to a population just under 17,000 in 1860. Unlike Troy, Kingston failed to develop a significant amount of modern manufacturing. Local quarries produced increasing amounts of bluestone and limestone, and much of the latter was processed in local lime and cement plants; but Kingston's economic development during this period is best described as commercial. Always a center of sorts for the mid-valley grain trade, Kingston became, after the construction of the canal and several plank roads, an important entrepôt for the Hudson's west bank and for the rapidly developing farmland just beyond the Catskills in Delaware and Chenango counties.[5]

The third town, Marlborough, was a thoroughly agricultural rectangle of land lying along the west bank of the Hudson, about twenty miles below Kingston and some seventy miles north of New York. Not all of Marlborough's men were farmers, of course, but the craftsmen, storekeepers, and professionals who resided in its two small villages did serve a population which was overwhelmingly agricultural through and well beyond the period considered here. Marlborough developed slowly in the eighteenth century, receiving most of its settlers from Westchester County and Long Island after 1750. By 1782, according to a local survey, there were just over 1,600 white inhabitants. By 1820, when the total population stood at about 2,250, some 60% of the acreage of the town had been improved by local farmers, most of whom appear to have been freeholders rather than tenants. Real pressure on the land, however, was just beginning. By 1855, more than 80% of Marlborough's potential farmland was improved, and a trend toward growing berries and other fruits for nearby urban markets and resorts was already under way. By 1860, Marlborough's population was just under 3,000.[6]

Let us turn first to a comparison of fertility in these three very different towns. As we would expect, the refined fertility ratio (that is, the number of children under 10 years of age per 1,000 women aged 16–44) declined rather dramatically in all three towns between 1800 and 1855; the decline was no more dramatic in the industrial city than in the rural township (Table 1). It is true that fertility declined somewhat earlier in the city than in the countryside, and that at all three census years the most urban of the towns displays the lowest ratio (Kingston in 1800, Troy in 1820 and 1855) while rural Marlborough displays the highest. In 1820, moreover, the differences between the fertility ratios of the three towns are quite pronounced, ranging from 1,198 in Troy to 1,751 in Marlborough. Still, the most striking figures in Table 1 are those which show that by 1855 these differences had nearly disappeared—that in all three towns the numbers of young children relative to the numbers of women of childbearing age were just about the same.

The reasons for reduced fertility in rural towns such as Marlborough are not difficult to locate; nor are they terribly different from the reasons for reduced fertility in cities. It is traditional to associate declining urban fertility with the increasing cost of living space in cities, and with the

Table 1 | Refined Birth Ratios: Troy, Kingston, and Marlborough, 1800, 1820, and 1855

Year:	Troy	Kingston	Marlborough
1800a	1,801	1,573	2,024
1820b	1,198	1,433	1,751
1855c	908	1,077	1,115

SOURCES: a. *Return of the Whole Number of Persons Within the Several Districts of the United States . . . (Washington, 1802).*
b. *Census for 1820 . . . (Washington, 1821).*
c. *Census of the State of New York for 1855 . . . (Albany, 1857).*

general economic burden of children who go to school rather than to work, who eat but do not earn. (It might be mentioned here that Troy's industries and Kingston's stores and quarries did not employ many children.) More recently, it has been recognized that similar spatial and economic pressures may operate in developing agricultural areas. Philip Greven, for example, has demonstrated the consequences of rural de-velopment in colonial Andover, Massachusetts, where the eventual al-location and domestication of nearly all of the township's arable land forced young men to seek opportunities elsewhere; more to the point, it caused many parents to begin to limit the numbers of children they would ultimately be called on to provide with livings.[7]

The pressure was not precisely the same as it was in the cities, for children were still assets during much of their dependency, but it was real and its effect was the same. To use Yasukichi Yasuba's phrase, the "availability of easily accessible land" was the crushing concern of those farmers who knew that the family farm could no longer withstand further subdivision, and who had no wish to sire a generation of sons thrown on the road and their own luck.[8] Where nearby land was availa-ble it could be purchased for younger sons, or even added to the original farm before subdivision. Where it was no longer available, or too expensive, farmers could marry later, could attempt to limit their offspring, and could do their best to find a place for those who did arrive. The declining birth rates that Yasuba and others have found in developing rural areas indicate how seriously farmers regarded this responsibility.

Was urbanization, then, only a minor component of the causes of fertility decline in the United States during the first half of the nineteenth century? I would suggest that the decline of fertility in the countryside was very closely bound up with the growth of cities and towns. For one thing, the emergence of urban markets and a transportation system capable of reaching them steadily increased the degree to which America's business-minded farmers (and I would exclude very few from this category) could participate in commercial agriculture. This commercialization, of course, served to fuel the expectations of rural folk, and to make it less and less acceptable to divide the family farm below the point of surplus production. But of greater significance is the fact that American farmers did not disperse evenly or randomly across the countryside. Good soil, water, terrain, and other natural considerations made some areas better than others, of course, and so did man-made phenomena such as cities, canals, and railroads. Rural development, east and west, followed the course of transportation routes to urban markets, and even brought new markets, in the form of regional distribution centers, into existence. Some land, in short, filled up before other land, and two of the primary factors shaping this uneven development of the rural landscape were the growth and distribution of cities. Marlborough, New York, developed as fully as it did because other places, primarily cities, began demanding its products, and because an urban-based system of transportation and finance permitted their shipment. Whether this is called urbanization or regional development (note that the commercialization of the land was a cause as well as an effect of nearby urban growth) seems trivial. What is important is the recognition that rural development, and with it the decline in rural fertility, occurred in the context of both nearby and distant urban growth.

Fertility ratios are rather abstract quantities which do not readily translate into real families. It may be useful, therefore, to take a second look at the women and children of the three towns, this time placing them within their own homes and using as our source the manuscript schedules of the U.S. census of 1860.[9] In Table 2, the married women of Troy, Kingston, and Marlborough are arranged into five-year age cohorts and are identified with the numbers of their children living with them. The resulting averages for each cohort are not quite perfect (for example, some "mothers" are really stepmothers), but they do provide a sufficiently accurate picture of the pattern of childbearing in the three towns.[10] In all three, the averages rise to somewhat above three children before tapering off in the 45–49 and 50–54 age cohorts. The decline among older women reflects the fact that their children were beginning to leave home and serves to remind us that we are probably not capturing the "completed" family in any of our cohorts. That is, since some children were born after their eldest siblings had already left home, we cannot claim that Table 2 reveals the total number of children raised by the mothers of Troy, Kingston, and Marlborough. What it does reveal,

Table 2 | **Average Number of Children in Household by Age of Mother (or Childless Wife): Troy, Kingston, and Marlborough, 1860**

Age of Mother:	Troy	Kingston	Marlborough
15–19	.46	.23	.13
20–24	1.05	1.01	.78
25–29	1.83	2.04	1.92
30–34	2.67	2.80	2.51
35–39	2.90	2.70	3.32
40–44	2.93	3.15	3.44
45–49	3.57	2.71	3.22
50–54	2.26a	2.39	2.21
55–59	1.20	2.26	1.21
60–64	1.31a	1.32	1.59
65–69	—	.52	.91a
70+	—	1.00a	.75a

a. n $\langle$ 20. Empty cells $\langle$ 10.

however, is that none of our towns, not even rural Marlborough, contained many households with great numbers of children. Two or three children under one roof was the rule rather than the exception in the countryside as well as the city.

The average sizes of households and families in the three towns are consistent with this fact. As Tables 3 and 4 demonstrate, households

Table 3 | **Average Household Size by Age of Household Head: Troy, Kingston, and Marlborough, 1860**

Age of household head:	Troy	Kingston	Marlborough
20–29	4.20	4.07	3.86
30–39	5.06	5.28	5.29
40–49	5.74	5.79	5.89
50–59	5.32	5.53	5.18
60+	5.18	4.98	4.56
All households	5.22	5.35	5.15

NOTE: Boarding houses, etc. are excluded.

averaged somewhat more than five persons in all three, and families (that is, related persons living within a single household) averaged between four and one-quarter and four and one-half. Both families and households "peaked" at the 40–49 age group cohort (which is based here on heads of household), where the average household approached six persons and the average family approached or exceeded five. It is only among these "approximately completed" families, incidentally, that the towns are arranged in order of size. But note that the differences are small, about as small, perhaps, as the differences among the refined fertility ratios of Table 1.

It may be argued that the existence of large numbers of highly fertile immigrants in urban populations obscures a real difference between the fertility of rural and urban natives. Troy and Kingston did have much higher proportions of immigrants in their populations than did rural

Table 4 | **Average Family Size by Age of Household Head: Troy, Kingston, and Marlborough, 1860**

Age of household head:	Troy	Kingston	Marlborough
20–29	3.49	3.47	3.31
30–39	4.37	4.59	4.57
40–49	4.98	5.10	5.17
50–59	4.28	4.70	4.42
60+	3.86	3.98	3.39
All families	4.27	4.52	4.33

Marlborough. Specifically, about half of the larger two towns, but only one-sixth of Marlborough, had come to the Hudson Valley from Ireland, Germany, England, Canada, and other countries. Many of these immigrants were Irish, and a majority conformed to the stereotype of the poor, unskilled, "dollar a day" laborer. But did they conform as well to the popular image of the Catholic Irishman as a prolific breeder of children? That this image was shared by some Kingstonians, at least, is indicated by the following excerpt from a piece of fictional humor in a Kingston newspaper, depicting, of all things, a census marshal's interview with a woman of "Balinale County, Longford, in ould Ireland," who has just startled the marshal by giving the ages of her fourth, fifth, and sixth children:

All three of them seventeen?

Yis shure, they were all thray uv them born twins; and then there's Kate, she's fourteen; and Biddy, she's twelve; and Dan O'Connel, he's ten [;] then comes Sukey, she's eight; and Luke, he's four; then Jim, he's two; and—*that's all at prisint!*

Why, Madam, you have a large family, and are fortunate so to have them all living for, I presume, you have had no death in your family circle.

And is it the graif uv me heart ye would now be raking up about me childer that is dead, waked and buried in ould Ireland! Hav'nt I lost four as swate babes as iver was born?[11]

Appropriately, it is the census marshal's own tabulations which give the lie to this image. In Table 5, Kingston's wives born in New York State, Ireland, and Germany are arranged into age cohorts and compared in terms of resident children. The differences are slight—indeed, we might even suggest a slightly higher birth rate among natives than among immigrants were it not for the likelihood that the immigrant averages are reduced more quickly by the departure of maturing children from the household. Let us consider native and immigrant fertility, then, to have been at approximately the same level.[12] To this we can add that about the same proportions of native and immigrant men were heads of household, and about the same proportions of native and immigrant adults (male and female) were married. Clearly, the presence of large numbers of foreign immigrants in the populations of Troy and Kingston does not distort the comparisons we have made between them and rural Marlborough. Nor, we may note in passing, does the somewhat more pronounced economic stratification of Troy and Kingston provide any difficulty—the average size of the households of those listing $100 or less in real and personal property on the 1860 census was almost exactly 4.7 persons in all three localities.

Fertility is the most obvious of those domestic phenomena affected by urban and economic development. In the American setting, at least, it also appears to be the most predictable.[13]

Table 5 | **Average Number of Children in Household by Birthplace and Age of Mother (or Childless Wife): Kingston, 1860**

| Age of Mother: | Birthplace of Mother | | |
	New York State	Ireland	Germany
15–19	.20	.43	.21a
20–24	1.00	.93	1.14
25–29	1.87	2.13	2.24
30–34	2.63	2.92	2.68
35–39	3.40	3.18	3.22
40–44	3.09	3.07	2.81
45–49	2.90	2.98	2.71
50–54	2.44	2.66	2.30
55–59	2.26	2.60	—*
60+	1.04	1.30	—*
n	(1,366)	(898)	(411)

a. Denominator $\langle$ 20.
*Denominator $\langle$ 10.

Only slightly less obvious, but considerably less apparent in its specific relationships with broader types of change, is the structure of households and families. Were extended-family households more characteristic of rural Marlborough than of Kingston and Troy? Did the larger towns more frequently augment their households with boarders, journeymen, apprentices, and servants? Did the cousins, in-laws, or boarders added to the basic nuclear family differ in any significant way between one locality and the others? What do these differences (or similarities) tell us about the interaction of economic development with the families of the city and the countryside? These questions are, it seems to me, logically prior to those which ask whether nuclear or more complex households are better suited to an urban-industrial society.

Table 6 provides a rough picture of the households of Troy, Kingston, and Marlborough in 1855.[14] Again, the similarities are far more striking than the differences. Approximately four-fifths of the households of each town were nuclear in structure, and in all three towns only a small percentage of households (ranging only from 4.8% in Troy to 7.6% in Marlborough) were extended to more than one relative beyond

Table 6 | **Family and Household Structure: Troy, Kingston, and Marlborough, 1855**

	Troy	Kingston	Marlborough
Family Structure (Extension)			
Nuclear	82.0%	80.2%	83.0%
Extended to one relative	13.2	13.2	9.4
Extended to two or more relatives	4.8	6.6	7.6
	100.0%	100.0%	100.0%
Household Structure (Augmentation)			
Family only	73.1%	72.6%	66.1%
Augmented to one nonrelative	14.2	14.7	19.7
Augmented to two or more nonrelatives	12.7	12.7	14.2
	100.0%	100.0%	100.0%
Household Structure (Overall)			
Nuclear family only	61.4%	60.3%	56.1%
One additional relative or nonrelative	19.1	19.0	22.2
Two or more additional relatives or nonrelatives	19.5	20.7	21.7
	100.0%	100.0%	100.0%
Number of households	643	2,744	513

the married pair and their children.[15] The proportions of augmented households were also quite similar, as were the proportions containing either nonrelatives or "additional" relatives. In all three towns, household augmentation was significantly more frequent than household extension, with one out of every seven or eight homes containing two or more nonrelatives, and another 14% to 20% containing one. Altogether, some 40% of the households of all three towns were extended or augmented, and approximately one in every five contained at least two persons other than the conjugal pair and their children.

These similarities of overall quantity need not imply that the specific patterns of household extension and augmentation were the same in all three towns. We might suppose, for example, that household extension followed the stem-family pattern in Marlborough, with one child (usually a son) remaining in the household, raising his own family there and ultimately succeeding his father as both household head and proprietor of the family farm. In Kingston and Troy, on the other hand, we might expect to find that most family extension resulted from the in-migration of various relatives, including brothers, sisters, cousins, nephews, and nieces, who had come to the city in search of a job and temporary quarters.[16] The overall quantity of extension could be quite similar under these conditions, but the underlying phenomena would obviously be quite different. Augmentation, too, might differ considerably between town and country. Rural boarders, perhaps, were hired hands who worked as well as lodged with the farm family, and who generally remained in the same household from one year to the next. Urban boarders, on the other hand, might have been far more transient, and far more peripheral to the life of the families from whom they rented quarters. In effect, both of these hypotheses claim that urban growth, but not rural development, altered the structure of the household, for the patterns they predict for Marlborough are regarded as traditionally rural ones.[17]

The pattern of family extension is probably most effectively revealed by examining the proportions of men and women bearing various relationships to each locality's heads of households. In the stem-family pattern we would expect to find relatively large numbers of sons, daughters-in-law, grandchildren, and, reflecting those households where the son has assumed control, relatively large numbers of mothers and fathers. In-migration, on the other hand, would produce larger proportions of brothers, sisters, cousins, nephews, and nieces of the household head. Given these assumptions, Table 7 suggests that we reject the idea that Marlborough extended its households through a stem-family inheritance system while Kingston and Troy extended theirs through in-migration. The overall patterns for the three towns are quite similar, and the differences that do exist do not point in the expected direction. There are higher proportions of resident sons and daughters in Marlborough, it is true, but this reflects the significantly higher mean age of the rural town's household heads (44, as compared

Table 7 | Household Status of All Inhabitants over Fifteen Years of Age: Troy, Kingston, and Marlborough, 1855

Relationship to Head of Household:	Troy	Kingston	Marlborough
Men			
Head of household	59.4%	58.1%	56.9%
Son	15.8	15.0	20.6
Grandson	—	—	0.3
Brother	1.7	3.2	2.5
Father	0.6	0.9	1.5
Nephew, uncle, cousin	0.6	0.4	0.4
In-law	1.5	1.6	0.4
Servant	0.1	1.4	0.3
Boarder, journeyman, or apprentice	20.3	19.3	17.1
	100.0%	99.9%	100.0%
Women			
Head of household	6.8%	5.3%	7.8%
Wife[a]	53.6	60.3	51.9
Daughter	13.3	12.7	20.7
Granddaughter	—	—	0.1
Sister	2.5	3.3	3.7
Mother	2.6	2.0	2.6
Niece, aunt, cousin	0.8	0.7	0.7
In-law	2.7	2.5	0.5
Servant	12.4	9.5	7.1
Boarder	5.4	3.7	4.9
	100.1%	100.0%	100.0%

a. A small proportion of wives (ca. 4%) are inappropriately classified as wives of household heads. These were wives of boarders and servants. The distortion is similar for all three towns.

with 38 in Kingston and 40 in Troy) rather than the continued residence of married children. In all three towns, nearly all of those listed on the census as sons or daughters were single young men and women in their teens or early twenties—indeed, the proportion married was slightly higher in Kingston and Troy, a fact further reflected in the somewhat higher proportions of male and female in-laws. In none of the towns were there many resident parents or grandchildren, while the most common type of family extension was the inclusion of siblings of the household head.

Neither Kingston, nor Marlborough, nor Troy, in short, seems to have maintained very many stem-family households in the mid-nineteenth century. Another indication of this is provided by Table 8, which arranges the household heads of all three towns into age cohorts. As Lutz K. Berkner recently has shown, the stem-family household fully reveals itself only during certain phases of the life cycle of the family—specifically, during the last years of the father's control, when his inheriting son has brought a wife and perhaps a child or two into the home, and during the first years of the son's control, while the father or mother remains. Aggregate proportions of nuclearity and extension, therefore, will often understate the significance of the stem family.[18] Table 8, however, reveals only a moderate degree of variation in nuclearity between the families of one age cohort and another. The proportion of nuclear-family households is high in all three of our towns for the youngest cohorts, as well as for those older cohorts whom we would expect to find at the head of nuclear families even if stem families were the rule. There is a noticeable decline among the oldest household heads, and this may very well reflect a degree of stem-family inheritance. Even so, it represents only a minor strain within the dominant

Table 8 | Age of Household Head by Family Structure: Troy, Kingston, and Marlborough, 1850

| | Percentage of Nuclear-Family Households | | |
Age of Head of Household:	Troy	Kingston	Marlborough
20–29	81.7	86.5	89.2
30–39	93.2	90.2	89.7
40–49	92.9	86.6	85.8
50–59	88.4	76.1	75.3
60–69	77.6	70.7	77.2
70+	72.7	69.4	71.9

nuclear pattern and is no more characteristic of the countryside than of the city.

The augmentation of households with boarders and other nonrelatives was a much more common phenomenon than family extension in all three of our towns. Moreover, it is here that we begin to find differences that appear to be significant, despite the fact that the proportions of nonrelatives in the populations of Troy, Kingston, and Marlborough were just about the same. For example, the male boarders, journeymen, and apprentices of the three towns were mostly young men, but they were significantly younger in Marlborough than in Troy (see Table 9). Occupational differences were more pronounced. In Marlborough, the large majority of boarders (71%) were unskilled workers, most of whom were farm laborers, while the boarders of Kingston and Troy were spread fairly evenly over the entire occupational structure. Troy's boarders, in fact, were somewhat underrepresented in manual, wage-earning jobs, particularly at the unskilled level. Consistent with this is the fact that Troy's boarders were also somewhat underrepresented among the foreign born, while Marlborough's were greatly overrepresented, especially among the Irish, who comprised 29% of the boarders but only 11% of the adult male population. Kingston again lay in-between, with a distribution more closely resembling Troy's than Marlborough's. Finally, the three towns varied considerably in the proportions of their male boarders who were themselves heads of families (that is, men who were married or who had children) and in the proportions of male boarders who lived in boarding houses rather than in private homes. Again, the differences are ordered according to the size of the town. Only 13% of Marlborough's male boarders were family heads, as compared with 14% in Kingston and 24% in Troy. Just under 10% of Marlborough's boarders lived in boarding houses, while almost 15% of Kingston's boarders and 31% of Troy's boarders lived in boarding houses and hotels.

The pattern of variation among the three towns could not be clearer. In rural Marlborough, boarding was essentially restricted to young, unmarried, hired farm hands, a disproportionate number of whom were of foreign birth. In Kingston and Troy, on the other hand, boarding was a far more generalized feature of social life, involving lawyers no less than laborers and natives no less than immigrants. Urban boarders were rather young as a group, but there were significant numbers of older men among them, and a substantial minority who were heads of families. In each of these respects, Troy, the largest of the three localities, was least like rural Marlborough.

It would appear, then, that the development of cities in the Hudson Valley did produce at least one significant difference between the domestic arrangements of its various localities. Boarding was nothing new, of course, and was not quantitatively more prevalent in cities than in the countryside, but it did develop along quite different lines in rural

Table 9 | Analysis of Male Boarders, Journeymen, and Apprentices: Troy, Kingston, and Marlborough, 1860

	Troy		Kingston		Marlborough	
Age	% of Boarders, etc.	% of All Men	% of Boarders	% of All Men	% of Boarders	% of All Men
16–29	57.5	43.5	60.3	40.6	72.6	39.9
30–49	33.3	42.4	30.2	45.2	20.1	40.4
50–69	6.6	12.0	7.1	12.6	6.1	16.3
70+	2.6	2.2	2.4	1.7	1.2	3.4
Total	100.0	100.1	100.0	100.1	100.0	100.0
Occupational Group						
Professionals	2.2	2.3	2.3	1.8	0.6	1.4
Merchants and manufacturers	13.6	13.4	5.2	8.6	1.8	5.4
Farmers	—	0.1	1.0	4.4	0.6	19.7
Clerical workers	16.2	8.6	5.9	4.3	3.0	1.5
Craftsmen	33.8	35.0	31.5	27.4	7.3	14.8
Semi-skilled workers	8.3	10.7	5.9	8.1	1.8	1.2
Unskilled workers	14.0	21.2	40.1	37.4	71.3	43.9
Other	2.6	2.6	0.4	1.2	0.6	2.4
No Occupation	9.2	6.1	7.8	6.7	12.8	9.7
Total	99.9	100.0	100.1	99.9	99.8	100.0

Table 9 | **Analysis of Male Boarders, Journeymen, and Apprentices: Troy, Kingston, and Marlborough, 1860 (continued)**

	Troy		Kingston		Marlborough	
Age	*% of Boarders, etc.*	*% of All Men*	*% of Boarders*	*% of All Men*	*% of Boarders*	*% of All Men*
Birthplace						
New York State	38.6	36.8	41.9	46.9	56.1	78.4
Other United States	16.7	12.2	2.9	3.1	3.1	3.2
Canada	4.4	4.1	0.3	0.3	—	—
England, Scotland	7.5	6.9	1.9	2.5	8.5	5.6
Ireland	27.2	35.6	35.8	31.7	29.3	10.8
Germany	5.3	3.9	13.9	14.3	2.4	1.7
Other	0.4	0.7	3.3	1.3	0.6	0.1
Total	100.1	100.2	100.0	100.1	100.0	99.8
% Heads of Families	23.7		13.9		12.9	
% in Boarding Houses	31.1		14.6		9.7	

and urban localities. On the other hand, there was one similarity between the boarders of Marlborough and the boarders of Kingston and Troy which may well have been more important than all of these differences. In all three towns boarders were extremely transient. As Table 10 indicates, more than 40% of the male boarders listed on the 1855 census had arrived in each of the towns within the previous two years, a figure which stands in striking contrast to the equivalent proportion for household heads, which in no town exceeded 20%. It is true that most of the remainder of Marlborough's boarders had been residents of the town for longer than a decade, but this proportion (44%) is considerably lower than the 73% pertaining to household heads. Moreover, only a small proportion of the boarders listed on the 1855 census remained to be listed again in 1860, and, more to the point, hardly any remained as boarders in the same households.

Table 11 summarizes an attempt to trace all of the male boarders of Marlborough and a sample of the male boarders of Kingston from 1855 to 1860. In both towns the apparent rate of out-migration was quite high, and half or more of those who did remain were no longer boarders by 1860.[19] Most were household heads, and it is interesting to note here the association between this transition and marriage in rural Marlborough, where the vast majority of boarders were single young men. Of the eleven boarders who had become household heads by 1860, only two had been married in 1855, but all eleven were married by 1860. Meanwhile, all nine of those who persisted as boarders persisted also in their bachelorhood. But the major point here is the very small number of boarders, in both towns, who remained in the same households over this five-year period. Only four boarders in each town, 3% of those identified in 1855, failed to pack their bags by 1860. In Kingston, three of these were residents of boarding houses, which leaves, from our sample of 131, only one who maintained quarters in a private home for as long as five years.

The fact that boarding was an institution of transiency in both the city and the countryside should cause us to modify the significance we might otherwise attach to the differing patterns of rural and urban boarding. With the possible exception of continuous migrants, boarding was for most a temporary phenomenon, facilitating either settlement into a new community, departure from the parental home, or both. As Modell and Hareven have found in a later period, most boarders looked past their temporary status to the time in the near future when they would establish households of their own. Very few children were raised in ''other

Table 10 | **Length of Local Residence, Adult Male Household Heads and Boarders: Troy, Kingston, and Marlborough, 1855**

Years of local residence	Troy		Kingston		Marlborough	
	Household heads	Boarders	Household heads	Boarders	Household heads	Boarders
0–2	14.4%	40.7%	19.7%	42.4%	10.1%	44.7%
3–5	17.2	21.4	24.8	29.6	8.5	4.9
6–10	23.5	16.1	21.0	13.7	8.5	6.8
11+	44.9	21.8	34.4	14.3	72.9	43.7
Total	100.0%	100.0%	99.9%	100.0%	100.0%	100.1%
n	639	243	2,466	767	435	103

people's" homes, or in boarding houses, and the role of any given boarder in the lives of the children of the household head was restricted to a few years at most.[20] The varying patterns of rural and urban boarding, in sum, do underscore real differences between cities and rural towns, but they do not demonstrate in themselves that these differences carried over in any significant way into family life.

Table 11 | Persistence of Boarders: Kingston and Marlborough, 1855–1860

	Kingston		Marlborough	
	n	%	n	%
Boarders, 1855	131[a]	100.0	131	100.0
Located in 1860 Census	30	22.9	22	16.8
Household Status, 1860:				
Boarders:				
In Same Private Household	1	0.8	4	3.1
In Same Boarding House	3	2.3	—	—
In a Different Household	11	8.4	5	3.8
Total Boarders	15	11.5	9	6.9
Heads of Household	13	9.9	11	8.4
Relatives of Head	2	1.5	2	1.5
Total Located in 1860	30	22.9	22	16.8

a. Represents a 16.7% systematic sample.

The same, of course, can be said of all the phenomena described in this paper, for we have raised only a few of the countless questions that can be asked about the family as a functioning institution. We have inquired into its structure, but not its life, and have found similarities where a functional analysis might have found differences. Nonetheless, the similarities we have found among the households and families of Troy, Kingston, and Marlborough are significant in themselves. They offer striking evidence that the distinction between "rural" and "urban" is most fruitfully conceived of in terms which include a due regard for the larger geographic contexts of economic and social development.

NOTES

1. Yasukichi Yasuba, *Birth Rates of the White Population in the United States, 1800–1860: An Economic Study,* The Johns Hopkins University Studies in Historical and Political Science, Series LXXIX, No. 2 (Baltimore, 1962); Colin Forster and G.S.L. Tucker, *Economic Opportunity and White American Fertility Ratios: 1800–1860* (New Haven and London, 1972). New York State has been examined, with similar results, in two articles by Wendell H. Bash: "Changing Birth Rates in Developing America: New York State, 1840–1875," Milbank Memorial Fund Quarterly, 41 (1963), 161–182; and "Differential Fertility in Madison County, New York, 1865," Ibid., 33 (1955), 161–186.

2. Bash does compare towns of different sizes in "Changing Birth Rates." A more thorough comparison, however, and one which leads to somewhat different conclusions, is John Modell, "Family and Fertility on the Indiana Frontier, 1820," American Quarterly, 23 (1971), 615–634.

3. As late as 1750 the colony of New York contained only some 73,000 inhabitants, of whom approximately 18,000 lived in Suffolk, Queens, Kings, and Richmond counties. Of those counties bordering the Hudson River, New York and Albany accounted for about 20,000 inhabitants, while some 35,000 were scattered along the intervening 150 miles of river valley. See Evarts B. Greene and Virginia D. Harrington, *American Population Before the Federal Census of 1790* (New York, 1932; reprinted Gloucester, Mass., 1966), 15.

4. The best history of Troy is Arthur J. Weise, *History of the City of Troy . . .* (Troy, 1876).

5. The standard history of Kingston is Marius Schoonmaker, *The History of Kingston, New York* (New York, 1888). Unfortunately, Schoonmaker's excellent book ends at 1820. The present brief summary of Kingston's development after that date is based on my own research into local newspapers and other records.

6. The single full-length history of Marlborough is C. M. Woolsey, *History of the Town of Marlborough, Ulster County, New York . . .* (Albany, 1908). Shorter sketches are included in Nathaniel Bartlett Sylvester, *History of Ulster County, New York . . .* (Philadelphia, 1880), II, 75–109, and Alphonso T. Clearwater, *The History of Ulster County, New York* (Kingston, N.Y., 1907), 287–305.

7. Philip Greven, *Four Generations: Population, Land and Family in Colonial Andover, Massachusetts* (Ithaca, N.Y., 1970).

8. Yasuba, *Birth Rates,* esp. 158–169.

9. The census schedules were recorded in their entirety for Kingston and Marlborough, while a 10% interval sample (every tenth household) was selected for Troy. The same procedure was followed for the New York State census of 1855. I would like to acknowledge my research assistant, Sheila Bryson, for her splendid work in the coding of the census schedules.

10. Children, for the most part, were easily identified with their own mothers on the census schedules.

11. *Ulster Republican,* December 18, 1850.

12. Differing child mortality rates would also affect these figures; unfortunately, there is no way of calculating accurate mortality rates for each ethnic group (or even for each town). Perhaps we should speak here only of numbers of children raised, rather than fertility. Bash finds higher birth rates among immigrants in "Differential Fertility in

Madison County," but Forster and Tucker argue quite persuasively that pre-Civil War immigrants had fewer children than did native Americans, in part because they arrived from nations (including Ireland) "in which family-building patterns were lower, not higher, than in the United States." See Forster and Tucker, *Economic Opportunity,* 70–82.

13. Compare American fertility studies with Michael Drake, ed., *Population in Industrialization* (London, 1969), particularly the essays by J. T. Krause: "Some Neglected Factors in the English Industrial Revolution," 103–117, and "English Population Movements Between 1700 and 1850," 118–127.

14. The New York State census of 1855 specifies the relationship of each individual to the head of the household. We will use the 1855 census in those tables which require this extra margin of accuracy.

15. The families referred to here are those which formed the "core" of their respective households, but not those headed by boarders, servants, journeymen, or apprentices. All "blood" and marital relations are included in the families of those listed as household heads, and "nuclear" is defined as the conjugal pair and their children.

16. Compare Lutz K. Berkner, "The Stem Family and the Developmental Cycle of the Peasant Household: An Eighteenth-Century Austrian Example," American Historical Review, 77 (1972), 398–418, with Michael Anderson, "Family, Household and the Industrial Revolution," in M. Anderson, *Sociology of the Family: Selected Readings* (Middlesex, England 1971), 78–96.

17. There is increasing realization of the fact that the stem family was not the only system of inheritance in rural America. For a recent discussion see James T. Lemon, *The Best Poor Man's Country: A Geographical Study of Early Southeastern Pennsylvania* (Baltimore and London, 1972), 91–94.

18. Berkner, "The Stem Family," 405–407.

19. Not all of those who were not located on the 1860 census out-migrated. Some died, some were incorrectly missed by the marshal, and some simply slipped through unnoticed in our attempt to link one census to the other. The fact that there are exactly 131 cases for both towns is a coincidence.

20. John Modell and Tamara K. Hareven, "Urbanization and the Malleable Household: An Examination of Boarding and Lodging in American Families," Journal of Marriage and the Family, 35 (1973), 467–479.

6

The Life Cycles and Household Structure of American Ethnic Groups: Irish, Germans, and Native-born Whites in Buffalo, New York, 1855

LAURENCE A. GLASCO

Despite increased interest in the ethnic dimension of American history, we still know relatively little about the social and economic characteristics of the immigrants themselves, especially their family patterns. And most of what we do know centers primarily around those who were both adult and male.[1] An understanding of ethnic groups—or of any population for that matter—should be based on all the component age and sex groupings: women as well as men; children and adolescents as well as adults.

Life-cycle analysis offers a useful method for doing this. The systematic age-related analysis of a population enables us to observe and compare the social characteristics of all its members as they pass through the age stations of childhood, adolescence, adulthood, and old age.[2]

The technique has other advantages as well. A division of the life cycle into separate stages can deepen our understanding of the two major themes of ethnic study: work and acculturation. If we relate stages of the life cycle to economic behavior and household organization, we can delineate patterns of "economic" and household cycles. Most of what we know in this area is based on the experiences of adult males. It is their occupation and income which is investigated in studies of ethnic stratification; it is they who are pictured as agents of change or acculturation, and the women as bastions of conservatism. In the present case, we have used life-cycle analysis to examine these issues, and have compared the age-related household and work experiences of men and women for each of three ethnic groups—Irish, Germans, and native-born whites—in a mid-nineteenth-century American city. The procedure helps to clarify how age and sex were related to the processes of ethnic stratification and acculturation.

Few studies have employed the method of life-cycle analysis because the sources are difficult to locate and utilize. The present study, using Buffalo, New York, as an example, takes the city's three major ethnic groups at one point in time, 1855, and describes their changing life situations in relation to age. It was possible to do this because the New York State manuscript census of 1855 provides not only the usual information on each person's age, sex, race, birthplace, and occupation, but also his or her marital condition and relationship to the head of the household. This material, transcribed and machine encoded for the city's entire population, enabled us to compare ethnic differences in the timed sequence by which both men and women passed through the various stages of childhood, adolescence, marriage, childbearing, and retirement, as well as corresponding household statuses of husband, wife, child, boarder, servant, and relative. Finally, it enabled us to trace and describe the age-related patterns of work and property ownership.

Such a description of the life cycle at one point in time cannot tell us whether any particular age cohort had previously followed, or in the future would follow, such patterns. That is, young children would not necessarily follow the example of their older brothers in regard to the timing or the sequence in which they left home, married, and established their own households. In fact, given the rapidly modernizing society of mid-nineteenth-century America, there is every chance that they would not. The complete answer to that question can be found only in cohort analysis, tracing the life cycles of specific age groups back in time and forward into the future. The form of analysis employed here, however, does tell us the age and age-related life patterns prevailing in a given period and provides a baseline from which to measure future deviations.

By the mid-nineteenth century, nationality virtually defined Buffalo's population and social structure. Like many northern cities at that time, Buffalo had a large, rapidly growing immigrant population jostling alongside a native-born, in-migrant population drawn mainly from New

England and the eastern part of New York State. Between 1845 and 1855 the city's population more than doubled, to over 70,000 residents, about one-fourth of whom were native-born, one-fifth Irish, and two-fifths German, the latter coming mainly from Bavaria and other southern principalities.

These residents had been attracted by the city's booming economy, based on the commerce of the Erie Canal and a rapidly growing manufacturing sector, especially of iron. Occupations tended to divide along ethnic lines, with Irish men holding many of the unskilled jobs along the docks, German men dominating the construction crafts, and native-born men controlling the finances, professions, and trade of the city.[3]

Ethnic differences of occupation and income were reflected in the life experiences of all members of society. As we will see, they extended through the entire life span, and included both the household and work cycles. Finally, as revealed by an examination of the household and work cycles, first of the men and then of the women, ethnic differences were as pronounced among young women as they were among adult men.

Native-born Men

The life cycle of native-born men reveals a rather prolonged childhood and adolescence. They did not begin to leave home until late adolescence, around age 19, and it was not until age 29 that virtually all had left the shelter of their parents' home. Many who left home, particularly if they were new to the city, became boarders. The practice of boarding, which has been associated generally with immigrants, involved one-third of all native-born men between the ages of 19 and 29, and over half of those present less than one year in the city. Most of these boarders—about four-fifths—were single, and less than one-half had a permanent occupation listed by the census. The longer they remained in the city, the less likely they were to board out. After residing in the city for five years, only about one-third of those in their early or late twenties and a fifth of those in their early thirties boarded out; among eight-year residents this was true of only 8% to 13% (Figure 1).

The typical native-born boarder lived with a family, almost always a native-born family, along with perhaps one or two other boarders who were also native-born. He was, in short, only semi-independent since in this situation his comings and goings were subject to supervision by the family with which he lived. The large, impersonal boarding house which characterized seaport towns housed less than half of the city's boarders. For the majority of young boarders, this practice was structured to provide a moderate amount of adult supervision, in a family setting, and to insulate the young men from intimate, unsupervised contact with the wider world.[4]

Figure 1: Native-born Males: Household Status by Age

Native-born men who had been in the city a few years seldom became boarders. Instead, they got married as soon as they left home and quickly established their own household. For this reason there was great variation in the average age at which native-born men got married. Marriage began as early as age 20 for about 10% of native-born men and did not include half of any age group until age 26.[5] Thereafter, the process speeded up and by age 28 three-fourths of that age group were married. Those who married early tended to delay the establishment of a separate household. Less than half the married men under age 24 had their own household. From age 25 on, however, three-fourths or more of married native-born men had their own households.

Once established, the native-born household was quite resistant to structural change. Half of the households consisted of husband and wife (with or without children); a fourth had one or more relatives; and a fifth had one or more boarders and roomers.[6] With only two exceptions, this distribution remained relatively unchanged as the household head grew older. When the household head was in his twenties he was slightly more likely to take in boarders: about a third took in boarders at that age, compared to a fourth of those in their thirties, forties, and fifties. When the household head reached old age, he was less likely to take boarders into his household, and more likely to take in relatives; about a fourth of household heads in their sixties took in boarders, compared to only 14% of those in their seventies. For the same age groups the proportion taking in relatives increased from 19% to 32%. Over the large middle range of age, however—the thirties, forties, fifties, and sixties—the native-born household was remarkably stable in form, with consistently close to half being nuclear, a fifth being extended, and a fourth being augmented.[7]

Although the native-born household head did not significantly alter the composition of his household with advancing age, he did change his status within that household by purchasing his own home. Almost a fourth of native-born family heads in their twenties owned real property. This proportion increased with age, and included two-fifths of those in their thirties, half of those in their forties and fifties, and three-fifths of those over sixty years of age.

Aiding him in the acquisition of his home was a clear occupational advantage. Native-born men dominated the white-collar, professional, and entrepreneurial positions in the city, and made up at least their share of the painters and mechanics. Moreover, they enjoyed these advantages over the entire course of their working years. There were not substantial age-related differences in their occupational chances. In their twenties, thirties, or forties, native-born men were likely to be clerks; when older, in their fifties and sixties, they tended to be entrepreneurs. Regardless of age, almost all native-born men were able to avoid the low-paying, unskilled position of day laborer. Moreover, the work career of native-born men extended over forty years. They began work fairly early, about age 16; by age 19 one-fourth were employed and by age 24 over half. As they aged, an increasing proportion of native-born men retired from the work force. Retirement began in their early sixties, when the percentage of men listed with an occupation decreased from 58% of those in their late fifties to 48% of those in their early sixties. For men in their late sixties the figure dropped to 40% and decreased still further among those in their seventies.

As they retired from the labor force, an increasing proportion ceased to head their own household. About one-third of native-born men over the age of sixty were living outside their own household, compared to about a tenth of those in their forties and fifties. Of those who did not maintain their own household, only a fifth went to live among possible strangers as a roomer or boarder. The great majority went to live with relatives. In over half of the cases, they lived with one of their children, while about 15% lived with an in-law.

This, then, briefly summarizes the age-related life experiences of native-born white men in a mid-nineteenth-century American city. Their household cycle was typically characterized by a prolonged childhood and adolescence, followed by a brief, relatively sheltered boarding experience, designed especially for those who were single, young, and new to the city. They generally married in their mid- to late twenties and began a family. During middle age their household consisted of a wife, two or three children and, for about half, either a relative or boarder, plus a servant. Increasing age brought its economic satisfactions. An examination of the economic cycle shows that they dominated the white-collar, professional, and enterpreneurial occupations, as well as certain of the skilled trades—especially metal working—and avoided the unskilled, day-laboring positions. This preferential occupational standing was enjoyed throughout the native-born man's occupational career. It paid off over the years. By the time they were in their sixties, about two-thirds continued to head their own household, and almost all of those who did so owned their own home. Most of the rest went to live with one of their children, so that only a few were left to live alone or to board out among strangers. All in all, the patterns suggest a fairly stable life experience.

Irish Men

To a remarkable degree the household cycle of Irish men resembled that of the native-born.[8] Like their native-born counterparts, Irish men began leaving home relatively late in adolescence, around age 19, although they completed the leaving process somewhat earlier, around age 25. As with the native-born, this amounted to just under a third of Irish men aged 19 to 29 and 40% of those aged 20 to 24 became boarders (Figure 2). Nearly all of these boarders were single and most were new to the city as well. Of Irish men aged 20 to 24 years, 70% of those present for less than one year were boarders, compared to a third among those present five years, and just over a tenth of those present eight years. Among those in their late twenties the corresponding decline was from 58% to between 7% and 12%. Again, as with the native-born, most Irish boarders lived with families of their own ethnic background, with perhaps one other boarder.

Irish men passed from a dependent to an independent status somewhat more quickly than native-born men. First, the process of leaving home was more accelerated, being virtually completed by age 25, compared to age 29 for the native-born. Second, the Irish boarding experience was somewhat shorter. Impressions to the contrary of boarding

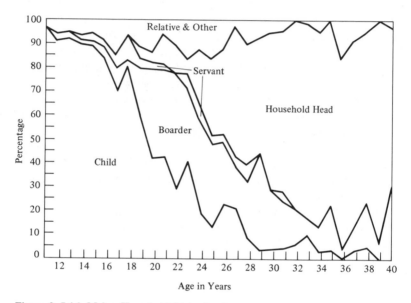

Figure 2: Irish Males: Household Status by Age

being primarily an immigrant phenomenon, boarding for Irish males was virtually over by the age of 27, whereas there were still a moderate number of native-born boarders in their early thirties.

The Irish marriage experience was similar too, but somewhat more compressed than that of native-born men. It began two years later (age 22) and was completed at about the same age—28 or 29. Irish married men achieved independence somewhat earlier, however, in that there was not a notable delay between marriage and the establishment of a separate household. Whereas only half the native-born men through age 23 headed their own household, two-thirds or more of Irish married men from age 22 (when they began marrying in substantial numbers) headed their own households.

In contrast to the native-born household, the Irish household was more likely to be nuclear in composition. Only 15% took in relatives and 13% took in roomers and boarders, compared to 25% and 20% respectively, for the native-born. The practice of taking in boarders did not vary with the age of the household head, and in this regard, too, the Irish pattern resembled the native-born.

The similarities between native-born and Irish break down in regard to the presence of relatives, however. The likelihood of an Irish household including relatives was clearly articulated to the life cycle. The proportion of Irish households containing extended kin declined from about 20% of those in their twenties to only about 10% of those in their forties; thereafter the trend reversed, such that older household heads were more likely to have relatives—about 15% of those in their sixties and 30% of those in their seventies. The causes of this inverted, or U-shaped, pattern are not clear. Possibly it is related to particular Irish migration patterns, in which young unmarried brothers and sisters came to America and set up a sibling household when young, which was followed by marriage in middle age and the establishment of independent households. This possibility, however, has not been tested.

The difference in the experience of Irish and native-born was also reflected in property ownership. Native-born household heads, as they grew older, were increasingly successful in buying their own home. This was not true for Irish men. Those owning real estate increased from 16% of those in their twenties to 26% of those in their thirties. The trend then stabilized, and ownership actually decreased among those over sixty years of age.

The reason for such a realtively low proportion of Irish home owners was their unfavorable occupational structure. Irish men dominated no specific occupation, but were overrepresented among teamsters, sailors, ship carpenters, and especially among unskilled day laborers. As a result, two-thirds of Irish family heads either were unskilled or —especially older men—had no occupation listed. Examination of this aspect of the economic cycle, furthermore, reveals that this maldistribution of occupational skills did not significantly vary with age; at no point in their working lives did a majority of Irish men have a chance for stable, well-paying work. The impact of this occupational pattern can be gauged by the fact that semi-skilled and skilled Irish workers were as successful as their native-born counterparts in acquiring property. This was not true for unskilled Irish laborers, suggesting the operation of cultural values as well in the matter of property acquisition.

To maintain even this position, many Irish men had to work past what was a normal retirement age for native-born men. Irish boys began working at about age 17, one year later than native-born boys. One-fourth were employed by age 19, and the proportion rose to one-half by the time they reached age 22. They worked substantially longer, however. By the early seventies, when only 14% of native-born men had a listed occupation, this was the case of one-third of Irish men.

In old age, the household status of Irish men came once again to resemble that of native-born men. Most were able to maintain their position as household heads. Indeed, the proportion who did so (three-fourths) exceeded that for native-born household heads (two-thirds). Of those who did not remain household heads, only about a fifth boarded out, and an insignificant number went to live with collateral kin. Almost half went to live with a child, and a third went to live with an in-law. In this way, their pattern resembled that of the native-born.

This, then, summarizes the age-related life experiences of Irish men. The greatest differences emerged in their economic cycle, specifically in the type of jobs held and the amount of property acquired over a lifetime. In certain respects there were striking, unexpected parallels in regard to their household cycles. They left home at about the same age, became boarders at about the same age and in about the same proportions, and in a similarly structured situation that provided adult supervision in a family setting and reduced contact with peers outside the ethnic group. Their households differed somewhat in composition, since fewer Irish families took in boarders or relatives. Yet the differences seem more one of degree than of kind.

There were similarities in the aging process as well. About the same proportion of Irish and native-born men headed their own households in old age, although a greater proportion of native-born men owned the dwelling in which they lived. Finally, the experience of those who left their households was similar: few of either group had to live among possible strangers in a boarding situation; a majority of both went to live with their children or, less frequently, with their in-laws.

German Men

At first glance, the life cycle of German men differed from that of native-born and Irish men. German men began leaving home at a substantially earlier age—16 years, compared to 19 years for the other two groups. Moreover, they practiced apprenticeship as an additional intermediate step between childhood and boarding or marriage. This practice was brought over from Germany and continued in Buffalo because of German domination of the city's crafts. It was most pronounced among young men between the ages of 18 and 22, when about one-fourth of German young men lived with a master craftsman (Figure 3).

Except for apprenticeship, the household cycle of German men broadly resembled that of the other two groups. About one-third of German young men between the ages of 21 and 24, and as many as 10% up to age 31, were boarders. The corresponding figures for those in their

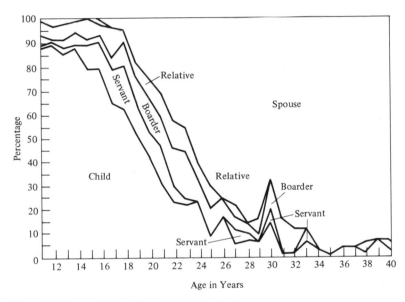

Figure 3: German Males: Household Status by Age

late teens and twenties were substantially lower (by about half) and were insignificant for most other age groups.

The marriage pattern for German men was compressed like that for Irish men, although it began and concluded about a year earlier, at ages 21 and 27, respectively.[9] Also like the Irish, German men experienced no delay in establishing their own household once they married.

Of the three ethnic groups, Germans had the most intensely nuclear household pattern. There existed few German boarding houses; boarders lived primarily with a single German family. Once established, the German household was only moderately subject to modification as the household head grew older. Only 8% of German families took in a roomer or boarder, and the figure varied very slightly over the life cycle of the household head. The percentage of family heads taking in relatives fell slowly, but steadily, from 11% of those in their twenties to 5% of those in their fifties; thereafter, the trend reversed, as 11% among those in their sixties headed extended households and 20% of those in their seventies. German households taking in boarders and roomers declined very slightly, but noticeably, among older members, from 12% of those in their twenties to 6% of those in their seventies.

German men experienced a fairly stable economic cycle and were substantially more successful than their Irish counterparts in buying a home. During their early adult years—the twenties and thirties—their patterns of home ownership were similar to those of natives, with about one-fourth and two-fifths of the family heads in those age categories owning their own homes. Thereafter, the German percentage stabilized while that of the native-born advanced, so that by the time they were sixty years or older, less than half of German family heads owned their own homes, compared to almost three-fifths of native-born family heads. If one allows for length of residence in the city (German family heads had been present eight years on the average, compared to thirteen years for the native-born), the differences disappear entirely. Finally, although home ownership among the Germans did not advance with old age as did that for the native-born, neither did it decline, as was the case for the Irish.

Part of the German success in acquiring a home, of course, can be attributed to their occupational patterns. Although they lacked any significant number of white-collar, professional, or entrepreneurial occupations, and over half of their family heads were unskilled or without occupation, they had a firm grip on the city's crafts and dominated many of the lucrative building trades. As a result, over a third of their family heads were skilled workers, compared to only a fifth of the native-born and a sixth of the Irish. There were proportionately more young skilled workers than older ones. Moreover, German men stayed longer in the labor force than either of the other two groups. At age 16, when native-born men were just entering the labor force and a year before Irish young men began to work, one-fourth of German boys were already employed. By age 20, almost half were listed with an occupation, a level not reached by the native-born and Irish until age 22. They also retired from the labor force at a later age than either of the other two groups. Whereas half of the native-born and Irish men retired in their early sixties, less than 40% of German men had retired before their late sixties.

Despite the undoubted significance of work, occupational patterns accounted for only part of the German success in acquiring property. Cultural preferences undoubtedly operated as well, for if one allows for differences in age and length of residence in the city, German family heads not only equaled, but often exceeded, their native-born and Irish counterparts in the proportion owning real property. It was particularly among unskilled workers that German family heads bested their ethnic competitors.

As with the Irish and native-born men, advanced age brought relatively few unsettling changes in their life patterns. About one German man in three past the age of sixty was not the head of his own household. The great majority (three-fifths) of those who were not household heads lived with a child or grandchild; somewhat over one-tenth lived with an in-law, and somewhat fewer than one in ten lived with a nephew or niece. Only 12% lived as a boarder or roomer.

The notable aspect of this comparison of age-related life experiences of native-born, Irish, and German men is that alongside the not unexpected socioeconomic differences—occupation and property ownership—there existed such remarkable similarities in the timing and form of their respective family cycles. As we will now see, it was the women who demonstrated the most striking and pervasive ethnic differences in their family and economic cycles.

Native-born Women

Native-born women began leaving home at age 16—several years before their brothers. Few left, however, to take a job; at no age did more than 5% of native-born women have an occupation listed in the census other than that of domestic servant. Few became servants. Only 12% to 17% of native-born women aged 16 to 19 were classified as domestic servants. By age 24, virtually none were domestics. Boarding was an equally rare experience, occurring primarily between the ages of 22 and 23 and even then involving less than one-fifth of the native-born women. Thus, except for a very brief period in their late teens, these women never lived in a household other than that of their parents (Figure 4).

Beginning at age 19 native-born women began to marry. By age 21 over half were listed as wives and by age 25 over three-fourths.[10] Most established their own household shortly after marrying. Three-fifths had done so between the ages of 19 and 22, and by age 27 virtually all had married. Native-born women delayed bearing children until a household

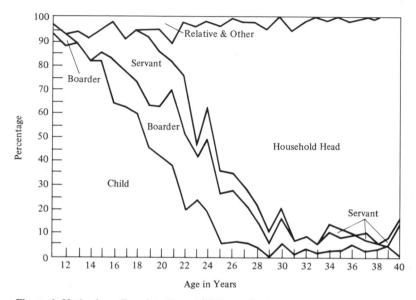

Figure 4: Native-born Females: Household Status by Age

was established. This conclusion is based on the following evidence: first, some 69% of native-born married women aged 20 to 24, and 89% of those aged 25 to 29, had their own households; second, there were 69 children aged 0–4 years per 100 married native-born women aged 20–24, and 91 children per 100 women aged 25–29 years. If the assumption is that most of these women had only one child under five years of age, this would mean that most of those without their own household had no children.

Even after they began to bear children, native-born women restricted their family size. They had a very low fertility ratio, only 585 children aged 0–4 years per 100 married women of childbearing years, 15–44.[11] They achieved this low rate by having most of their children before age 35. The fertility rate was 188 for native-born women in their late teens, 685 for women in their early twenties. It peaked at 910 for those in their late twenties and then declined rapidly, to 600 and 452 among women in their early and late thirties and to only 286 among those in their early forties. All this suggests a conscious pattern of limited childbearing.

Had native-born women not restricted their childbearing years, their households would have become rather large, and would have remained so, until the women reached middle age. As noted above, children of native-born parents did not leave home until late adolescence—the boys around age 19 and the girls around age 16 or 17. Thus, a native-born woman who began raising children in her mid-twenties could not expect them even to begin leaving until she was in her forties. During such a sixteen-year fertile period, if she gave birth every other year (the rate to be expected for a population not practicing birth control, but engaged in breast feeding), she would have had seven or eight children before the oldest daughters began leaving home. An examination of age-specific family size, however, shows that native-born families peaked in size while the family head was in his late thirties, with two to three children—2.56 on the average. Such a low figure reveals the extent to which most native-born women limited their family size.

As they aged, the death of the husband and/or financial pressures meant that fewer women were able to maintain their previous status as wife in an independent household. The first major decline in the proportion listed as "spouse" of their own household occurred among those in their early fifties. Prior to that, over two-thirds of any particular age group were so listed; after age sixty only about a fifth. What happened to the others? Of the women over sixty years of age who were not living with their husbands in their own households, only a few (16%) became household heads in their own right, half went to live with one of their children, and slightly less than a fifth went to live with in-laws. As with the men, a negligible percentage lived as boarders or with collateral kin.

Irish Women

While the life cycles of Irish and native-born men converged at several points, the pattern for Irish and native-born women was one of sharp and persistent differences. The divergence began in early adolescence. At age 17, when native-born women were just beginning to leave home, over half of the Irish girls had already left theirs to take on domestic work, starting as early as 11 years of age; and by age 21 virtually all of them were living apart from their parents. This was not true of native-born women until age 25. Whereas only a few native-born women ever lived outside the household of either their parents or of their husbands, live-in domestic service claimed the energies of more than one-fourth of Irish girls between the ages of 13 and 25, and from half to two-thirds of those aged 18 to 21 years (Figure 5).

Domestic service was closely related to at least two demographic

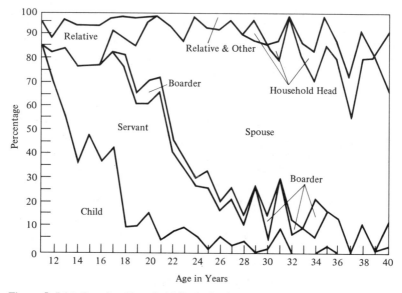

Figure 5: Irish Females: Household Status by Age

factors—age and length of residence in the city. Undoubtedly, Irish parents did not want their daughters to work as live-in domestics. These girls typically lived and worked among native-born families who themselves had adolescent sons living at home. Those who were new to the city, however, were unable to keep even their very young daughters out of domestic service. One-fourth of Irish girls aged 10 to 14 who were present in the city for one year or less worked as live-in domestics, compared to less than 15% of those present more than three years. The corresponding drop among those aged 15 to 19 was equally dramatic, from 75% to 32%. Among older girls, however, those in their early twenties, the decline was only from 52% to 39%; among those in their late twenties the decline was from about 30% to about 15%. Domestic service was the female counterpart of boarding out for the men and was much more widely practiced. Regardless of how long they had been in the city, however, domestic service was not a permanent feature of Irish women's lives. Beginning at age 21 Irish girls rapidly left such work and by age 26 virtually none were so employed.

Irish girls left domestic service in their late teens in order to get married. One-fourth were married by age 19, half by age 21, and three-fourths by age 25. Despite domestic service (or perhaps financially because of it), Irish women caught up with their native-born counterparts in terms of age at marriage. As with the native-born women, about half of those who married early set up their own household. By age 22 over four-fifths of married Irish women had their own, independent household.

By contrast to the severely restricted overall fertility rate of native women, Irish women had a fertility rate high enough to suggest virtually unregulated childbearing. The Irish figure was 100 for married women 15–44, almost double that of native-born women. Inspection of the age-specific fertility rates for Irish women in comparison to their native-born counterparts reinforces this impression. Thus, among married Irish women aged 15 to 19 the fertility rate was 313, or about two-thirds higher than that for native-born women of the same age. Among Irish women in their twenties and early thirties the fertility rate was much higher, 1,130 among those aged 25 to 29, and 1,290 among those aged 30 to 34 years. The latter figure was over twice as high as that for native-born women of the same age. Not until their late thirties did the Irish rate decline. It fell to 927 among the 35 to 39 age group and to 446 among the 40 to 44 age group. By the late thirties, however, simple biological restraints would have been operating, as many women drew toward the end of their fertile period.

Despite higher fertility rates and longer periods of childbearing, Irish families were not substantially larger than native-born families. Irish families had an average of 2.37 children, not significantly higher than the figure of 2.06 for native-born families. Moreover, native-born families peaked in the average number of children living at home with 2.56; Irish families peaked (at age 50) with 3.43. The maximum average differences between the two, then, were just one child. The only plausible explanation of this small divergence in family size in light of such major differences in fertility is related to the household cycle, by which native-born families kept their children home until late adolescence, whereas Irish families sent their children, particularly their young girls, out for a prolonged period of domestic service. Domestic service, then, served as an important regulator of Irish family size.

In describing the transition to old age for men, whether native-born or Irish, we focused on the age group over sixty because that was the period of major shifts in household status. The same was true for native-born women. For Irish women, however, shifts in household status began much earlier—in the age group 41 to 60. Beginning in their forties, the Irish woman's household began to break up. Only half of Irish women in their forties and fifties were wives living in their own households compared to three-fifths of native-born women. Similarly, one-fourth of all Irish women in that age bracket headed their own household, compared to less than 15% of native-born women. The reasons for this unusually high number of female-headed households among the Irish is not clear. It is possible that Irish men had a higher death rate than Irish women, but in the 41 to 60 age group there were 604 men compared to 565 women, suggesting that mortality alone is not a sufficient cause. Whatever the cause—death, separation, or divorce—it is clear that many middle-aged Irish women did not remarry.

Among older women, those over sixty years of age, Irish women continued to head a disproportionate number of households. About a fourth of those not living with a husband headed their own household (compared to 16% among the native-born). Half had gone to live with children, another 15% had gone to live with other in-laws, and an insignificant proportion boarded.

The life cycle of Irish women, therefore, diverged substantially from that of native-born women. The differences emerged in early adolescence, as most Irish girls went to live and work as servants in native-born households. This prolonged period of domestic service, however, was not a permanent part of their lives. Between the ages of 20 and 24, most Irish girls left that service in order to get married. At that point their age-related life experiences diverged again from the native-born pattern. Irish mothers had a much higher rate of childbearing, lasting over a longer period of time. While native-born mothers kept their daughters home until the time for them to marry, this was not possible for most Irish mothers. Perhaps out of both economic necessity and considerations of space in the house, their daughters spent most of their adolescence living with, and working for, those native-born families. During much of the middle and later years, Irish women were more likely than native-born women to head their own households, a type of independence which they probably did not relish. An insignificant number of Irish women were listed in the census with an occupation, reflecting the fact that Buffalo was not a city with an industry which could provide outside sources of income for working women. We may assume, however, that these women heading households did work; it probably only consisted of such poorly remunerative work as taking in other people's laundry.

German Women

Like Irish girls, German girls left home at a very early age. The transition began at the age of 11 years, but was more gradual. Not until age 23, two years after almost all Irish girls had left home, was it completed (Figure 6).

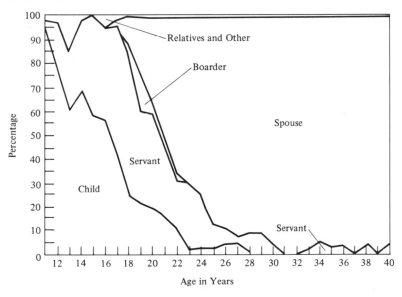

Figure 6: German Females: Household Status by Age

As with the Irish, nearly all German girls at some point during their adolescence served as live-in domestics, almost invariably for native-born families. For the Germans, however, the length of service was shorter. Only between the ages of 17 and 18 did as many as two-thirds work in such a capacity, a figure which characterized Irish women in the age group from 18 to 21. Finally, German girls married and helped to establish a household earlier than either Irish or native-born girls. They began at age 17 (two or three years before the Irish), and by age 25 over 80% were listed as wives of household heads, compared to only 60% of Irish women and 70% of native-born women. After marriage, never more than 5% were listed with an occupation.

As with the Irish, once German women married, they experienced little or no delay in setting up a household. Nor was there any delay in beginning a family. German women aged 15 to 44 had the same overall fertility rate as Irish women, but a review of age-specific fertility shows that among the young and the old, German women had a higher rate than the Irish, and among the middle childbearing years, a rate only slightly under that of the Irish. As with the Irish, the suggestion is that their childbearing was regulated primarily by biological consideration.

Despite their high, prolonged fertility, the German family averaged just over two children (2.13), somewhat more than native-born families (2.06), and less than Irish families (2.37). The explanation is not related to age differences between the groups, for the average number of children present in German families peaked among family heads 45 years old at just over three children (3.08), again not substantially higher than the peak for native-born families at 2.56 and below the Irish figure of 3.43. As with the Irish, family size was regulated by sending children out of the household. German girls went into domestic service among the native-born; German boys became apprentices for German master craftsmen. Among the Germans, then, both domestic service and apprenticeship served as important regulators of effective family size.

As they aged, German women were more fortunate than either native-born or Irish women in remaining spouses in their own households. Among those over sixty years of age, over a third had that status, compared to a fifth or less among the native-born and Irish. Of those whose position changed, about a fifth became household heads in their own right, half went to live with their children and 14% went to live with in-laws. Thus, as with the other ethnic groups, boarding or living with collateral kin was seldom resorted to by the elderly.

Conclusion

Irish, Germans, and native-born whites, then, had distinctive life cycles. This was true for both the men and the women, but the men's patterns differed primarily in their economic cycles, while the women's patterns differed in terms of both the economic and the household cycles.

Among the men the household cycle was more notable for similarities than for differences among the ethnic groups. The most impressive differences among the men involved not the timing, but the content, of their life cycles. Thus, throughout their working lives, native-born men dominated the white-collar and entrepreneurial occupations, virtually to the exclusion of immigrant men; the ranks of the unskilled were composed largely of immigrant men, and most of the crafts, especially in the construction industry, were dominated by Germans. Occupational differences among them were largely indepedent of age.

Age-related patterns, and ethnic differences in those patterns, were also pronounced for the men in terms of property ownership. A substantial proportion of each group owned their own homes, but the differences were nonetheless substantial—one-fourth of the Irish, two-fifths of the Germans, and over two-fifths of the native-born. Moreover, the differences became even greater as the household head aged, reflecting presumably age-related differences in the earning potential among the types of occupations.

It was among the women that there existed the most consistent ethnic differences in life cycles. The years of "adolescence" for immigrant girls were strikingly different, not only from their native-born counterparts, but also from their brothers. For an extended period of time they lived and worked with native-born families. Their brothers, however, were never exposed to an intimate living situation with persons of another ethnic group. They remained home until late adolescence, boarded among families of the same nationality, married a girl also of the same nationality, and established a household usually in an ethnically homogeneous neighborhood. Their only chance for contact with the native-born occurred in the work situation, but, given the degree of occupational specialization along ethnic lines, this was probably neither extensive nor significant.

This early departure of girls from their parents' household was functional, both in terms of their later marriage prospects being increased from the earnings and especially as a regulator of the household size. In this way, although Irish and German fertility rates were almost double that for the native-born, and although the childbearing period for them extended ten years longer, immigrant families were not substantially larger than those of the native-born population.

The implications of these age-related sex differences are enormous, especially for the question of acculturation. The contact of immigrant girls with native-born families occurred at an impressionable age, when patterns of behavior, dress, language, and cultural values were still being learned. For foreign-language groups like the Germans, in particular, the girls probably learned English before their brothers. For the second generation it would be they who taught and translated such behavior to their children, years before the schools did their work. For working-class populations of immigrant background, the institution of domestic service was probably as important a force for acculturation as the more widely known institutions of work and schooling. These are only some of the perspectives that a comparative life-cycle analysis can offer for all of a community's members, young and old, male and female.

NOTES

1. Earlier historical studies of immigration give scant treatment to family composition or to age-related aspects of immigrant adjustment. A partial exception would be Oscar Handlin, *Boston's Immigrants: A Study in Acculturation* (Cambridge, Mass., 1941, 1959), which describes a wide range of social characteristics of Boston's Irish immigrants. The focus of much subsequent history, particularly the "new" urban history, has been on occupation and geographic mobility. Only lately has attention shifted to studies of the family and household. See Tamara K. Hareven, "The History of the Family as an Interdisciplinary Field," Journal of Interdisciplinary History, 2 (1970); Journal of Marriage and the Family, 35 (1973); Michael Gordon, ed., *The American Family in Social-Historical Perspective* (New York, 1973); Peter Laslett and Richard Wall, eds., *The Household and Family in Past Time* (Cambridge, England, 1972).

2. Paul C. Glick and Robert Parke, Jr., "New Approaches in Studying the Life Cycle of the Family," Demography, 2 (1965), 187–202, summarizes much of the sociological literature on the life cycle applied to the family. Tamara K. Hareven, "The Family as Process: The Historical Study of the Family Cycle," Journal of Social History (March, 1974), 322–329, urges historians to adapt, in a creative fashion, this analytical tool for their own purposes. There are no studies comparing the life cycles of ethnic groups in nineteenth-century America, but see Robert V. Wells, "Demographic Change and the Life Cycle of American Families," Journal of Interdisciplinary History, 2 (1971), 273–282; Howard P. Chudacoff, "The Non-Private Newlyweds: Familial Extension in the First Stage of the Family Cycle, Providence, Rhode Island, 1864–1865 and 1879–1880," paper submitted to the MSSB Conference on Family History, Williams College, July, 1974. Because of lack of space, not all the tables were included in this paper. For tables see Laurence A. Glasco, "Ethnicity and Social Structure: Irish, Germans and Native-Born of Buffalo, N. Y., 1850–1860," Ph.D. dissertation, State University of New York at Buffalo, 1973; esp. ch. 3, "Household and Family Structure."

3. Laurence A. Glasco, "Ethnicity and Occupation in the Mid-19th Century: Irish, Germans and Native-born Whites in Buffalo, N.Y.," paper delivered at the Conference on Immigrants in Industrial America, Eleutherian Mills Historical Library and the Balch Institute, November, 1973; Theodore Hershberg et al., "Occupation and Ethnicity in Five Nineteenth-Century Cities: A Collaborative Inquiry," Historical Methods Newsletter, 7 (1974), 174–216.

4. Michael Anderson found that in mid-nineteenth-century Preston, England, about half of the lodgers were single and between the ages of 15 and 24. Only one-fifth lived in a household containing more than five lodgers. Anderson, *Family Structure in Nineteenth*

Century Lancashire (Cambridge, England, 1971), 47. Compare with John Modell and Tamara K. Hareven, "Urbanization and the Malleable Household: An Examination of Boarding and Lodging in American Families," Journal of Marriage and the Family, 35 (1973) 478–479.

5. The same as in 1890 for all white males in the United States. See Paul C. Glick and Robert Parke, Jr., "New Approaches in Studying the Life Cycle of the Family," Demography, 2 (1965), 189.

6. These figures for relatives and lodgers are almost identical to those for Preston, England. Anderson, *Family Structure in Nineteenth Century Lancashire,* 46.

7. The distribution of households with relatives and boarders—one-fourth and one-fifth, respectively—does not quite agree with the distribution of extended and augmented households—one-fifth and one-fourth, respectively—because the classification "augmented" includes households which contained both relatives and boarders.

8. Unfortunately, the printed U.S. census does not provide information of the family and household characteristics of immigrants. For information on the Irish, see K. H. Connell, *The Population of Ireland, 1750–1845* (Oxford, England, 1950).

9. John Knodel, "Law, Marriage and Illegitimacy in Nineteenth-Century Germany," Population Studies, 20 (1966–1967), 279–294, deals with the effects on marriage age and illegitimacy of marriage restriction by various German states.

10. From the late eighteenth century onward, this has been the median age at marriage for American women. Wells, "Demographic Change and the Life Cycle of American Families," 280 ff. Cf. Tamara K. Hareven and Maris A. Vinovskis, "Marital Fertility, Ethnicity and Occupation in Urban Families: An Analysis of South Boston and the South End in 1880," paper presented at the MSSB Conference on Family History, Williams College, July, 1974.

11. A rate only moderately below that for other cities of its size in the mid-nineteenth century. Warren S. Thompson and P. K. Whelpton, *Population Trends in the U.S.* (New York, 1933), 263, 279.

7

Family and Business in a Small City: Poughkeepsie, New York, 1850–1880

SALLY GRIFFEN AND
CLYDE GRIFFEN

Before his death in 1869 Matthew Vassar took three of his nephews into partnership and entrusted them with the active management of his brewery, then Poughkeepsie's richest firm. Matthew Vassar, Jr., Oliver Booth, and James Harbottle had different parents, grew up in different households, and always maintained separate residences in the city, but their social as well as their business lives intertwined. The Vassar brewery is perhaps the most important example in Poughkeepsie of family partnerships which united the interests of several city households.

In the last few years much historical and sociological debate has focused on Talcott Parsons' contention that the social mobility characteristic of modern industrial societies is incompatible with a traditional extended family and that the evolution of the nuclear family was a highly functional adaptation to the opportunities and demands of the industrial order. Few observers challenge Parsons' contention that the classical extended family is antithetical to social mobility. But

Authors' Note: *We are indebted to Robert W. Lovett, Curator of Manuscripts, Baker Library, Harvard University, for facilitating our use of the credit ledgers for Poughkeepsie in the Dun and Bradstreet collection, an invaluable source for nineteenth-century social as well as economic history.*

sociologists such as Marvin B. Sussman and Eugene Litwak have pointed out that modified extended-family relationships, far from being incompatible with intergenerational mobility, may be a more functional adaptation than the isolated nuclear family.[1]

The present essay, which is based on a study of business arrangements between relatives by blood and marriage in Poughkeepsie, New York, in the three decades after 1850, offers evidence that the extended family played an important role in business entrepreneurship. As in many other nineteenth-century cities, nuclear household structure predominated in Poughkeepsie. But the formal household structure did not mean the absence of kinship ties and a "help" pattern similar to that of today. At the same time, family members arranged their financial assistance, partnerships, and succession in ownership in ways that did not interfere with personal mobility. These kin relations seem to have been largely instrumental. Individual opportunity or security took precedence over family solidarity and reputation.

We interpret these family arrangements as a rational adaptation to the insecurity of a highly competitive business environment. Moreover, they are consonant with the individualism ascribed to Americans by mid-century, an individualism often viewed by historians as the capitalist ethos freed from feudal inheritances. Since this relationship appears throughout our systematic evidence on Poughkeepsie's businesses from the 1840s to the 1880s, our essay cannot pursue questions of causation or timing of change in the relationships among values, environment, and behavior. It does suggest that, in the short run, families tend to adapt their business behavior to the character of the immediate environment. Whatever the differences in their value systems or in the recency of their involvement in the city's business life, families of immigrants as well as of natives, of former artisans as well as of long-established retailers, show remarkably similar tendencies in business behavior.

To help define the meaning of these tendencies, this essay begins with the provocative contrast between American business and the French family firm offered by David Landes and John Sawyer during the early 1850s. This contrast presumed to characterize both large and small business in the two countries.[2] Because of the very limited empirical foundation, especially for small business, the description of the French family firm serves our investigation as an ideal type which calls attention by comparison to characteristics of American enterprise presumed to be distinctive.

According to Landes, the values of growth and competition dominated American enterprise whereas dynastic considerations motivated the French family firm. Managed on the same principles as the bourgeois household, the *maison* also expressed the survival of preindustrial aristocratic values among the bourgeoisie. The French firm existed for the family, preferring its independence, honor, and security to the risks of a too-ardent pursuit of riches. The firm avoided dependence on credit wherever possible since that gave outsiders some control over family affairs. The family also sought to avoid extreme competition and risk-taking, because failure in business meant a permanent stain on its reputation.

Landes argued that differences in value systems explained differences in patterns of entrepreneurship between the nations. This argument provoked controversy over the specific causation of entrepreneurship which largely neglected Landes' contrast between the United States and France. In the meantime, however, one American scholar outside the controversy—sociologist Daniel Bell—drew on the work of Landes in generalizing boldly about the relation of the family to enterprise in America. We have not advanced much beyond his broad and largely unsubstantiated assertions.

Bell argued that "family capitalism has entrenched itself in many middle-sized enterprises and left its mark on so many cities," but "never succeeded in establishing its hegemony in the area of large-scale capital industries."[3] Unlike France, America never experienced a full development of family capitalism, especially continuity in ownership. The ease of alienating land made it difficult for family founders "to impose their wishes regarding the conservation of property upon successive generations." And, according to Bell, the United States has had "a tradition—or at least a myth—whereby the son does not succeed the father but strikes out for himself."

Bell's presumption that family capitalism, if not possessed of all of the values attributed to the French family firm, entrenched itself in middle-sized enterprise in the United States raises questions about Landes' contrast. For example, is the prevalence of the family firm largely a function of the size of enterprise? Have small shopowners —the businessmen least studied in all modern capitalist nations—been far more preoccupied even in France with day-to-day tactics of survival than with the reputation of the family and its continuity in business? Have local urban economies in the United States typically seen more turnover in firms than their French counterparts in size and diversification?

These comparative questions point up the importance of close examination of the relationship between family business behavior and the particular urban environments in which it occurs before we can begin to assess adequately the interaction of both with social values. Until we have such studies for a variety of urban environments, we will not get much beyond postulates like those of Landes and Bell about how values influence business arrangements among family members.

For a beginning study of this kind, Poughkeepsie at mid-century has the advantage of not being a highly specialized economy which might project the peculiarities of one or a few industries as representative of urban enterprise generally. A center for retail and wholesale trade for its vicinity in the Hudson Valley, Poughkeepsie also had a diversity of manufactures, ranging from small craft-related firms to factories with several hundred employees. Correspondingly, however, it cannot be used to assess the adequacy of the stereotype of the mill town proposed by Bell: "the domination, by the leading family, of the towns in which the family enterprise resided."

Our interpretation of family behavior in business in Poughkeepsie derives from two complementary analyses. A preliminary analysis of the careers of city businessmen, their recruitment, subsequent occupational and property mobility, and length of life of their firms comes from our larger study of occupational mobility in Poughkeepsie.[4] We present here only those findings which describe the business environment most succinctly. Credit reports prepared for 1,530 individual firms by the Mercantile Agency and then by R. G. Dun and Company, predecessors of Dun and Bradstreet, provide the evidence for analysis of family involvement in business.[5] They show frequent family assistance and partnerships in Poughkeepsie firms, but—as with most quantitative results—whether this frequency seems high or low depends on one's expectations. It may seem high if one assumes that in a mobile society the majority of enterprises will not depend in any significant way on family support. We do not make that assumption, and we do not find the frequency of family involvement as important as its character.

We will argue that the majority of business arrangements between family members in Poughkeepsie appear to have been expedient and temporary, designed for immediate profit or protection of individual property. The most common exceptions to this generalization were family partnerships in large firms where substantial capital was at stake. Even members of these family firms, however, often behaved in ways which seem to us incompatible with the cautious, dynastic mentality

Landes postulates for France. In smaller businesses proprietors often used both the firm and members of their families opportunistically in the struggle for survival with few apparent scruples about damaging the reputation of either. In a highly competitive business environment this flexible, instrumental attitude undoubtedly saved many ventures which otherwise might have failed and consequently have taken away the livelihoods of immediate families of the proprietors.

High mortality has characterized businesses in Poughkeepsie since at least the 1840s. A classic investigation which traced the length of life of individual firms through annual city directories found that between 1843 and 1873 alone, 60% disappeared in less than four years.[6] Our analysis of occupational and property mobility provides abundant additional evidence of the constant change and insecurity within Poughkeepsie's business community.

At any census during the three decades after 1850, one-fourth or more of the city's proprietors had been employed at manual work ten years previous. This reportage underestimates the frequency with which skilled and unskilled manual workers started small retail and service ventures; about one-tenth of the shopowners evaluated by Dun and Company never appear in the census as anything but holders of manual jobs unrelated to their businesses. The census analysis, moreover, does not include proprietors not employed in Poughkeepsie a decade earlier, largely newcomers to the city.

Only a small minority of those who achieved proprietorship subsequently lost status by shifting to manual work in Poughkeepsie. Many more left the city amid evidence that their businesses had not prospered. Moreover, continuity in occupational status within the city did not ensure continuity in the same line of business either by the proprietor himself or by his children, the hallmark of the French family firm. Continuity between generations was especially weak in Poughkeepsie. Among merchants, grocers, hotelkeepers, and saloonkeepers who had sons employed in the city for at least two census decades, sons who never reported the same occupation as their fathers constituted 57%, 68%, and 92%, respectively. Another 6% to 16% of all but the sons of saloonkeepers reported their fathers' occupations only as a first job.

Furthermore, continuity in occupational status did not ensure retention of, let alone increase in, prosperity. If one uses the Dun and Company estimates of worth, of the 183 firms reported for more than 10 years for which several estimates are available, 41% show a C.O.D. rating.[7] Greater age does not improve the prospect much: one-third of those firms surviving twenty years or more ended up in serious trouble and another one-tenth suffered fluctuations and reversals during their existence.

Smaller firms as expected show shorter lives on the average. Some 56% of all firms rated "worth nothing" or "small," reported for less than four years, are compared to a mere 6% of firms whose highest estimated worth exceeded $25,000. But a significant minority of the richest firms were short lived—17% surviving less than ten years—and a similar minority of marginal firms managed to stay afloat for some time—15% being reported for a decade or more. Outright failure, whether foreclosure by the sheriff, voluntary assignment, or declaration under the bankruptcy act, punctuated the careers of 24% of the firms ever reported by Dun and Company. But of the 371 failures recorded, slightly over half did not result in terminations of the business, 40% surviving for three years or more and 20% for ten years or more. Firms which went under more than once account for 6% of the total.

In so competitive and unstable a business environment, the proprietor who showed too rigid a concern for the honor and reputation of his family handicapped himself in the struggle for survival. We are persuaded that the local lawyers and merchants who served as Dun and Company's correspondents at mid-century did not err in emphasizing the frequency with which arrangements between relatives were used to fend off creditors. In general, the thoroughness of the correspondents' investigations is impressive. Some types of information were gathered more systematically than others, however.

The reports provide quite complete information on the family relationship, if any, of current partners and also on the ownership of property by all proprietors and any close relatives resident in the city. Correspondents covered the entire range of the city's enterprises. Indeed, the kinds of firms least treated in most historical sources, the small, the marginal, or the temporarily precarious firms, receive fuller description in credit reports than do large, well-established enterprises.

Unfortunately, the correspondents reported only sporadically on the sources of capital for business. The most tentative part, therefore, of a survey of the role of family in business based on credit reports concerns capital supply. The first reports on some firms occurred years after their establishment, and these rarely gave much detail on the previous history. Other firms, such as saloons and repair shops, usually began so modestly that capital supply did not merit comment. The proprietors had little property and their business required little capital beyond small credits from wholesalers. Eliminating all proprietors worth $1,000 or less and those for whom no estimate of worth appears, we find that local correspondents commented explicitly on the sources of capital for 249, or 32%, of the remaining firms.

The family clearly predominated as a known source of capital for these more substantial firms.[8] At least one partner in 153 of the 249 firms, or 61%, depended on relatives for part or all of his investment in the business. Often rich relatives endorsed notes for their kin rather than turning over their own capital directly.[9] An additional 99 cases of succession in the ownership of enterprises, mostly from father to son, should be considered as a transfer of capital to relatives. Succession by a relative usually involved inheritance of goods, sometimes money, and, at the very least, the firm's good will.[10]

Among the 532 firms worth $1,000 or more whose sources of capital remain unknown, it seems probable that family assistance accounted for a much smaller proportion than among the known. At least 179 of these firms belonged to proprietors who had been or still worked as skilled craftsmen. In all likelihood their skill served as their most important form of capital initially. Other firms appear to have been founded by clerks, largely out of their savings from previous employment, and by men coming into the city who had been engaged in business elsewhere. All firms, whatever their worth, relied extensively on credit from wholesalers as well as on money raised from the mortgaging of real estate, if they owned any.[11]

Because information on the origin of capital covers only a minority of the firms evaluated, no definitive conclusion can be reached on the role of family. But examination of those firms assisted by family members does show the ways in which families used or did not use their money to promote the family interest over individual interests. Parents predominated among related financial backers, accounting for 64% of the total. But there were enough cases of brothers, brothers-in-law, uncles, cousins, and more distant relatives to indicate some sense of solidarity among family members and some concern for their individual welfare.

Thus, a Dun correspondent expected Stephen Merritt, partner in a bookstore, to receive a large inheritance from his uncle, who in the meantime assisted the firm financially. Philip Klady, a German brewer, gave his nephew Charles a small loan of $600 which Charles combined with personal savings to start a grocery. Uncles resident elsewhere sometimes helped out. Jeweller David Ainsley's uncle in Newburgh, down the river, gave him $2,000 to start his business. Robert Taylor's uncle in New York City endorsed his notes for him.[12]

Occasionally, relatives deliberately made what the market regarded as a bad investment. Hezekiah Sherwood's uncle continued to endorse for his nephew, a druggist, despite losses from previous endorsements. Bank cashier Walter Fonda bought the stock of his insolvent brother-in-law, butcher Ebeneezer Cary, and set him up in business again in order to give Cary something to do.[13]

But assistance in the form of capital did not necessarily mean promotion of family business interests over individual interests, even in the more common and intimate assistance of sons by parents and of husbands by wives. Thus, while many fathers did take their sons into the family business and pass it along to them, one-fifth of all sons who became partners with their fathers chose to leave rather than to continue in the family business. Other fathers provided capital to set their sons up in businesses which had no connection with the family or with its current source of income.

To be sure, some of these fathers, who were wealthy farmers or gentlemen living on inheritances, had to provide their sons with careers apart from the family because they did not have enterprises to pass on. Nevertheless, they enabled their sons to achieve a different career and financial independence, perhaps with the hope that the sons would increase the family fortunes through diversification. David B. Lent, Sr., a rich landowner, financed three sons and a son-in-law in separate businesses. He backed one son in a partnership in dry goods and another in a plaster mill. He endorsed all of the paper of a third son, who failed in the manufacture of bedsteads. When his son-in-law went into the gas-fitting business, Lent also signed for him at local banks. Rather than husbanding the family estate or concentrating it in one enterprise, the gentleman dispersed it in several directions.[14]

More persuasive evidence on the lack of subordination of children to family business interests comes from the number of fathers who presided over flourishing enterprises yet financed sons entering unrelated lines. John P. Adriance, owner of the huge Buckeye Mower and Reaper Works, twice enabled his son James to buy into different local bookselling firms as a partner. A rich dry goods merchant, James Bowne, financed two of his sons in different businesses: Charles in a partnership in drugs and James, Jr., in an unsuccessful coal yard of his own.[15]

Whether the father was a gentleman or a businessman, his willingness to provide sons with money or ready credit gave other entrepreneurs a source of capital in some instances. Francis Stevens' father gave him $10,000 to invest in the Eureka Mower and Reaper, providing the chief source of money for that firm. The credit report noted that Stevens was "not much posted in the ways of the world, refined gentleman, regular habits, but may have visionary ideas of business at present." John Auger, a mechanic recently arrived in Poughkeepsie, persuaded 24-year-old George Burnap to go in with him to produce a steel axle and spring for buggies which Auger had patented. The local correspondent commented that George, son of a very rich lawyer and banker, "has no means of his own. Watch carefully. The firm is good only as long as Burnap's father chooses to support them." A year later, the report added, "His business doesn't pay, seems to be a sort of White Elephant, and he makes ends meet only by the assistance of his father."[16]

Whether parental assistance to sons beginning new businesses represented anything like a conscious policy of encouraging diversified family investment cannot be determined, of course, in any systematic way from credit reports. A few families in Poughkeepsie numbered proprietors in several lines of business, and it could be argued that the more successful of these were simply embryonic versions of great family clans controlling a variety of enterprises. Certainly empire-building tendencies have not been uncommon among leading families in many cities and towns throughout our history. Yet what evidence we have on the nature of these new ventures suggests in the majority of cases response to individual circumstances rather than any policy of family aggrandizement. It seems probable that attitudes toward the financial assistance of sons differ in tendency between families with modest fortunes and those with great wealth, the former more often practicing as well as preaching an ideology of individualism, the latter more preoccupied with perpetuating their obvious collective power.

As one might expect, following an independent line was even more common among sons-in-law, including those who received money from their wives rather than directly from their parents-in-law. In only 5 cases did sons-in-law succeed to a business; in only 14 cases did their fathers-in-law take them into partnership. By contrast, wives and their fathers put up the capital for 47 sons-in-law. Occasionally a son-in-law who had been taken in as a partner left the firm after a few years and set up business for himself in exactly the same line, as Augustus Koch did in clothing. His brother-in-law remained in the old firm, presumably in direct competition. On the other hand, James Marvin, who married the daughter of a bedspring manufacturer, left his father-in-law's firm to start a complementary enterprise, a mattress factory.[17]

Typically, a father-in-law aided his daughter's husband in an entirely different line of business. The German owner of a successful pottery works gave his native son-in-law a line of credit to the extent of $1,000 at the New York house where he bought linens for his new shirt factory.[18] Many of the wives who gave money to their husbands' businesses had received that money from fathers still active and prospering in commerce or manufacturing. Marriage to a rich wife often did not secure a niche in an already established firm, but, looking at his situation positively, a son-in-law might reasonably hope to receive financial aid from his wife's family while remaining separate and independent in business.

Much of the assistance, however, had some strings attached. In many cases the backers tried to secure themselves against possible loss, often through chattel or real estate mortgages. Livery stable owner Azor B. Lewis held a chattel mortgage on his sons' horses and carriages after he turned the business over to them. When the sons failed in 1876, this property reverted to him. Even a very wealthy man like the retired Irish merchant Edward Hunter covered his gifts to his son, a dry goods merchant, by both chattel and real estate mortgages.[19]

Other parents went to court and had their sons sold out at forced sales to recover the amounts they had loaned them. The father of a fancy goods dealer sold out his son and took all the tangible assets; other creditors received nothing.[20] Families aided relatives, but normally they did not do so to their own detriment. When commenting on businesses financed by families, the author of a treatise on mercantile credit cautioned, "It is generally only a question of time when the aforesaid relatives become solicitous about the business and its success, and they must be secured, and it is usually understood in the beginning that they shall not lose by the venture, no matter who else loses. Of course, the general creditor gets left."[21]

Wives often proved as jealous of their capital as other relatives. Isaac Sherrill's wife gave him money outright which Sherrill then placed in his own name; and Charles Barnes's wife gave Barnes the capital to buy out his father in the furniture business. But other wives exercised varying degrees of caution or control. Some apparently let their husbands have small amounts of money from time to time for their businesses. The local correspondent thought an English merchant tailor's wife paid for all he bought.[22]

Other wives kept some form of control over the businesses they had helped financially. Mrs. Theodore Allen became the "company," the silent partner, in the hardware business run by her husband and brother. Another spouse loaned her husband and father-in-law about $5,000 for their dry goods firm. Subsequently, she became alarmed about the downhill trend and had the sheriff close them up. In the extreme situation, a never-very-successful crockery merchant remained completely dependent on his wife and her rich family. He could not touch a dollar, said the local correspondent, without their approval.[23]

Such care in securing capital can be seen as a means of husbanding the family resources. Yet the contrast with the businessmen described by Landes is obvious. In France businessmen considered bankruptcy a blot on the family honor, a disgrace to be avoided at all costs. In Poughkeepsie, by contrast, relatives supplying capital worried more about protecting their investment than about family honor. And American businessmen seemed to have few scruples about using their families as means of evading creditors whenever their businesses seemed precarious or on the brink of failure. In the Darwinian jungle of small business in the United States, survival frequently involved use of family relationships, founded in trust, to take advantage of loopholes in the law. These legal dodges allowed proprietors to stave off bankruptcy or at least to manage their insolvency so that some property would be salvaged for their family's security or for a fresh start in business.

When feminists mounted their campaign in New York State for the Married Women's Property Act of 1848 and the subsequent act of 1860, they probably did not foresee one of the chief uses to which those acts would be put. The act of 1848 gave wives legal control of their premarital and inherited property; the act of 1860 gave them control of property acquired during the course of marriage.[24] While these acts fulfilled one of the feminists' purposes—that of preventing spendthrift husbands from running through their wives' property—they also provided a means of securing the future of the nuclear family no matter how risky the business venture. Businessmen could put their dwellings, land, bank stocks, and other assets not involved in their businesses in their wives' names and, therefore, beyond the reach of creditors. Or, if a wife already had property, she could keep it and, in addition, take title to these outside assets of her husband.[25] Thus, the nuclear family could be shielded from the vicissitudes of the business cycle and even from the consequences of failure due to bad management.

Faced with the prospect of insolvency, many businessmen transferred their business assets to their wives or children through hastily arranged chattel mortgages or bills of sale covering merchandise, fixtures, and equipment. When failure came, a member of the family who had not contracted for the goods would hold title to them and so not be liable to creditors. Such transfers could be declared illegal by the courts if too obviously fraudulent and made too close to the time of failure, but more often than not they succeeded.

A German brewer gave a real estate mortgage to his wife in 1879 which the local correspondent suspected of being a bluff. In 1882 with the business doing poorly, his wife was found to own all of his stock, security for the mortgage. A liquor dealer transferred all of his property to his wife just before he failed; he claimed that he did so only to secure her for money he had borrowed. When it turned out that a grocer's wife owned everything after his failure, he claimed she had inherited the property she owned. An investigation by the local correspondent, however, disclosed a deed conveying the property to her shortly before he got into trouble.[26]

Wives, and less commonly parents, also made it possible for men to continue in business when they had been declared bankrupt but had not been discharged from their former debts by their creditors. Men resumed business as agents for their wives, usually having transferred their property to the wives before their failure. The wives as principals would now be liable for the debts of the firm, but their property could not be seized to pay off their husbands' old debts. The amount of autonomy a man had in this situation depended on his wife.

A treatise on credit generalized about this kind of agency: "The logical conclusion in regard to this stamp of individuals is that the acquisition of property by any means, and the comfort of their families, at all hazards, is the chief aim before them, and they do not scruple to attain these results, even at the loss of character and name."[27]

Doing business as agent for one's wife usually was a tactic of small businessmen struggling to survive. But its disreputability among creditors should not blind us to its frequency in that numerous world of small shopkeepers, neighborhood grocers and saloonkeepers, marginal hardware and shoe shops, or back-street variety stores. The American petit bourgeoisie in the nineteenth century offered many examples, which credit reporters never tired of praising, of the small dealer who pays his every debt regardless of the burden to himself and to his family. But such scrupulousness and preoccupation with family honor did not predominate. At the other extreme, family members demonstrated their inventiveness by frustrating the attempts of creditors to fix financial responsibility within their enterprise.

To the wonder and chagrin of local correspondents, a German locksmith's family by frequent shifting of ownership managed to keep their once prosperous hardware store afloat after the father's failure in 1875, continuing to do a fair business and to earn more than a bare livelihood despite a wholly adverse credit rating. In 1880 the correspondent observed that the family ownerships "have turned over several times in the past few years in order to evade creditors and the stock of goods is now claimed by a son who is running the business as his own. . . . The style is changed whenever the one in charge becomes unable to pay his bills." Six years later the situation remained unchanged: "If you see the father, the business belongs to the mother; if you see her, it belongs to the father; if you see both, it belongs to the son."[28]

The family proved most useful in all of these legal maneuverings because of trust between its members. Family members could betray that trust—wives could leave their husbands and parents could let their children remain stranded—but the assumption apparently was that they would not or, at least, that relationships outside the family would be even less trustworthy. The same need for trust and loyalty in a mobile society undoubtedly accounts for the frequency of family members in business partnerships in the city. No less than 48% of the firms ever run as partnerships in Poughkeepsie brought together relatives at one time or another.

The frequency of family members as partners increases with the estimated worth of the firm, but the tendency shows diminishing strength at higher levels of estimated worth with a slight reversal at the very top. Thus, 46% of the firms ever rated at more than $25,000 had at least 2 family members as partners for some period of their life compared to 36% of the firms rated between $10,000 and $25,000. Among firms estimated at between $50,000 and $100,000 a slightly higher proportion—48%—involved family partnerships, but among the 27 richest firms in the city worth $100,000 or more the proportion drops to 44% with another 4% accounted for by incorporated firms and the remainder by single proprietorships and nonfamily partnerships. As these figures indicate, the family partnership did not typify either Poughkeepsie's smaller firms—comparable to the French boutique —nor the relatively few richest firms which Bell might classify as "middle-sized enterprises."

Nuclear family relationships predominated among partners; 106 partnerships joined fathers and sons and 113 joined brothers.[29] Practically all of the remaining 37 partnerships involved in-laws. Moreover, in another 44 cases sons succeeded to their fathers' businesses without ever having been partners. They probably had been active, but subordinate, in the firm before their fathers died. Of those who had been partners with their fathers, 45 succeeded to the business eventually, making a total of 89 firms which passed from one generation to another within the same family.

Firms involving partnerships of family members tended to be among the more successful in the city, an obvious economic inducement to sons to join or to succeed their fathers. Still, as noted earlier, a fifth of these partnerships proved temporary, the sons deciding to leave the family business. Moreover, examination of these father and son partnerships suggests that fathers did not choose to use their economic power to try to keep their sons in prolonged dependence on them.

Especially striking in this regard are the relatively young ages at which fathers admitted their sons to partnerships and the ages at which sons assumed full control of the business on their fathers' retirement or death. While the elevation of sons to partnership did not mean that they had achieved equal financial standing with their fathers, it did express a legal and symbolic equality.

Sons shared in the profits and could sign notes and conduct transactions in the name of the firm. If sons turned out to be incompetent, they could dissipate the father's capital by signing notes recklessly, by ordering too much merchandise, or by granting too much credit. The sons of a dealer in toys and fancy and sporting goods did just that. In 1871 the family enterprise won an A-1 rating as a large and paying business; in 1878 the local correspondent commented that the father, now by himself in business, "Was at one time worth considerable property, but his sons are fast and used it all up."[30]

By admitting sons to partnership, fathers expressed trust in their sons' abilities while granting them a measure of independence.[31] This kind of recognition came early to the sons of businessmen in Poughkeepsie; of the 70 who joined their fathers as partners for whom we can find age data, 39% were between 25 and 29 years of age while 40% were under 25 and only 21% were over 30. A long apprenticeship in the business inculcating caution and prudence does not seem to have been very common.

The ages at full succession to businesses fall later, of course.

Nevertheless, 54% of the sons who succeeded their fathers had done so by age thirty. Differences do appear between sons who succeeded their fathers after having been in partnership with them and those who succeeded without any experience as a partner. Those who had been partners normally did not take over the business before age thirty; 67% did so after age thirty, with 23% not succeeding until their forties. By contrast, 76% of those who never experienced partnership with their fathers controlled the business by age thirty.

The earlier successions often resulted from the death of the father, but not invariably. Valentine Frank turned his prosperous business over to his sons when they were only 24 and 26; he continued to supply them with capital, but they legally constituted the principals in the brewery. Similarly, another German took over his father's clothing business when he was 26 and his father only 49 years of age; his father, according to the report, gave him the stock and the profits of the business.[32]

Partnerships among brothers were more numerous than those between fathers and sons. They also proved more transient. Over half—53%—lasted for five years or less, and they usually dissolved because of a mutual agreement.[33] Brothers who found it difficult to work together or who felt that the partnership limited their individual opportunity did not hesitate to extricate themselves from an unpromising situation. Seneca Lake and his brother began as joint proprietors of a barbershop; after two years they dissolved the partnership and set up separate and competing shops. Two German brothers who launched a cigar store repeated the pattern, each managing his own store after four years together.[34]

Sometimes brothers gave up their partnership in order to seize new opportunities. The sons of Elisha Sterling, an iron merchant, purchased their father's business with help from a relative and continued together for five years. When one of them decided to go to Wisconsin as an employee for a firm there, the other remained as sole proprietor of what had been a family business. An Irishman left his brothers in the soap and candle factory to set up for himself in dry goods. He may have considered himself well out of the family enterprise; one of his brothers drank so much that his business affairs had to be run by a committee.[35]

A minority of partnerships among brothers proved both long-lived and successful; 13% continued for fifteen years or more, and most of these for more than twenty years. Just as firms which passed from father to son tended to be among the more prosperous, so these more enduring partnerships between brothers belonged to the city's more successful firms. All of them had an estimated worth of more than $10,000. Some of them, such as the Reynolds firm, represented brothers who had inherited the business from their fathers and who would pass it on in turn to their sons. Others, like the Pelton carpet factory, had been founded by brothers who stayed together as the firm increased in prosperity, and the nearly thirty-year partnership was broken only by the death of one brother.[36]

Several families in Poughkeepsie did perpetuate large enterprises for two generations or more; relying primarily on relatives for partners or officers and for capital. The Reynolds, Adriance, Innis, Arnold, and Vassar connections come closest to resembling Daniel Bell's description of "family capitalism." But they cannot be said to have dominated Poughkeepsie's economy, politics, or social life although they obviously had influence in each sphere. Their fortunes were substantial, ranging from several hundred thousand dollars to more than a million dollars, but no more so than those of several self-made men who recently had come to the city. No one family connection or cluster of them commanded anything like the overwhelming superiority of resources of the DuPonts in Wilmington or even the power of the mill-owning families of Fall River.

Nor did these few families generally keep their principal enterprises alive and under family control for the longer run.[37] All but one of the large manufacturers of the sixties and seventies had been sold out by the turn of the century or simply closed up, victims of obsolescence and competition. Even during their prosperity, family members responsible for these firms did not always hesitate to seek large amounts of money outside the firm and the family.

The managing partner of one largely family enterprise, himself a former bank president and mayor of the city, accumulated debts of more than $100,000 with local banks and friends. To the alarm of his creditors, reduction of the debt progressed extremely slowly although the firm's volume of business had never been greater. Ultimate payment in full seemed so uncertain that his friends on the board of directors of the bank of which he had been president believed "that a compromise of 50% would be allowed were a cash settlement offered at that rate." This is a far cry from the self-sufficiency and caution attributed to the maison.[38]

Even among substantial family firms which seem most probably exempt from any spirit of opportunism, notions of family honor and financial responsibility often proved flexible in practice, accommodating a well-developed capitalistic spirit rather than expressing the precapitalistic mentality David Landes describes in French firms. Some prominent families, to be sure, had more rigid notions, preferring loss of profit or even property to loss of reputation. Evaluating the business run by Mrs. Leason Holdridge's husband, a local correspondent commented, "In case of trouble, her family, noted for pride of name and position, would not allow debts to go unpaid."[39] In the seventies such probity already seemed a little old-fashioned and more the exception than the rule.

By the middle of the nineteenth century at least, the testimony of credit reports for this one small city suggests that the character of the local business environment, its competitiveness and insecurity, strongly influenced family business arrangements. The social values which seem to underlie these arrangements are those historians commonly have ascribed to nineteenth-century America, those of a capitalism without a feudal past. However the immigrants, natives, former artisans, old merchants, and manufacturing entrepreneurs who made up Poughkeepsie's proprietorial class pursued different values outside their business lives, they met the typical insecurity—stated positively, the opportunity—of urban economies throughout the Northeast by mid-century with that mixture of individualism, opportunism, and ingenuity whose extreme expression appears in the image of the Yankee trader.

NOTES

1. Eugene Litwak, "Occupational Mobility and Extended Family Cohesion," American Sociological Review, XXV (1960); Marvin B. Sussman, "The Help Pattern in the Middle Class Family," American Sociological Review, XVIII (1953); and Sussman and Lee Burchinal, "Kin Family Network: Unheralded Structure in Current Conceptualizations of Family Functioning," Marriage and Family Living, XXIV (1962); Robert P. Stuckert, "Occupational Mobility and Family Relationships," Social Forces, XLI (1963). For a highly critical view of Litwak and Sussman see Geoffrey Gibson, "Kin Family Network: Overheralded Structure in Past Conceptualizations of Family Functioning," Journal of Marriage and the Family, XXXIV (1972). For a similar view that kinship aid in nineteenth-century England was functional, but also highly instrumental, see Michael Anderson, *Family Structure in Nineteenth Century Lancashire* (Cambridge, 1971).

2. David Landes, "French Business and the Businessman: A Social and Cultural Analysis," in Edward M. Earle, ed., *Modern France* (Princeton, 1951), 336, 348; see also John Sawyer, "The Entrepreneur and the Social Order: France and the United States," in William Miller, ed., *Men in Business* (Cambridge, 1952).

3. Daniel Bell, "The Breakup of Family Capitalism," in *The End of Ideology* (New York, 1961), 41–42.

4. Forthcoming under the title: *Natives and Newcomers: The Ordering of Opportunity in Poughkeepsie, New York, 1850–1880*.

5. The 159 firms headed by women and first reported by 1880 have not been included in this essay. These firms tended to be so marginal and specialized, primarily dressmaking and millinery shops, that to include them would distort some of the totals. The Mercantile Agency, organized in 1841 by Lewis Tappan, bore that name until 1859 when it became R. G. Dun and Company. Dun remained proprietor until his death in 1900. The reports for Poughkeepsie begin in 1844, and like the volumes for other cities deposited in Baker Library, they end in 1890. For a description of the reporters and their reporting, see the commemorative work by Roy Foulke, *The Sinews of American Commerce* (New York, 1941), Part Four.

6. R. G. and A. R. Hutchinson and Mabel Newcomer, "A Study in Business Mortality: Length of Life of Business Enterprises in Poughkeepsie, New York, 1843–1936," American Economic Review, XXVIII (1938).

7. Of the 1,530 businesses evaluated, the estimated worth of a little more than two-fifths never exceeded $1,000; nearly two-fifths fell between $1,000 and $10,000; one-tenth fell between $10,000 and $25,000, and only one-tenth exceeded $25,000 in any report. "Estimated worth" in the credit reports refers to all assets which could be reached by creditors, if necessary. A C.O.D. (cash on delivery) rating indicates that the individual or firm is regarded as financially worthless and therefore not worthy of any credit.

8. Sources of capital other than the family were various. Many businessmen took out real estate mortgages; some swapped land for the stock of a business; some had already been successful in other business ventures.

9. The importance of this assurance in making credit available appears in the frequent comment of local correspondents that a certain young businessman's notes should be accepted only when his rich father has endorsed them. See the entries in the Mercantile Agency ledgers for Ellsworth and Briman, Hardware, 114, 126–127 (1868); Morgan Farnum, Drugs, 23 (1865); Henry Morris, Stoves, 77 (1849); Palmer and Marble, Sash and Blind Mfr., 74: 401, 519, 521, (1882); Arthur Wilkinson, Cigars, 99 (1855). All credit report citations hereafter follow the sequence of initials of the proprietor or partnership, type of business, page of the ledger and, in parentheses, the year of the specific report. Pages in the two volumes for Poughkeepsie, numbers 73 and 74 in the Baker Library collection, are numbered sequentially with the exception of pages 400–499 which conclude volume 73 and the repetitious pages 400–499 which begin volume 74. We include volume numbers only for these repeated pages. "Mfr." abbreviates manufacturer.

10. HF, Insurance, 1 (1868); G & TH, Jewelry, 333 (1875); MM, Wagon Mfr., 249 (1871); JR, Hotel, 57 (1867).

11. D, C & M, Dry Goods, 395 (1875); F, S & Co., Overalls Mfr., 373 (1880); D & E, Fancy Goods, 175 (1875); MG, Hotel, 125 (1870); PMH, Drugs, 123 (1868); JS & Son, Livery, 241 (1870).

12. F & M, 187, 341 (1873); CK, 422, 465 (1879); A & M, 270 (1973); RT, 34, 41 (1858).

13. HS, Drugs, 570 (1882); EC, 293, 338, 521, 525 (1881).

14. GBL, 62 (1844); JRL, 248 (1870); DBL, Jr., 102 (1855); CW, 98 (1855).

15. H & A, 158, 227, 474 (1870); R & A, 237, 302–303 (1872); R, G & B, 270, 413 (1875, 1877); JJB, Jr., 160 (1868).

16. EM & R Co., 130, 231, 264 (1868, 1871); A & B, Carriage Mfrs., 205, 265, (1870, 1871).

17. JJB & Co., 116, 74: 429 (1865, 1882); JM, 74: 427, 641 (1876).

18. D Bros., 74: 424, 539, 631 (1882).

19. AB & OPL, 124, 228, (1868, 1877); JH, 232, 233, 542 (1870, 1879, 1881). The chattel mortgage on stock in trade was a more extreme measure than the mortgage on real estate since the former almost always affected credit.

20. BV, 369 (1875); see also SKD & Son, Hats, 54, 176, 177, 293, 369 (1875) and JT, Grocery, 242, 74: 418, 521 (1878, 1880).

21. P. R. Earling, *Whom to Trust* (Chicago, 1890), 92.

22. B, H & Co., Leather, 563, 572 (1882); LB, Furniture, 277, 74: 423, 543 (1876); GKL, 93, 129 (1855).

23. A & Co., 305, 74: 477, 512 (1875, 1880, 1883); JW and WFM, 287, 74: 451 (1879); LH, 122, 123, 74: 430 (1870).

24. Beard and Profatt both point out that the common law restrictions on a married woman's property could be overturned in equity proceedings. Since only the very rich were likely to take advantage of the relief afforded by equity, the legislative acts, by removing the common law restraints on the married woman's possession of property, enabled all women to retain their property despite their husbands' debts. Eleanor Hays, *Morning Star: A Biography of Lucy Stone* (New York, 1961) 78–79, 168–172; Yuri Suhl, *Ernestine L. Rose and the Battle for Human Rights* (New York, 1959), 200–214; George Bayles, *Women and New York Law* (New York, 1911), 51–55; John Proffat, *Women Before the Law* (New York, 1874), 73–78; Mary Beard, *Woman as a Force in History* (New York, 1946), 138–144.

25. This device was especially important in New York State, which did not have a generous homestead law. Texas, for example, allowed the bankrupt $5,000 for the property on which the homestead stood and the homestead, whatever its value. James Hagerty, *Mercantile Credit* (New York, 1913), 331–332.

26. FG, 210, 226, 74: 402 (1879, 1882); EP, 255, 298, 344 (1884); HG, 162 (1870).

27. Earling, *Whom to Trust,* 132. Thirty-three men appear as agents for their wives, not including cases where ownership shifted frequently within the family; twenty of these did so immediately after a failure. For examples, see WCB, Meat, Coal, 200, 74: 440 (1872, 1876); SB, Plumbing, 26, 294, 350 (1875, 1876); AD, Fancy Goods, 239 (1870).

28. FH, 376, 377, 506, 552 (1876, 1880, 1886).

29. These figures include an overlap of ten firms run by partnerships of father and sons, but later of brothers; so the total number of firms covered by the two tabulations is 208.

30. WCB & Sons, 68, 93, 199, 296, 297 (1871, 1872, 1878).

31. The credit reports do not clarify absolutely whether family businesses were partnerships or corporations. The vast majority may be presumed to be partnerships since the reports specify corporations generally and name the officers within them.

32. VF, 246, 74: 459, 669 (1879); IH, 87, 178, 396 (1876). Data on age at succession come from the manuscript population schedules of the federal census; the analysis included only those individuals we could find in the census, a majority of those evaluated in the credit reports.

33. Dissolution refers to those cases in which one brother left a firm leaving the other brother still in charge of the business. The longer brothers were in business together the less likely they were to dissolve the partnership.

34. G & Bros., 16, 106, 308, 409 (1858, 1860); SL, 44, 520–521 (1876–1878).

35. D & Bros., 186, 74: 440–441, 677 (1879).

36. WW & JR, Flour and provisions, 75, 95, 189, 379, 74: 421, 630 (1844, 1853, 1866); G & CP, 6, 23, 76, 85, 82 (1849, 1868, 1878).

37. Frederic C. Jaher, in his preliminary findings about the Boston Brahmins, similarly notes a decreasing tendency for sons to follow their fathers into business and to maintain entrepreneurial vigor in those instances when they did succeed to the family business. See his ''Businessmen and Gentlemen,'' *Explorations in Entrepreneurial History,* 4 (1966–1967), 17–35.

38. G, S & I, Dye Wood Mfr., 11, 344 (1864, 1880–1881, 1883).

39. LH, 122, 123, 74: 430 (1870).

8

Urbanization and the Malleable Household: An Examination of Boarding and Lodging in American Families

JOHN MODELL AND TAMARA K. HAREVEN

The challenges to traditional values posed by the urbanization of American society included by the late nineteenth century a new and widespread doubt that the family was capable of withstanding the pressures to which it was exposed. One aspect of family life upon which this lack of faith focused was the common practice of taking into the household boarders or lodgers.[1] What once had seemed a genial practice, a way of providing at once temporary accommodation and a family setting for those who lacked their own ménage, now seemed a threat to the institution of the family itself. James Quayle Dealey expressed the setting of the anxiety nicely in 1912, when his *Family in Its Sociological Aspects* likened even the modern urban family (biologically defined) to "a temporary meeting place for boarding and lodging," where strangers entered while family members passed large portions of their time on the streets or in other company.[2] By this time, however, boarding and lodging within the family had been under attack for a quarter of a

Author's Note: *Modell wishes to thank Winifred Bolin, whose student work on lodgers has contributed insight into their importance. Hareven is grateful to Stuart Blumin, Maris Vinovskis, Richard Jensen, Stephen Shedd, and Randolph Langenbach for their advice and expert help. Research on the Boston data in this essay was supported in part by the Clark University Graduate Research Fund, and the Clark Computer Fund.*

century, and a somewhat diffuse but nevertheless damning bill of particulars had been drawn up against it. The present paper seeks to suggest the social and economic significance of this transit of values, while exploring the extent and functions of the institution of boarding within the family.[3]

Family governance was the lynchpin of the Puritan theory of social control, as it was in less dramatic form of the whole English tradition carried over into the American republic.[4] In its multiple functions as a workshop, a church, an asylum, and a reformatory, the Colonial family included boarders as well as servants and apprentices and dependent strangers. The presence of strangers in the household was accepted as a normal part of family organization. Town governments customarily boarded the homeless, poor, or juveniles with families for a fee. The first federal census, taken in 1790, showed a very small proportion of persons living alone (3.7% of households were of one person only, as compared with nearly 20% in 1970). Even a frontier state in 1820, peopled almost entirely by newcomers to the region, saw all but 2.7% of its white households with two or more living together.[5]

Inspection of census enumerators' manuscripts from 1850 onward reveals large numbers of persons recorded as ''lodgers'' in established households of otherwise predominantly nuclear structure who were either juveniles, distant relatives, apparently unrelated persons of similar village origin or from the same foreign land, or young men sharing a trade with the household head. Occasionally they constituted an entire family group in the household. Studies now in progress for rural and urban communities in the decade before the civil war show around one in five families with lodgers. Blumin has found an average of 17 to 20% of all households augmented by one or more non-kin members in three Hudson Valley communities—Troy, Marlborough and Kingston —while Glasco has found that about 21% of all native households and 15% of all Irish households in Buffalo in the 1850s were augmented by strangers. A figure of 15.7% has been computed for Detroit in 1880.[6] Boston neighborhoods in the same period show from 10 to 30% of households containing strangers in the family.

The nineteenth-century American family was an accommodating and flexible institution, as had been its eighteenth- and seventeenth-century predecessors.[7] Lodging was one major rubric under which its biologically-defined limits were breached by an instrumental relationship based on economic and service exchange.

Yet by the end of the nineteenth century such Progressive moralists as

Lawrence Veiller, the housing reformer, had created both a new name for the old practice—"the lodger evil"—and a behavioral measure for it: "room overcrowding as we know it in America," Veiller wrote, "is almost entirely wrapped up with the lodger evil."[8] In matter of fact, Veiller was quite wrong; but in any case, the lodger evil could not *really* be measured spatially. A speaker at the 1910 biennial session of the National Conference of Jewish Charities revealed this neatly when he argued that "above all the keeping of lodgers, other than those related by blood ties to the family, should be prohibited absolutely," and went on to explain the dangers of overcrowding just as though biologically related persons required less space than unrelated individuals.[9] Social, not physical, space was the question.

It was a matter of privacy, and middle-class definitions of privacy were tightening. Carol Aronovici, another housing reformer, spoke with horror of "this widespread practice of exposing the private life of the heads of the family and that of the young girls to the presence of men in no way connected by blood relationships with the members of the household."[10] Still another reformer saw fit to record the statements made to her by "little girls" that "the men (boarders) are nasty and lift up our skirts."[11] For (according to a government report) when strangers become members of the household

. . . the close quarters often destroy all privacy, and the lodger or boarder becomes practically a member of the family. . . . While such conditions, through custom and long usage, lose the startling effect they would have to one unused to them, they cannot help but blunt a girl's sense of proper relations with the other sex and foster standards which are not acceptable in this country.[12]

Sexuality rampant, or potentially so when and if the family failed to socialize its young properly, that was the fear.[13] The context of this fear of family breakdown was that which underlay so many middle-class fears of the period: that the conditions of rapid urbanization were making life on its traditional basis impossible, an anxiety visible (again with sexual overtones) as well in the literature of the period dealing with women's work, the tragic end of the prostitute, and the vast library of progressive discussion of the immigrant.

Veiller's rich fantasy about what went on in the teeming immigrant tenements need hardly be rehearsed here, but it is significant that it surfaced (among other places) in his appeal for widely expanded police powers to stamp out "the lodger evil," which he mainly identified with immigrants. Aronovici was so convinced of this linkage that she contradicted her own empirical findings in her study of Saint Paul, Minnesota, housing conditions (which found that in "striking contrast to the ordinary conception of the lodger evil," foreign-born residents were not particularly disposed to taking in lodgers) to assert that "the main reasons for the evil are to be found in the gregarious habits of the foreign elements."[14]

The fear expressed by social workers and reformers, of family deterioration and breakdown under the impact of lodging and boarding, was closely associated with a general fear of the disintegration of traditional primary groups under the pressures of urban life. While earlier the guardians of social norms had used boarding as a safety valve, they had come to view it as a manifestation of social breakdown in the urban environment. This association of the practice of boarding with the social deterioration of the city was reinforced in reformers' minds by the actual transformations in housing patterns which they were witnessing in their own environment. In Boston, for example, the South End was changing from an elegant bay-front, town-house neighborhood into a boarding and lodging and tenement district through the subdivision of three- to five-story row houses and their conversion into multiple-family apartments, or into one-family houses with lodgers and boarders on the top floors. Aside from its impact on the family, lodging and boarding was clearly associated with the decline of neighborhoods and with social disorder.

By the early twentieth century, thus, the ideal of the lodger-free household was associated in the minds of social workers and reformers with that of the upright, decent working girl, that of the acculturated immigrant family, and indeed with the whole set of values encompassing the well-ordered family, the wisely budgeted household, and the child protected from the most corrupting of life's threats. Since progressives believed that the future belonged to the young and acted accordingly, they turned their reforming attention to the family, bewailing its imminent demise. In part their approach was surgical: to cut out from the family those strangers whose presence apparently placed its integrity, cohesion, and socializing values under strain.

Yet families—even native-born families—did not on the whole conform to the reformers' prescription for nearly half a century. From a wide variety of sources, one gets the impression that for half a century and probably more the proportion of urban households which *at any particular point in time* had boarders or lodgers was between 15 and 20%. For 1920 we find for such varied cities as Chicago, Wilkes-Barre, Passaic, and Rochester figures at roughly this level. When in 1930 the Census Bureau first published uniform statistics on lodging in large cities, the proportion of urban American families who kept boarders was 11.4%. At this date, Chicago's percentage had increased during the decade, while Rochester's had declined.[15]

Lodging in families was on the decline by the 1930's, despite the fact that in the short run the Depression worked to increase the tendency of established families to take in boarders. The 11.4% overall figure for 1930 was down to 9.0% for 1940. By 1970, even a city with a very "high" incidence of boarding in families, like San Francisco, had a shade under 4.5% of families with boarders, with most cities considerably under this figure.[16] The institution of boarding in families was, at last, disappearing.

We have already implied our point of view about boarders and lodgers in the family: that the practice was, like cityward migration itself, one institutionalized mode of the "social equalization of the size of the family," in Irene B. Taeuber's felicitous phrase.[17] From this perspective, change-over-time figures for the incidence of boarding pose two questions. First, in view of the middle-class opposition to the practice, why did this vehicle for family equalization persist as long as it did and as late as it did, given the ample opportunities for institutional alternatives to have developed? And second, why did the ultimate decline of boarding and lodging come when at last it did?

In its urban, nineteenth-century manifestation, boarding in families was an adaptation of a traditional middle-class practice[18] to a situation in which large numbers of new urbanites, both foreign- and native-born, usually young and with shallow resources, were thrown into a chaotic housing market. Confusion, economic considerations, and the need for socialization into the ways of the city all made a quasi-familial setting a very attractive proposition to the newcomer, the more so when he had in common with the family in which he would temporarily settle origin, ethnicity, occupation, or kinship.

We can look at the Rhode Island state censuses of 1885 and 1895 for some insight into the local conditions conducive to boarding in the family. To do so we will have to shift our focus momentarily from the family itself, for the "boarders and lodgers" figure on the Rhode Island censuses included lodgers under the same head, whether they were living in families or in boarding houses. This, however, is not troublesome if we allow that these two categories (from the point of view of the lodger) essentially competed within a single market, that is, were substitutable goods. The town-to-town range of boarders enumerated per household was tremendous: a firm minimum was found in the declining agricultural town of Foster, whose ratio of lodgers to families implied that perhaps 3% of Foster families took in these strangers in 1885 and perhaps 4% in 1895. The maximum figures are a bit less certain, because in each year one town (each on the seacoast) had what seem quite inflated figures for boarders. If we exclude these, we find maxima of 44 and 43 lodgers per 100 families for the two years, implying that about 25 or 30% of families in the two years had boarders at the time of the census, if the usual quota of lodgers per household (about 1.5 as a mean) obtained in Barrington, the locus of the maxima. Barrington posed quite a contrast to Foster: its steadily growing population was engaged during this period in a changeover from a fairly agricultural setting to one which was very substantially industrial.

Looking systematically at the Rhode Island town figures, we find strong and significant positive correlations between the lodging ratio and such characteristic aspects of industrial urbanization as five-year population gain, proportion of manufacturing employees in the local labor force, and proportion of the local population born in foreign countries. The last mentioned is the strongest of the three, highly significant in both years, accounting for about half the town-to-town variation in 1885 and about a quarter in 1895.[19] The correlation observed in the Rhode Island materials can and should be explained quite simply: the kind of town the foreign-born came to was the same kind of town potential lodgers both foreign and native came to.

Statewide data for Massachusetts in 1885 permit us to refine these clues somewhat, by computing the ratios by age, sex, and nativity, between boarders and lodgers, and those living in households as non-lineal kin (brothers or sisters, uncles or aunts, nephews or nieces, and cousins)—roughly as a measure of "taste" for living as boarders rather than as extended family members.[20] Having had relatively less time in which to develop kinship networks, the foreign-born of both sexes had higher ratios for boarders to extended family relationships, overall, but taking this into consideration, the patterns are age- and sex-specific, rather than varying by nativity.

For both native- and foreign-born males, there was a broad peak of preference for boarding extending from the 20 to 29 category through the 40 to 49 category, peaking slightly among those 30 to 39; ratios are about 4.5 times as many boarders as extended kin for the native-born, about 5.75 times for the foreign-born. Among women, the peak is in the 20 to 29 group, and it is a sharp peak, declining quickly on either side, with the peak ratio about three times for the native-born but only 2.1 for the foreign-born. The overall lower ratios for females than for males speaks eloquently of a lingering societal preference for family governance for women, while the sharp peak ratio for the women is no doubt parallel to their brief exposure to ''independent'' existence in the labor force. Among males of both nativities, both the height and the breadth of the peak of preference for lodging points to the extent to which an economic relationship served instead of a possibly traditional familial one for all but those at the opposite ends of the age continuum. The young and the old, of course, included high proportions of the dependent, for whom familial relationships were evidently considered preferable. That the age- and sex-specific patterns were parallel for the native-and the foreign-born indicates yet again how thoroughly by 1885 the institution of boarding had become part of the American social structure.

When we turn from aggregate data for the state to individual data for Boston, we discover that in boarding as in many other areas, America was a multi-layered society. An analysis of family and household structure and residential patterns in select Boston neighborhoods in 1880 corroborates the general patterns found in the state data, but also reveals significant differences.[21]

The Boston data show conclusively that boarding with families was far more pervasively a native American phenomenon than an immigrant practice. The Irish, Boston's largest immigrant group, included the lowest percentage of boarders in the neighborhoods studied. The highest concentration of boarders was among natives of Massachusetts (38%) and among natives of Maine, New Hampshire, and Vermont, many of whom were recent arrivals to the city (19.3%). In Boston's South End, where the Irish comprised about 31% of the entire population studied, Irish boarders made up only 10% of all boarders sampled. The Boston data support our hypothesis that boarding was a *migrant* rather than a foreign immigrant practice: individuals who showed the highest tendency to board were newest to the city. Immigrants from abroad, however, resorted to boarding as a temporary measure until they settled in their own households in other parts of the city or in other towns. For native Americans on the other hand, lodging was a regular and long-term alternative to the nuclear or extended family. (In the South End, 30% of all households studied had boarders. Only 15% included extended kin.)

Whether a temporary measure or a longer-lasting arrangement, boarding was a function of the life cycle. It was most prevalent among unmarried men and women, most of whom were employed in the central downtown area. About 37% of all boarders in the entire Boston sample studied were in the age group 20 to 29, and about 27.5% in the age group 30 to 39—a significantly higher concentration than in the rest of the population sample, where these age groups comprised 22% and 19% respectively. There were no significant differences in age grouping between men and women. While the largest part of this group boarded in the interim between their departure from their parents' households to the establishment of a household of their own, others continued to board through their thirties and forties. Children under 14 and teenagers were least represented in the boarding population (6.5% for those below 14, and 8.2% for the age group 14 to 19). Where they appeared as boarders, they were generally members of an entire family which boarded in the household. Such families consisted generally of parents in their late twenties or thirties with one or more children, or more frequently of widows or single women with their children. This type of boarding was most common among the Irish in the group studied (Irish boarders included 12% children under 14), which suggests their tendency to board in family clusters, no doubt in part a function of the higher mortality of Irish males.

A comparison of the age distribution of boarders and lodgers with that of the heads of households with whom they boarded shows a marked decline in the tendency of individuals in their forties to board. The data reveal, in fact, a role reversal at this stage. Rather than board or live with extended kin, men and women in their forties tended to head their own households and to take in boarders. One-third of all boarders studied were living with household heads in their forties. This practice appears to be particularly widespread in the South End, which housed the highest concentration of female-headed households in the neighborhoods studied, as well as the highest number of widows over forty. Female-headed households constituted 28% of all households studied in the South End. Of these, 39% took in boarders, in contrast to male-headed households, of which only 26.5% took in boarders.

A correlation of individuals with the heads of households with whom they boarded showed a clear pattern of bunching by age groups. While the largest proportion of boarders, regardless of age, lived with heads of households in the 40 to 50 age group, there was generally a "generation gap" between boarders and their heads. Most boarders under 35 tended to live in households headed by individuals who were their seniors by 15 years or more. This age pattern clearly suggests that the practice of

Table 1 | **Observed Frequency of Selected Ethnic Matches, Boston (South End) Boarders with Their Household Heads, Compared with "Expected" Frequency of Matches, 1880 (N = 645)**

	Same US state category*	Same foreign country	Different U.S. state category	Different foreign country	Boarder US head FB	Boarder FB, head US
	%	%	%	%	%	%
Observed	22.3	13.5	27.4	4.5	17.8	14.5
"Expected"	15.7	3.5	27.7	8.1	24.2	20.8
Ratio, observed: "expected"	1.43:1	3.81:1	0.99:1	0.56:1	0.74:1	0.70:1

*State categories are: Massachusetts; Maine–Vermont–New Hampshire; Connecticut–Rhode Island; rest of United States.

boarding and of taking in boarders was a function of the life cycle. A conservative estimate would suggest that at least one-third to one-half of all individuals were likely to experience both—boarding in their early adulthood and taking in boarders at a later stage of life.

The desire for independence from family ties was no doubt a major factor in the decision of boarders to pay rent rather than live with their kin in an extended household arrangement. Young men and women in their twenties, employed in semi-skilled or skilled jobs, preferred boarding with a strange family, over their own, because the exchange of rent and services was defined in strict economic terms. Boarding offered the advantages of a family setting, without the affective and lasting obligations that are woven into family relationships.[22] It also often placed them into a peer-group relationship with fellow boarders, an association which they sometimes carried over from their place of employment. Location in the city was an equally important consideration. In Boston, boarders and lodgers constituted 25% of the entire population of the centrally-located South End, which had become by then the city's primary boarding and lodging center. By contrast, in South Boston, a predominantly Irish section removed from the center of the city and thus inconvenient to the location of most jobs held by newcomers, only 5% of the groups studied were lodgers and boarders.

Boarding and lodging patterns in the South End reveal a distinct tendency toward ethnic clustering, and a lesser though nevertheless significant tendency toward occupational clustering. A comparison of each of about 700 boarders in Boston's South End with the head of household with whom he boarded suggests strong connections between the boarders' places of origin and those of their household heads. Table 1 presents these data in the form of a comparison between the matchings observed in the Boston data and those which would have been "expected" had boarders from different origins simply placed themselves at random in the homes of those offering space. The highest ratio of observed to expected frequencies is seen—understandably enough—in the category "same foreign country," in which nearly four times the number of exact matches was found as one would expect by chance alone. Among foreign nationalities, the highest concentrations of matches appeared among the Irish and the Canadians (principally from the Maritimes). Of Irish boarders, nearly six in ten were found living in households with Irish heads. Yet Irish-headed households with boarders had fellow Irishmen as boarders in only 35% of the cases, a number which contrasts sharply with a 60% figure for Canadian-headed homes with boarders sharing their nativity. But only 38% of Canadian boarders were lodged in Canadian-headed homes. The orderly quality of this rather complicated pattern is attested to by noting that Irish-headed families tended most often (40% of the time) to take in Massachusetts-born persons, no doubt often second-generation Irishmen, while Canadian boarders apparently had little trouble in situating themselves in the homes of the New England–born, whom they evidently sufficiently resembled to make fitting boarders.

Table 1 shows, too, a distinct clustering pattern by state, and a distinct avoidance pattern for three combinations. Of these, matches of different foreign nativity groups were the rarest, while foreigners mingled with the New England-born at roughly three-fourths the "expected" rate, both for foreign boarders in native households and native boarders in foreign households. The intensity of ethnic clustering is revealed not only in the comparison of boarders to their heads of households, but also among fellow boarders. In households containing several boarders, all boarders were frequently from the same place of origin, even if the head of household was not.

Occupational clustering (based upon data excluding all matches in which either boarder or household head had no occupation listed) was weaker, but reasonably convincing, especially in view of the broad occupational categories employed (professional; semi-professional; white collar; skilled; semi-skilled; and unskilled). Exact occupational matches occurred 1.14 times as frequently as would be expected by chance, while near-matches (between adjacent occupational categories) appeared 1.06 times the "expected" frequency. Among those where matching was more distant, surprisingly, it was slightly more likely that boarders would *exceed* their household head in status (0.92 times the chance likelihood) than would *be exceeded by* the head (0.87 times chance likelihood). The differences here are slight, but suggestive: boarders and their households sought out appropriate matches, no doubt utilizing the pricing mechanism as well as outright rejection. A perfect occupational match was seemingly optimal, but a near-match would also serve without being offensive to either party. Where no match or near-match was achieved (as in about 45% of the cases) boarders more frequently accepted accommodations with a less well-placed family than the reverse.[23]

By the beginning of the twentieth century Boston's South End was christened by one of its dedicated social workers as "The City Wilderness." As a tenement and lodging-house section in the commercial and entertainment center of the city, the South End already showed most of its "wilderness" characteristics by 1880. It was a polyglot section, a depository for most newly-arrived immigrants, an area containing a patch-work of ethnic enclaves, highly populated by unskilled and semi-skilled workers, and showing the highest proportion of unmarried and widowed persons in the city. It also housed the city's highest concentration of boarders and lodgers. This neighborhood can serve, therefore, as an excellent test for the stigma of social breakdown and anomie attached to boarding. Yet boarders in the South End were representative of the entire population groups studied, differing only in age and in marital status. They included a higher proportion of individuals in their twenties and thirties, and, in this age group, they were more frequently unmarried than the rest of the population studied. The overall occupational distribution for the South End lodgers is not substantially different from that of the neighborhood as a whole. The persistence of lodgers in the city parallels that of heads of households studied, and their lodging pattern is not random; it gives every impression of a sensible and orderly accommodation to urban life.

Families took in boarders primarily for economic considerations, which in turn depended in part on the characteristics of the housing market and in part on the uncertainties of income in a period of high morbidity and mortality and oppressive cyclical unemployment. Families which were prepared to accept lodgers: (1) were able to receive a "brokerage fee" for adapting the predominantly large dwelling units to the needs of usually single immigrants, usually from their own social level and of a similar standard of living; (2) realized income for work performed by the wife *within the home,* varying with the amount of effort the housewife wished to devote, reflected in the quantity, "quality," and duration of accommodations offered,[24] (3) benefited by a gain in flexibility in terms of their potential family income, available even in times of sickness or unemployment; (4) were in a position to stabilize their income through the family life cycle by moving a paying guest into the room once inhabited by a son or daughter who had left the home; (5) afforded widows and single women in their forties, fifties, and sixties an opportunity to maintain their own households rather than to live with their kin.

In an industrializing, rapidly urbanizing society, however, boarding was so widespread as to be reasonably considered indispensable: it was, in fact, far more common than the aggregate momentary estimate of 15 to 20% would suggest. For in nineteenth-century cities the practice of boarding in families was closely articulated to the life cycles both of the boarders and of the families which took them in. Figure 1 is admittedly based upon two entirely different and strictly noncomparable sets of data, one of which suffers from unrepresentative sampling techniques, the other of which suffers from a too-broad definition of the variable "boarder." Nevertheless, if the exact figures the graph suggests are

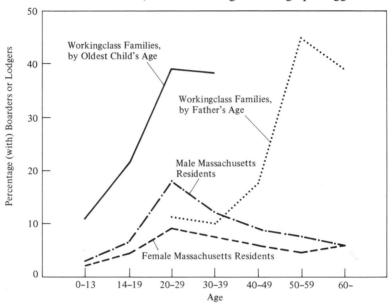

Figure 1. Proportion of Native-born Massachusetts Residents Who Are Living as Boarders or Lodgers, 1885, by Sex and Age; and Proportion of Native Working-class Families which Have Boarders or Lodgers, 1890, by Age of Male Household Head and by Age of Oldest Child in the Family[a]

imperfect, its implications are unmistakable, and of great importance: boarding in families in industrial America in the late nineteenth century was the province of young men of an age just to have left their parents' homes, and was an arrangement entered into and provided by household heads who were of an age to have just lost a son from the residential

[a]**Source:** Massachusetts, Bureau of the Statistics of Labor (1887); U.S. Bureau of Labor (1892), and see text footnote 13. The 1895 Massachusetts state census gives substantially similar patterns. The working-class family sample excludes those families with no children in the household.

family to an independent residence. It was *plausibly* a surrogate family—in the psychological sense. But in terms of an economic calculus, it was *almost precisely this*. Or rather, in Taeuber's terms, it was a social equalization of the family which operated *directly* by the exchange of a young-adult person and a portion of his young-adult income from his family of orientation to what might be called his family of re-orientation—re-orientation to the city, to a job, to a new neighborhood, to independence. It was a transfer from a family (often rural, whether domestic or foreign) with excess sons or daughters (or insufficient economic base) to one (usually urban) with excess room (or present or anticipated economic need). And often both the excess room and the present or anticipated economic need can have come from the departure from the household of a newly independent son.[25]

The *economic* logic of boarding for the family life cycle can be examined by manipulating the household budget materials collected by the Commissioner of Labor in his 1890 study of the standard of living in working-class families.[26] The central fact of this economic logic was that taking the sample of working-class families *as a whole*, family expenses varied somewhat less widely than did fathers' incomes, while *over the life cycle* average expenses changed markedly without corresponding changes in fathers' incomes. Families thus suffered a double economic squeeze: a relatively mild one from the greater "chance" variability of income as compared with expenditures; and a severe and regular one, from the tendency for costs to outstrip fathers' incomes as families passed through their life cycles.

Mean fathers' incomes varied less than $100 over the life cycle, while expenses even for families of nuclear composition varied almost $200. And the cyclical developments did not match in direction! The problem of the mismatch of income to outgo was no doubt a daily concern to the working classes, a potent motive for family decisions.[27] One answer to this mismatch was occupational mobility (excluded, of course, from these data as from all cross-sectional samples though of obvious theoretical relevance); another was age-graded pay scales (demonstrably rare in nineteenth-century industrial employment); another common answer was the early employment of youth; women's work was equally logical, but less common. Taking in a boarder was still another response, from an economic point of view not largely different from sending a child out to work, as Table 2 suggests.

With the data at hand we are in a position to make a rough partitioning of the "causes" of boarding (from the point of view of families taking them in) into those enforced by immediate economic need, and those brought about either by anticipated needs or as a product of culture directly. Table 3 seeks to supply some insight into the mix of immediate economic motives, and other motives, by examining the proportion of working-class families with lodgers at various life-cycle stages, holding the current gap between father's income and family expenses constant. Cases in many of the cells of the table are admittedly rather few, but the story is clear nonetheless: the logic of the life cycle dominates, and though the economic squeeze is still of some influence, it plays *directly* a relatively minor role, even as it intervenes potently (as Table 2 suggested) between the life-cycle stage and household malleability.

Why did families more advanced in the life cycle show by far the greatest tendency to take in boarders and lodgers, even when they did not have immediate budgetary reasons for doing so? Figure 1 provided one clue. Another may be seen by noting that as families passed through their life cycle they also tended to acquire their own houses, rising from a base level of around 10% at the earlier stages to 15 and 21% home owners at the final two life-cycle stages. Thernstrom has suggested the meaning of this tendency for an earlier period, and his reasoning would seem to apply for turn-of-the-century workingmen as well.[28] He documented the agonizingly slow accumulative process leading up to the purchase of a house, and the modicum of security it offered in a highly insecure industrial environment, despite the obligations it entailed. Since mortgage costs considerably exceeded rentals at this time, such security was clearly at a substantial premium.[29] Aging—the life cycle—was a dynamic development, in which foresight and anxiety no less than calculation played a part, to which the family's function and composition had to bend.

By the 1930's, most of the conditions which had made boarding in families an arrangement of widespread functionality had at last begun to disappear. The Depression decade, for one thing, interrupted the flow of both foreign and domestic migrants to cities. A sharp decline in demand for urban housing thus followed sharply a changed supply situation, for in the prosperity of the 1920's urban housing construction began to catch up with demand, which had outrun it for many decades.[30]

The later 1930's and the subsequent decades saw the elaboration of the welfare state, among the consequences of which was to remove some of the need for just such a source of supplementary family income as boarding offered. Cyclical unemployment, sickness, and old age all had at least partial answers in the new provisions. So, too (though for

Table 2 | Economic Characteristics Associated with Stages in the Life Cycle, Native Working-class Families in the Industrial North, 1890 [a]

	Childless[b]	Young bearing[b]	Middle bearing[b]	Middle stopped bearing[b]	Older bearing[b]	Older stopped bearing[b]
Mean family expenses (only nuclear families here)	$480	$576	$580	$635	$661	$641
Mean fathers' incomes (all families with fathers)	$484	$409	$494	$504	$475	$421
Implied deficit	$ 4	$167	$ 86	$131	$186	$220
Mean income from children	0	0	$ 21	$ 88	$185	$249
Mean income from wife	$ 43	$ 26	$ 15	$ 34	$ 11	$ 10
Proportion of families with paying lodgers	10.9%	20.0%	9.8%	10.6%	35.2%	35.6%
N	137	30	511	132	75	129

[a] Commissioner of Labor household budget sample, described in note 13.

[b] The life-cycle categories are based upon the age of the youngest child of the household ("bearing" when a child younger than 5 years is present) and the age of the male household head ("young" is under 25 years, "middle" 25–44, "older" 45 years or older).

Table 3 | **Proportion of Native Working-class Families with Boarders by Life Cycle and Relation of Father's Income to Family Expenses (Excluding Estimated Expenses for Boarder), 1890 (Per cent shown is based on number of cases in cell, shown in parentheses)**

	Childless	Young bearing	Middle bearing	Middle stopped bearing	Older bearing	Older stopped bearing
	%	%	%	%	%	%
Deficit of $100 or more	18.2 (22)	12.5 (8)	13.6 (118)	10.4 (48)	39.5 (43)	42.1 (88)
Deficit of $99 to surplus of $99	11.8 (76)	21.0 (19)	9.6 (322)	14.3 (63)	29.6 (27)	25.9 (27)
Surplus of $100 or more	5.1 (39)	33.3 (3)	4.2 (71)	0.0 (21)	25.0 (4)	14.3 (14)

different reasons), covert women's work became needless, as profitable and honorable jobs outside the home opened up during and after World War II. Correspondingly, added duties within the home seemed increasingly onerous to housewives.

At the same time, privacy, both within and without the family, was being redefined, partly, but only partly, in ways congruent with the hopes of the urban progressives decades earlier, due more than anything to the previously unimagined prosperity which reached down to the level of the workingman. Seeley, Sim, and Loosely (1956), for example, point to the extraordinary demands for *individual* privacy within the household.[31] The arrangements of such ideal households, urban as well as suburban, hardly left room—social or physical—for a lodger. And the concurrently changing definition of permissible sexuality —permissible, however, only as highly private acts—called for a great deal of apartness, most especially for the unmarried young adult —formerly the most typical lodger. As one-person households became the ideal for this stage in the life cycle, prosperity made the maintenance of such settings possible. As from the supply side, so from the demand side, boarding and lodging in the family became obsolete.

We began this excursion into the workings of an almost forgotten family institution by looking at middle-class reformers' criticisms directed toward it, and at the quantitative spatial metaphor—room overcrowding—which they employed in condemning it. We are now in a position to contemplate the literal justness of this aspect of the criticism, again basing our discussion on the 1890 Bureau of Labor Statistics data, which included an item on number of rooms occupied by each renter family. With these we are able to compute, for each life-cycle stage, a room-to-person quotient for each family, subdivided into those families consisting only of heads and their children and those who had lodgers. The findings are unequivocal. For *all but one life-cycle stage,* families who had lodgers had *more* rooms per person when we exclude their lodgers from the calculation than families without lodgers. But when the lodgers are included in our divisors, then the *non-lodger* families had more room, in all but one life-cycle stage.[32] In other words, though the progressives were correct in asserting that some crowding was a concomitant of taking in lodgers, they did not recognize that lodgers were on the whole taken in where there was some "excess" room in being.[33]

Accepting a lodger into the family was not evidence of incipient family disorganization, as reformers feared, nor a helter-skelter piling of individuals upon one another without regard to privacy. The largest discrepancy between families with and without lodgers in rooms-per-person (with lodgers counted) in *any* life-cycle stage was 31% for younger families just in the childbearing stage. Yet this discrepancy was scarcely greater than that found *between* life-cycle stages, *for non-boarder families,* even if we exclude the spatially plush childless stage. The median additional crowding in lodger families was only 16%; there was a trade-off, to be sure, but a narrow one. Lodging in the family was a vehicle by which urban Americans gained control of their environment, not one by which they lost it.

Although the hostility and anxiety expressed by reformers toward lodging and boarding was misplaced, their fears were a response to major historical changes in the role of the institution and its relationship to the family which had taken place over an entire century. Under the impact of urbanization in the nineteenth century, the functions of asylum which had previously been assigned to the family by the town authorities were gradually transferred to institutions established specifically for the care of the young, the poor, the dependent, and the delinquent. By mid-nineteenth century the urban family lost its cachet as a rehabilitative haven for "boarded out" poor and dependent strangers.

From 1850 the influx of foreign immigrants and rural migrants into American cities overwhelmed the available housing facilities. Middle-class boarding, a voluntary practice, for individuals in certain stages of the life cycle or in certain occupational groups, was overshadowed by the emergence of lower-class boarding. By the 1880s, family boarding lost both its official use for social control, as well as its middle-class respectability. It became identified exclusively (if erroneously) as a lower-class practice, and was attacked in the context of tenement squalor and the poverty of immigrant life.

In this instance the demonology of boarding is characteristic of the entire theory of family breakdown under the impact of industrialization and urbanization. Sociologists who have promoted this thesis have cited the surrender to other institutions in society of functions which had been exclusive to the family as proof for family breakdown. Though by the end of the nineteenth century boarding had, indeed, lost its "formal" poor-relief function, in a society which even at the turn of the century was still familistic, boarding was still chosen (no doubt consciously in many instances) as a family surrogate.

The family was not fragile, but malleable. That so many misunderstood this distinction is itself symptomatic, for reformers who bewailed the imminent breakup of the family had displaced their concern from the hardness of life inherent in the industrial system to an institution that not only was a sensible response to industrialization but, in cushioning the shock of urban life for newcomers, was decidedly humane.

NOTES

1. We shall use the terms "lodger" and "boarder" synonymously in this paper. Although currently their meaning is somewhat distinct—the former term implying meals as well as bed taken in the family—nineteenth-century usage was less distinct. One distinction that *is* intended here is between boarding (or lodging) *within families,* the subject of the paper, and that in houses specialized for the purpose. The latter is itself a significant development, one of which contemporaries were relatively aware. For an excellent contemporary study see Albert B. Wolfe, *The Lodging House Problem in Boston* (Cambridge, 1906).

2. James Q. Dealey, *The Family in Its Sociological Aspects* (Boston, 1912), pp. 90–91.

3. The present paper owes much to John Modell's "Strangers in the Family," an earlier treatment of the boarding and lodging theme delivered at the Clark University Conference on the History of the Family, April, 1972, and to Tamara K. Hareven, "Social Change and Family Patterns in Nineteenth-Century Boston," delivered at the Organization of American Historians, Washington, D.C., April, 1972.

4. Edmund S. Morgan, *The Puritan Family* (Boston, 1944); John Demos, *A Little Commonwealth; Family Life in Plymouth Colony* (New York, 1970); Bernard Farber, *Guardians of Virtue, Salem Families in 1800* (New York, 1972), chap. 2; David Flaherty, *Privacy in Colonial New England* (Charlottesville, 1972), chap. 2.

5. W. S. Rossiter, compiler, *A Century of Population Growth* (Washington, 1909); U.S. Bureau of the Census, *Census of Housing: 1970* (Washington, 1972); John Modell, "Family and Fertility on the Indiana Frontier," *American Quarterly,* 23 (1971), pp. 615–634.

6. Stuart Blumin, "Rip Van Winkle's Grandchildren: Family and Household in the Hudson Valley, 1800–1860," in this collection; Laurence Glasco, "The Life Cycles and Household Structure of American Ethnic Groups," in this collection; Susan E. Bloomberg, et al., "A Census Probe into Nineteenth-Century Family History: Southern Michigan, 1850–1880," *Journal of Social History,* 5 (1971), p. 39.

7. "The problems of mutual observation by lodgers and family were neither new nor unusual [in colonial New England]. The most common remedy was for a family gradually to accept a boarder into the intimacy of the family." (Flaherty, *Privacy in Colonial New England,* p. 69.)

8. Lawrence Veiller, "Room Overcrowding and the Lodger Evil," in *Housing Problems in America: Proceedings of the Second National Conference on Housing, Philadelphia* (1912), p. 60.

9. Robert H. Bremner, et al., eds., *Children and Youth in America,* II, first part (Cambridge, 1971), p. 355.

10. Carol Aronovici, *Housing Conditions in Fall River,* Associated Charities Housing Committee (unpublished), p. 5.

11. Johanna Von Wagner, *Teaching the Tenant,* National Housing Association Publications, No. 8, 2nd ed. (1914), p. 10.

12. U.S. Bureau of Labor, *Report on Conditions of Women and Child Wage-Earners in the United States,* 5, Senate Document 645, 61st Congress, 2nd session (1910), p. 62.

13. W. I. Thomas, *The Unadjusted Girl* (Boston, 1923), pp. 13–14; W. I. Thomas and Florian Znaniecki, *The Polish Peasant in Europe and America,* II (New York, 1958, reprint), pp. 1723–1725; Clifford R. Shaw in collaboration with Maurice E. Moore, *The Natural History of a Delinquent Career* (Chicago, 1931), p. 44.

14. Carol Aronovici, *Housing Conditions in the City of Saint Paul* (Saint Paul, 1917), pp. 51–52.

15. Day Monroe, *Chicago Families* (Chicago, 1932), pp. 154, 191–99; Bertha M. Nienburg, *The Woman Home-Maker in the City* (Washington, U.S. Bureau of the Census, 1932), p. 25; U.S. Department of Labor, Women's Bureau, *Bulletin 23: The Family Status of Breadwinning Women* (Washington, 1925), pp. 57–58; U.S. Bureau of the Census, *Fifteenth Census of the United States, Population, VI, Families* (Washington, 1933), p. 67. We touch here only upon the questions of ethnicity and the relationship of boarding to the socioeconomic integration of the immigrant to native patterns. A few empirical points, however, should be noted. First, several sets of data confirm the absence of a substantial direct correlation between foreign birth and propensity to take in lodgers when other relevant factors are accounted for. Initial insights into this question are available in the standard-of-living data presented by states in U.S. Bureau of Labor (1904) and in the United States Census of 1930, which shows that in most cities the foreign-born had a lower proportion of families with boarders than native whites. A final tantalizing suggestion arises from the juxtaposition of the Immigration Commission's finding (1911) that (holding city and ethnic group constant) the longer the immigrant had been in America the less likely he was to have a lodger, with that discovered in 1920 census data for Passaic, where the *reverse* pattern obtained. U.S. Bureau of Labor, *Eighteenth Annual Report of the Commissioner of Labor, 1903* (Washington, 1904); U.S. Immigration Commission, Reports, Vol. 26, *Immigrants in Cities,* Sen. Doc. 338, 61st Congress, 2nd session (1911); U.S. Department of Labor, Women's Bureau, *Bulletin 23,* p. 34.

16. U.S. Bureau of the Census, *Sixteenth Census of the United States: 1940, Population and Housing. Families, General Characteristics* (Washington, 1943), p. 28; Everett S. Lee, et al., *Demographic Profiles of the United States* (Oak Ridge, Tenn., 1971–72), *passim.*

17. Irene B. Taeuber, "Change and Transition in Family Structures," in *The Family in Transition,* Fogarty International Center Proceedings (Washington, 1969), p. 5.

18. Charles Strickland, "A Transcendental Father: The Child-Rearing Practices of Bronson Alcott," *Perspectives in American History,* 3 (1969), p. 30, for example, reports that the Bronson family readily (though, in the end, unhappily) resorted to taking in juvenile boarders when the family "was hovering between genteel poverty and outright destitution," and thus remained on the more desirable side of that line.

19. To make much of the problem of multicollinearity in multiple regressions based on such indicators would be fruitless though justified from a statistical point of view. Dependent and independent variables alike are imperfect here, and used more for what they suggest than for the assessment of causal relationships.

20. Massachusetts Bureau of the Statistics of Labor, *Census of Massachusetts: 1885* (Boston, 1887), pp. 470–85.

21. The individual data on boarders and lodgers for Boston are part of a larger study of family and ethnicity in nineteenth-century Boston. The study is based on an analysis of family and residential patterns of approximately 6,000 individuals selected by household from the manuscript schedules of the 1880 Federal Census. The households were sampled from four distinct neighborhoods, representing a variety of ethnic compositions, different socioeconomic groups, and varying lengths of residence in the city. In the South End, the most ethnically complex neighborhood in the city, the households were chosen by stratified samples, in proportion to the ethnic composition of the neighborhood. The entire sample consisted of 3,363 males and 3,960 females. The total South End population sampled consisted of 3,314 individuals, of which 700 were listed as "boarders." Except where the entire Boston population sample is mentioned specifically, most data on boarders and lodgers cited in this article are based on this group of 700.

The heads of household and individuals sampled from the 1880 census (the only one which designates relationship to the household) were traced backward and forward through city directories to their earliest as well as most recent listing in the directory. They were also traced back to the censuses of 1870, 1860, and 1850, wherever this was possible. The findings presented in this paper represent data observations rather than the result of statistical manipulation and are among the earlier materials to be derived from the long-range project.

22. There is no doubt that, in certain instances, individuals designated as boarders might have been relatives who had entered a boarding relationship. Unfortunately, the census listings provide no systematic clues to such relationships.

23. In this context, we should note that while the *incidence* of boarding was somewhat greater among families of lower socioeconomic strata, this was only relatively true. Absolutely, one can say that boarding was practiced by families at all economic levels. (See Monroe, *Chicago Families,* pp. 191, 194.)

24. Apparently, it would be an error to assume that on the whole families chose whether women would work outside the home or take in boarders, since they both could do both and did do so, according to 1930 census data. At that time, it would seem, families with homemakers gainfully employed outside the home were *more* likely to have boarders than the national average (although only slightly more), with especially high proportions of boarders admitted to families where the gainfully employed homemaker was an older woman, a servant or waitress, or a professional worker. (U.S. Women's Bureau, *Bulletin 148. The Employed Woman Homemaker in the United States* (Washington, 1936), p. 22.)

25. These speculations are obviously just that, and call for empirical verification.

26. The data here employed consist of 1,048 family budgets of factory workers, with information on ages, household composition, nativity, and details of income and expenditure. Over 5,000 such budgets—potentially magnificent social documents—are published in U.S. Bureau of Labor's *Seventh Annual Report of the Commissioner of Labor, 1891,* II, part 3 (Washington, 1892). The Commissioner of Labor does not specify his sampling techniques, which we may assume were born of convenience rather than statistical sophistication. In order to obtain as homogeneous a sample as possible—to observe as clearly as possible the workings of family composition, life-cycle, and budgetary considerations —we have included only 1,048 American-born workers in major industries living in northern and midwestern states. For present purposes, we have further excluded from analysis families headed by widows.

27. A brilliant exposition of this nineteenth-century dilemma (in an English setting), together with an impressive theoretical framework, is Michael Anderson's *Family and Kinship in Nineteenth-Century Lancashire* (Cambridge, 1972). We could cite this volume at many places in this essay, but can best suggest our debt to it by urging that our readers avail themselves of it.

28. Stephan Thernstrom, *Poverty and Progress* (Cambridge, 1964).

29. U.S. Bureau of Labor, *Eighteenth Annual Report.*

30. Manuel Gottlieb, *Estimates of Residential Building, United States 1840–1939,* National Bureau of Economic Research, Technical Paper 17 (1964), chapts. 2–4; Burnham O. Campbell, *Population Change and Building Cycles* (Urban, Ill., 1966).

31. John R. Seeley, et al., *Crestwood Heights: The Culture of Suburban Life* (New York, 1956).

32. The formulae treated all household members as requiring the same amount of room, regardless of their age.

33. Note, too, that the exclusion of families which owned houses (but whose rooms were not counted in the data) biases the sample *against* roominess in the boarder families, since in five of the six life-cycle stages home-owning families were more likely to have boarders than were renters—which makes sense, since they (one imagines) had more room and higher monetary obligations to worry about. (But in Boston's South End, with few exceptions, heads of households taking in boarders did not own the houses they lived in.)

9

Family Time and Industrial Time: Family and Work in a Planned Corporation Town, 1900–1924

TAMARA K. HAREVEN

The role of the family in the adaptation of workers to industrial life, a central concern for sociologists for some time, has only recently excited the imagination of historians. In his now classic analysis of working-class culture in early industrial England, E. P. Thompson dramatized the theory of family breakdown in the industrial revolution: "Each stage in industrial differentiation and specialization struck also at the family

Author's Note: *This paper is part of a book in progress on "The Laborers of Manchester, New Hampshire, 1880–1940: The Role of Family and Ethnicity in Adjustment to Urban, Industrial Life." The project was supported by Grant No. RO 8963–73–500 from the National Endowment for the Humanities, and by a research grant from the Merrimack Valley Textile Museum, with matching funds from Amoskeag Industries, the Cogswell Benevolent Trust, and the Norwin and Elizabeth Bean Foundation. The oral history interviews were supported by the New Hampshire Council for the Humanities and the United Textile Workers. I am indebted to Dr. Thomas Leavitt, Director of the Merrimack Valley Textile Museum, whose initial support helped launch this project. Research was carried out at the Manchester Historic Association and the Baker Library, Graduate School of Business Administration, Harvard University. I am indebted to Randolph Langenbach for his important discoveries in the history of the Amoskeag Corporation in his own study of the architectural and urban planning history of the Amoskeag Mills. Herbert Gutman, David Montgomery, Maris Vinovskis, John Modell, Howard Chudacoff, Daniel Walkowitz, and David Grimsted provided valuable criticisms.*

economy, disturbing customary relations between man and wife, parents and children, and differentiating more sharply 'work' and 'life.' Meanwhile, the family was roughly torn apart each morning by the factory bell.'' Recent scholarship has challenged the prevailing thesis that the family was a passive victim in the process of industrialization. Neil Smelser has shown that during the early years of the industrial revolution in Britain, working-class families carried their own habits into the factory setting and often continued to function as units. In a later study, Michael Anderson has documented the active role which the family group had in the process of migration from rural Lancashire and Ireland to the large textile communities, and in the workers' adaptation to new industrial conditions. William Goode went further to argue that the family was an independent agent in the process of industrialization. Rather than being a passive recipient of social and economic change, the family acted as a catalyst in activating changes in the larger society.[1]

This revisionist sociological view of the role of the family in the process of industrialization has been reinforced by the work of some labor historians. Following the route of cultural anthropologists, they have demonstrated that workers, while adapting to the industrial system, also succeeded in modifying it in terms of their previous cultural traditions and work habits. The continuous influx of immigrants from the same or similar backgrounds tended to reinforce the impact of preindustrial immigrant traditions on the new system.[2]

Several recent historical studies have emphasized the active role of the family in the migration process and its function as a source of continuity and stability under the pressures of adjustment to new conditions. Some of these studies now argue that not only did the family not break down, it in fact retained active control over the careers of its members. As the transmitter of premigration culture, the family kept ethnic traditions alive, and its cultural heritage guided the family in its adaptation to new conditions.[3]

Such revisions of the stereotypes of family passivity and breakdown in the industrial process have engendered new extremes. The filiopietism which has been emerging over the past years tends to exaggerate the strength of the immigrant or working-class family and its autonomy as an institution. This neo-romantic interpretation of the role of the family could easily result in another stereotype, as removed from historical reality as earlier ones.

Now that the ghosts of social breakdown are being exorcised from historical scholarship, we must ask: to what degree, under varying circumstances, was the family in control of its own decisions, and to what degree was its behavior guided by external pressures and incentives? To answer these questions it is necessary to study more closely the family's role in the industrial environment, an approach which must be *contextual* as well as *dynamic*. Contrary to the prevalent approach which studies the family in isolation in the household, it is necessary to see the family as it actually existed in constant interaction with other social processes and institutions.[4]

For laborers such an approach links family organization and traditions to the experience of industrial work. It takes into account the interrelationships between the family and technological change, the work process, demands for work discipline, job mobility, ethnicity, and economic behavior within the framework of industrial capitalism. Such a model by necessity views the "family" as a process which unfolds over its entire cycle rather than as a constant at one point in time. It takes into account the fact that family structures, functions, relationships, and needs differed at each stage of the family cycle and that these internal changes were related to larger societal processes.[5]

If the term "industrial time" designates the new time schedules and work discipline imposed by the industrial system, "family time" refers to the internal and external timing of family behavior at different stages of individual and family development, particularly to the timing of major demographic events. An understanding of how the two different times affected each other, the areas in which they conflicted or reinforced each other, provides a model for the study of the family's role in the larger society. While families responded to external pressures and adjusted their timing accordingly, they also often timed their own behavior in accordance with their internal "clock." It is the historian's task to determine to what degree, under what changing circumstances, the family's behavior was timed in response to external conditions, and to what degree it moved in accordance with the family's internal and traditional timepiece.[6]

This essay will explore the family's interaction with the industrial system on two levels: it will first examine the workers' adjustment to industrial life. Secondly, it will examine the internal timing of family behavior along the family cycle in response to the external pressures and demands of the world of work.

This exploration focuses on the experiences of French-Canadian immigrant laborers of the Amoskeag Manufacturing Company in Manchester, New Hampshire, at the peak of the corporation's industrial development during the first two decades of the twentieth century. At the turn of the century Manchester had 70,000 inhabitants and was the seat of the world's largest textile mill—The Amoskeag Corporation—which employed an average of 14,000 workers each year in the period preceding World War I.[7]

Originally developed by the Amoskeag Corporation as a planned New England textile community, Manchester, unlike its sister communities of Lawrence and Lowell, continued to be dominated by the corporation that originally founded it in the 1830s.[8] Similar to the textile manufacturing towns on which it was patterned, the Amoskeag Corporation recruited its early labor force from rural New Englanders. From the 1850s on, immigrants from England, Scotland, and Ireland began to replace native American workers. In the 1870s, following the textile industry's discovery of the French Canadians as the most "industrious" and "docile" labor force, the corporation embarked on the systematic recruitment of laborers from Quebec. By 1900, French Canadians constituted about 40% of the labor force in the mill, and about one-half of the city's population. While their migration continued through the first two decades of the twentieth century, the corporation was also absorbing small numbers of Germans and Swedes, followed by increasing numbers of Polish and Greek immigrants in the second decade of the twentieth century.[9]

As a planned industrial town, Manchester did not experience the classic problems of social disorganization generally attributed to urban living. The carefully designed and maintained corporation space, encompassing the mill yard and housing for a large segment of the work force, enclosed the workers in a total environment. From the late nineteenth century on, Manchester developed cohesive ethnic neighborhoods which were organized along kinship and ethnic lines, and which surrounded the corporation housing, radiating east, south, and west of the mill yard.[10] The problems that Manchester's laborers were facing, therefore, did not derive from urban anomie, but rather from the pressures of industrial work and discipline. These conditions allow the historian to examine the role of the family in the process of industrialization without the interference of factors generally connected with the pressures of life in a large city.

The surviving historical record utilized for this study is unusually rich, allowing an exploration of conditions and developments from the perspectives of the workers as well as the corporation. The unique collection of cumulative, individual employee files which were re-

corded for the period 1910–1936 provides detailed data for the reconstruction of the workers' careers. Particularly important are the entries
in each employee file listing the reasons for his or her leaving the job, as
well as the reasons given by overseers for the dismissal of workers. The
linkage of this data with marriage and insurance records, as well as with
oral histories, permitted a reconstruction of the workers' life and work
histories with a wealth of information unavailable in census records.[11]

Family Interaction with the Corporation

In their day-by-day relationships, the corporation and the family were
two interacting institutions. Although the two were not equals, they
were exercising checks and balances on each other. In a paternalistic
system such as that of the Amoskeag Mills, the corporation not only
perceived itself as a family, but also was aware of the family's powerful
role in the workers' lives and consciously attempted to utilize that force
as an instrument to control the workers. It therefore relied on the family
to recruit the workers and to socialize them into industrial work.[12]

The Amoskeag Corporation and its immigrant workers demonstrated
a remarkable fit in their respective ideologies of work and social hierarchy and authority. Nineteenth-century paternalistic ideology, still alive
in twentieth-century Manchester, viewed industrial management as a
family affair. In the tradition of industrial paternalism the corporation
perceived itself as a large family, and the workers within it as its
children. "More than 15,000 persons work in these mills. . . . It is true
that the large company to which they sell their labor treats them as its
own children," read a typical corporation advertisement in French-
Canadian newspapers. The corporation's own management and organization were structured along family and kinship lines. Even in the early
part of the twentieth century, when workers were hired as individuals,
the corporation continued to employ entire families where possible.
Family hiring was more advantageous to the corporation since the effort
invested in recruitment and transportation could be maximized through
the number of textile workers provided by one family. This also held
true for housing arrangements where the corporations preferred to
utilize the space by placing families with several working members in
the corporation tenements.[13]

In the beginning of the twentieth century, the corporation embarked
on a series of new employee welfare programs. With the exception of
the superannuation of a limited number of older workers, these pro-

grams were aimed primarily at the workers' families, rather than at individuals. They included a home ownership plan for workers who had stayed in the corporation's employ five years or longer, a playground and dental care program for children, and a visiting nurse and home instruction program for mothers. Management hoped to socialize the children through these programs, to Americanize the workers, and to develop a permanent, stable, and loyal industrial labor force. The new welfare program introduced in 1910 was combined with an efficiency program which, under the influence of Taylorism, tried to centralize and rationalize hiring policies, and to increase the speed of production.[14]

Corporate paternalism struck a responsive chord in newly arrived immigrant workers. The work ethic and customs of a preindustrial culture were woven around the traditional view of the family as a work unit. The workers transferred this tradition into the industrial system and realigned their family work relationships in accordance with the needs and expectations of industrial work. This is not to argue that the tasks and division of labor which the French-Canadian farm family had traditionally carried out in rural Quebec were automatically transferred to the American industrial system. Child labor in the factory, the work of mothers outside the home, and the regimentation of life to an industrial schedule were all novel experiences.[15]

The basic tradition of family work and of the economic role of each member, however, was carried over from the agricultural background. The important continuity was in the perception and experience of the family as a work unit, even when the locations of the job and the work process were different. Daughters and wives who had earlier contributed to the family's economic efforts on the farm transferred these work roles to industrial labor. Even though the tasks they were performing differed from those in their premigration setting, the basic traditional assumptions that guided family work roles were not disrupted.[16] The one area of conflict concerned the issue of women's work. French-Canadian customs, reinforced by the Catholic Church, regarded women's work outside the home as a threat to the family. This did not stop two-thirds of all married French-Canadian women in the town from working in the factory. In their own minds, they reconciled the conflict by arguing that their work was temporary. Many, however, claimed such temporary conditions till the end of their lives. Married women continued to work over their entire careers with intermittent interruptions for childbirth.[17]

The relationship between the workers and the corporation was one of mutual interaction. The degree of their cooperation or withdrawal depended on a variety of factors for each: on the corporation's side, the relationship was governed by the availability of the labor force and by the fluctuation of the textile market. In periods of labor shortage prior to World War I, when the corporation had to compete with other industries over the labor supply in the city, it was forced to tolerate the autonomous behavior of the workers and their resistance to modernization. On the other hand, during its continuous decline in the post-World-War-I period, and until its shutdown in 1936, the corporation's gradual curtailment of its labor force allowed the workers less freedom to manipulate the system.[18]

The workers were by no means equals to the corporation in this balance of power, but they were able to exercise a certain degree of autonomy under limited conditions. The workers' response depended on the changing work conditions and demands of the corporation, and on individual and family considerations. The availability of alternative employment opportunities in the city, economic needs, traditional work habits, and family values all influenced their behavior. Demographic patterns had a crucial impact on the workers' careers, especially those of women. The degree of their dependence on industrial work or independence from it, especially mobility in and out of the mill, was determined by individual and family needs which changed over the stages of the family's development. Particularly significant in this scheme was the shifting margin of poverty and subsistence at different stages of the family cycle. Unmarried individuals in their late twenties had a different attitude toward work than fathers of families of five, for example, or widows in their fifties.[19]

This model suggests, therefore, that both the worker's family and the corporation were flexible institutions. Their relationships and patterns of interaction fluctuated and changed over time, in response to internal conditions as well as under the impact of larger historical processes. The family was most effective in making an impact on work patterns in two areas: (1) it facilitated the adjustment of its members by acting as a labor recruiter, a housing agent, and as a source of support in critical life situations, and (2) it exercised its own controls, even if limited ones, against the corporation by encouraging labor turnover, by influencing the job placement of its members, and by affecting job control in the daily routine of work.

The Role of Family and Kin in Industrial Adjustment

Acting as a conveyor belt, facilitating the workers' movements and cushioning the shock of adjustment, the family and the kin group served as the labor recruiters, the organizers of migration routes, and housing agents. Within the factory, the family group directed the work choices of its members, influenced their placement in different departments, and prepared them for industrial work. Kinship ties were especially instrumental in facilitating the workers' experimentation with alternative careers.[20]

French-Canadians were streaming to Manchester in response to systematic recruitment propaganda issued out of Manchester through their own ethnic organizations and through communications from relatives. Their kin met them on arrival, placed them on their first job, and located them as temporary boarders until they found a corporation flat or rented an apartment in the growing French-Canadian section of the city's West Side.[21]

Chain migration through the kin group was not limited to Manchester. Kinship networks were pervasive throughout the entire industrial region in New England. The presence of clusters of kin in a variety of New England industrial towns offered laborers of the Amoskeag Mills the opportunity to migrate through a series of mill towns with the hope of improving their conditions. Their migration was not terminal. It followed a circuitous route through other textile mills in Maine, southern Massachusetts, and Rhode Island, where relatives were working.[22] Workers moved back and forth, from Manchester to Quebec and back to Manchester. Leaving the mills often for two or three summer months, they visited relatives in the Quebec countryside or took on temporary jobs, only to return again to the textile mills in Manchester.

Family ties thus formed a network of employment opportunities as well as temporary and permanent stations for migration. A reconstitution of the migration patterns on the basis of the employee records of the Amoskeag Company suggests that prior to 1922 about one-fourth of the employees studied immigrated to the other New England mill towns in search of better jobs. In most of these instances, the presence of relatives in other towns facilitated their temporary sojourns. Migration did not destroy the family and kin group. It transposed a formerly localized family pattern over an entire industrial region in New England.[23]

Flexibility in corporation employment policy, which emanated primarily from the need for cheap labor, enabled the family to exercise some controls over the recruitment and placement of its members. The continuous informality in corporation hiring policies, and especially the overseers' autonomy in their departments, facilitated personal connections between overseers and the workers' relatives. The character of a department was basically determined by its overseer, and a workroom frequently containing 100 or more workers was still identified by the overseer's name. Workers continued to obtain jobs directly from the overseer, even after the introduction of a formal employment office.[24] When there was a vacancy in a workroom, the overseers generally filled it by asking one of the workers to bring in someone he knew. Most workers ignored the employment office and turned directly to the overseers for jobs and the placement of relatives. Since the workers were continuously coming and going, this informal placement network was quite extensive.

The family group thus infiltrated the mill and made its direct impact on the composition of the workrooms. Kin and ethnic clusters developed in most departments. Members of one family often clustered in a variety of jobs, working near each other in the same room, and childhood friends, cousins, and neighbors often worked side by side for years. About one-fourth of all French-Canadian workers studied in this group met their spouses in the mill and continued to work there after marriage.[25]

Such arrangements enabled the workers to exercise some controls over the work pace. Especially following World War I, as the corporation accelerated its pressures for speed-ups, workers assisted relatives and friends in meeting quotas, even if it meant a loss in pay on their own piece-rate work. The presence of relatives reinforced the workers' collective strength in resisting corporation pressure, especially when the demand for speed-up became overwhelming. The pervasiveness of family groups also enabled the workers to try out different jobs in various departments by passing for one of their relatives, to take turns going to work, and to substitute for each other by switching their employee passes, or by having several members utilize the same pass.

From the late 1920's on, the corporation was becoming nervous about the ethnic and kin alignment in the workrooms: "Refrain from requesting the employment of relatives of persons in charge of units in the same units," read the instruction of management to overseers. An inspector reporting his conversation with various overseers to the management concluded: "For instance, I did not believe it was really good for any unit of the mill to be wholly comprised of relatives and friends of the operatives also of the same race.'' In that particular workroom, 90% of the labor force was made up of the same ethnic group.[26]

The strength and resilience which workers derived from their families was reinforced by ethnic ties. Ethnicity provided the major organizational scheme for the workers' adjustment to the pressures of the factory work and life in the city. The ethnic group offered the commonality of a cultural heritage, language, residential cohesion, entertainment and rituals, religious ties, and mutual benefit associations. Most of the work and residential patterns were organized around the laborers' family and ethnic ties. Tight-knit clusters of ethnic residential areas appeared in Manchester from the 1880s on.[27] Ethnic enclaves developed in the corporation housing as well. Although corporation flats had to be secured through individual family applications, residents managed to cluster along ethnic lines in corporation housing in the same manner in which they succeeded in aligning themselves in the workroom. Officially, applications for residence in corporation housing had to be submitted long in advance, and workers had to wait their turn. In reality, friends and relatives notified prospective tenants of vacancies and managed to secure those flats ahead of their turn through the help of acquaintances in the office. Sons of former workers recall the invisible, but clearly reinforced, boundaries between ethnic youth gangs in the corporation tenements.[28]

Family Time: The Stages of the Family Cycle

Internal family considerations and demographic conditions, but primarily economic need, influenced the patterns of the workers' persistence and migration. In the pre-World-War-I period, families decided who of their members would go to work, what son or daughter should start first, at what point the wife should stop, when she should return to work, and who should explore alternative employment outside the mill.

This process of family decision-making emerges both in the analysis of the employment files, where workers frequently cited family reasons for leaving their jobs, as well as in the oral history interviews. Aside from involuntary reasons such as illness, accidents, retirement, and death, laborers left because: ''husband did not want wife to work,'' ''wife did not approve of husband's work in the night shift,'' ''parents want son to go back to school,'' ''girl takes care of young children at home.'' As long as the employment system was flexible, family members could decide whose labor was needed to maintain the family's income, who should work in the mill, who should stay home, and what department or workroom he or she should be sent to.[29]

What factors governed the family's decision on the timing of entrance into the labor force, taking on new family obligations, or migration into new areas? What were the internal and external factors which directed the family's interaction with the world of work?

The timing of behavior followed the family life cycle and was governed by the external pressures of the industrial system. The decision as to when people were leaving home, marrying, giving birth to their first child, spacing the births of their subsequent children, or sending their children to work or to school were timed by the internal clock of family traditions as well as by the external pressures of the factory system and by economic needs. Historians are only now beginning to unravel what specific processes were involved in this timing, and how they varied among different socioeconomic and cultural groups under different circumstances.[30]

For the French-Canadian immigrants, industrial work meant family employment. It is not surprising, therefore, that they were recognized as textile workers par excellence. French Canadians had the highest birth rate of all industrial workers in the United States. Their large numbers of children made them particularly suitable for family employment. In New England their average family size was 7.2, while the Irish, a group also well known for high fertility, had an average of 5 members per family. French Canadians also boasted the highest average number of family members working in the textile industry (3.9). Large family size which had served well the work needs of farmers continued to be an asset in industrial work in the late nineteenth century.

Changing conditions in the textile industry from the early part of the nineteenth century, however, dictated a modification of demographic behavior after the end of the nineteenth century.[31] The first major impact of the industrial system on demographic behavior was in the postponement of marriage, particularly for women. By the second decade of the twentieth century, women who had migrated to Manchester in their teens and second-generation immigrant women began to delay their marriage until their late twenties or early thirties. This was a direct response to the conditions of industrial work. Because much of the family's income depended on the work of more than one member, marriage did not offer an escape from work outside the home.[32]

Postponement of marriage was also dictated to women by their own parents. Since single women workers carried a significant share of the burden of their families' support from the moment they were able to work, parents counted on their daughters' wages as an essential addition to the family income. As unmarried daughters sixteen and older began to work full-time, their parents and younger siblings were gradually withdrawing from work. Several investigations of New England textile towns, including Manchester, which were carried out by the U.S. Bureau of Labor Statistics, revealed that while sons committed only 83% of their income to their parents' budgets, daughters delivered 95% of their pay. Parents tried to influence daughters to delay their marriage in order to continue to rely on them as a source of income.[33]

Aside from economic need, women also worked because they enjoyed their occupations. Numerous testimonies in the oral history interviews provide this insight, which has escaped historians who rely on quantitative data only. "I loved my work," said one retired weaver (now 94 years old). Work in the mills provided an experience of partnership and sociability which was organized along sex lines, but which nevertheless carried a family ambiance into the workrooms. "We were all like a family," remarked another retired worker.[34]

For most young immigrant women workers, marriage did not provide an escape from industrial work; it actually added the new burden of housekeeping and childrearing to factory labor. Caught between the traditional definition of sex roles in their own culture and the economic needs of their family, women found themselves working in the mill as well as tending to their domestic tasks. Most female textile workers continued to work after marriage until giving birth, and returned to the mill as soon as they weaned their infants. They worked until the birth of their next child and then stopped temporarily, only to return again.[35] The woman's mother next door, or an aging aunt, or other female relative provided day care. Where no relatives were available, women either left their children with a neighbor or deposited them each day at the orphanage, which, in addition to its regular inmates, by necessity took in children of working mothers.

About one-half of the married men working in the Amoskeag Mills also had their wives working with them, in order to supplement the family income. This experience was not unique to Manchester. It was characteristic of employment patterns in the textile and shoe industries in general, which in 1930, for example, had the highest ratio of females to males ten years and above reporting gainful employment.[36]

Once they had children, however, women's careers became more checkered and less stable. Married women with children made up the major proportion of the Amoskeag Mills' reserve labor force. While the group of regularly employed workers consisted of a higher percentage of young women under age 35, the reserve labor force included a higher percentage of women between the ages of 35 and 55. There was no comparable age discrepancy between males in the regular and the reserve force. Among workers older than 55, there was no major difference in the percentage of men and women in the reserve labor force.[37]

The pattern of the work cycle of married women was thus articulated to the family cycle: during their childbearing and childrearing years, women did not work to their full capacity. For family reasons as well as corporation needs, they found themselves in the reserve labor force, rather than as regular workers. During the period of optimal family earnings, when their children were grown, but still living at home and working, the women worked only occasionally. The marriage or departure of the last child drove the mothers back to the mill. This explains why one finds a much higher proportion of married women aged 55 and up on the regular labor force, rather than on the reserve. The most intensive periods in the employment of married women came before age 35 and after age 55. In the intervening periods, their intermittent work patterns depended on the availability of temporary jobs in the mill. Prior to 1922, there was almost always a job to be found in one department or another. After the strike, as a consequence of gradual and continuous curtailment, married women were most vulnerable to permanent job loss if they left work to raise children.

One of the important functions of delayed marriage, especially in the second generation of immigrants, was a curtailment in the number of children born. In some respects, this decline in fertility was a manifestation of a gradual secularization and relaxation of traditional norms. It also represented, however, changing conditions in the employment market. With the passing of the New Hampshire Child Labor Law in 1905, the employment of children under 16 became increasingly risky. In this case, the corporation decided to comply with the new law, since it had nothing to lose at a time when changes in production and experimentation with efficiency made the work of young children obsolete. The decline in the child labor market turned large numbers of children into economic burdens on the family. It was advantageous, therefore, to limit the number of children, especially since childbirth impaired the mother's effectiveness as a breadwinner; it imposed on her patterns of intermittent employment and therefore undermined her chances of occupational advancement.[38]

Even though they were not actually entering factory work before age 16, children were socialized to the work experience in the mill at an early age. Industrial labor became part of their lives even before they actually worked. The experience of their parents, and the proximity of their homes to the mills, prevented any real separation between the world of childhood and the world of work. Children carrying lunch pails to the mills at the noon hour were a familiar part of the Manchester scene, where schoolchildren earned their first money by bringing lunches from the boarding houses to the mills. Most youths attending high school worked regularly in the mills during the summer. The expectations that children would have to work as soon as the law permitted were strongly impressed on them from an early age by their parents. The family economy, as well as the family's work ethic, was built around the assumption that children would contribute to the family's economic effort from the earliest opportunity.

By the time they entered the mill, young people had become familiar with the entire work process. Parents and older brothers and sisters provided a variety of models of occupational behavior. Oral history interviews have revealed consistently that most young boys and girls commencing work in the mills learned initial tasks from relatives rather than from strangers. An informal family apprenticeship system was thus infused into the formal structure of the world's largest textile mill.

When they came to take their first job, the children were already familiar with the names of overseers and second hands, knew the gossip about various transactions in the workrooms, and were familiar with a number of shortcuts and tricks. They also knew from an early age that the Amoskeag Corporation was the single largest employer in the city and that they could not afford to be blackballed by the Amoskeag Company, because they would not be able to find work anywhere else in northern New England.

Work roles along sex lines were also inculcated at an early age. Girls knew that, until their marriage, their work would be regulated by parents and that most of their income would be plowed back into the family's resources. They were also prepared for the fact that if the family could afford to send any of its children to school after age fourteen, the boys would go first. Within the limited occupational structure of the mill town, they were prepared for the fact that the highest rank of skill a woman could aspire to would be that of a weaver, while men could hope to become loom fixers, expert dye mixers, master mechanics, and eventually even overseer, the most coveted position.

This advance knowledge of the limits of opportunity cast the daughter into the role of back-up person for the son's career. It meant that her work would serve to facilitate her brother's occupational mobility. Girls were directed to the mill and were expected to work steadily, in order to plug the holes in the family's income, so that their brothers could afford the flexibility of experimentation in search of better occupations. As long as the daughter maintained a consistent income, the sons could afford the freedom to transfer from one department to another in the mill, or could take the risk of experimenting with outside jobs. It is not surprising, therefore, that unmarried women under thirty (who might generally be expected to have a higher turnover on the job) showed a higher persistence rate except for situations where they moved because they followed future husbands or parents to another mill town or to another job.[39]

Commencement of work did not mean independence from parental and family controls. Young men and women working in the mill continued to live in their parents' or relatives' households until marriage. Those without parents boarded with relatives, usually with married brothers and sisters or with aunts and uncles under similar arrangements. They were paying, in effect, for their room and board and were using the remainder of their pay for supplies and personal savings. While in large commercial cities young men and women tended to leave their homes and to board with strangers, industrial workers in Manchester continued to live at home or with relatives until they married. They rarely boarded with strangers. Only those men and women in their twenties and thirties who had no relatives in the city turned to corporation or commercial boarding houses.[40]

Family regulation of the individual careers of its members significantly cut down initiative for migration and experimentation with other occupations. The employment of several members in the same enterprise made the entire family vulnerable to fluctuations of the labor market and the shifting of occupational opportunities. During periods of layoff and curtailment of production, an entire family group found itself without work. This particular vulnerability was dramatized during the strike of 1922, when whole families were unemployed and on the verge of starvation during the nine-month shutdown of the mills. The strike clearly revealed that workers who had spouses or other relatives employed in the shoe industry were more inclined to strike than those whose entire source of support depended on the textile industry. Disagreement over the strike tore families apart. Brothers and sisters stopped talking to each other after their initial disagreement over whether they should strike. The almost total dependency of entire families on the textile industry deprived them of the opportunity of assisting each other during that critical situation.[41]

Conclusion

Family or surrogate family organization thus provided the central organizing scheme in the workers' living and work experience. These arrangements had their own built-in flexibilities which were governed by the family's decisions, or by external pressures, as conditions might dictate. On what basis the family made its decisions and what considerations and motives were involved in the decision are questions still open for exploration.

Immigrant families in factory towns timed their behavior by the internal clocks which were wound by their traditional customs, as well as by the factory bells. Under what circumstances did they respond to their traditional rhythms of time, and under what circumstances did they conform to industrial time? This is one of the key issues of social, cultural, and economic history. The data in this study suggest that at certain stages of their cycle families were more independent than at other stages, and that the differences in their behavior at different points in time were governed by internal family conditions as well as by the pressures and requirements of the industrial system. While these tentative conclusions await careful testing and further detailed research, it is clear now that the family was a flexible institution, and that given the historical circumstances or the opportunity structure, it was a dependent agent at certain times and an independent agent at other times.

While sociologists have been arguing that the isolated nuclear family was the form most fit for the industrial environment, this study suggests that the most adaptable family type was the extended family. With elaborate kin networks in Manchester as well as in Quebec, and with extensions in several other industrial New England towns, such families were best able to offer their members flexibility in the immigration process and in adaptation to new industrial conditions. Their major strength was in their ability to manage their resources and to direct their members into the labor force in accordance with their own needs.[42]

Despite the sophisticated structures of industrial capitalism, families continued to function as production units, even though the workplace shifted from the home to the industrial plant. Within the limited flexibility of a corporation-controlled factory town, the family could continue to make its own labor force decisions and to maintain controls over the careers of its members, as long as the market was open. Migration to an urban setting and industrial work did not drastically challenge paternal authority and traditional sex roles.

The family's interaction with the system was based on co-operation and mutual exploitation of needs and opportunities. The family succumbed to the pressures of industrial work during periods of labor surplus, but maintained its own controls during periods of labor shortage. It offered its members important resources to fall back on during times of crisis or critical life situations. While it prepared its children for industrial work, it also cushioned them from the potential shock and disruptions which they encountered under new industrial conditions. In its effort to protect its members from such exposures, the family developed its own defense system and brought its cultural traditions to bear on its environment and the industrial system.

The immigrant laborers of Manchester, New Hampshire, offer the historian the rare opportunity to explore intensively a group of industrial villagers living in a twentieth-century city still dominated by nineteenth-century paternalism. Several unique facets of their experience might lead us to question the feasibility of generalizing on the experience of the family and industrial work: patterns of family employment were different in the textile industry, which is female-intensive, than in steel communities, where women's occupations were segregated from male occupations. [43] Secondly, the continuation of paternalism in a community this size is not typical of American industrial towns in general. Finally, the particular immigrant group studied here in detail—the French Canadians—had the flexibility of "commuting" to and from the homeland, which other immigrants did not enjoy.

Despite the unique conditions of Manchester, it is possible to generalize from its experience about most early twentieth-century textile communities in the northeastern United States. It is not surprising that the patterns found in Manchester have strong parallels in mid-nineteenth-century Lancashire, England, and in the late-nineteenth-century Stockport, England, and Amiens, France—all of which were centers for the textile industry. [44] What is more surprising is that the kin and family patterns described in this study bear resemblance to patterns found in London's Bethnal Green and Boston's West End in the 1950s. [45]

This study does not provide a universal interpretation of the interaction of the family with the world of work. Instead, it invites historians to pursue these questions in a variety of communities under different historical conditions in order to derive deeper insights into the relationship between the family and the process of industrialization.

NOTES

1. E. P. Thompson, *The Making of the English Working Class* (New York, 1963); Neil Smelser, *Social Change and the Industrial Revolution* (Chicago, 1959); Michael Anderson, *Family and Kinship in Nineteenth-Century Lancashire* (Cambridge, 1972); William Goode, *World Revolution and Family Patterns* (New York, 1963). See also, Sidney Greenfield, "Industrialization and the Family in Sociological Theory," *American Journal of Sociology,* 67 (1961), 312–322.

2. For crucial revisions of traditional working-class historiography, see Thompson, *The Making of the English Working Class;* Herbert Gutman, "Work, Culture and Society in Industrializing America, 1819–1918," American Historical Review, 78 (1973), 531–588; David Montgomery, "Immigrant Workers and Scientific Management," in *Proceedings of the Conference on Immigrants in Industry, Eleutherian Mills, 1973* (forthcoming). On recent working-class historiography, see Paul Faler, "Working-Class Historiography," Radical America, 3 (1969), and Robert H. Zieger, "Workers and Scholars: Recent Trends in American Labor Historiography," Labor History, 13 (1972).

3. The most well-documented work in support of this thesis is Michael Anderson, *Family Structure in Nineteenth-Century Lancashire* (Cambridge, 1973). Specifically on American immigrant families, see Virginia Y. McLaughlin, "Patterns of Work and Family Organization: Buffalo's Italians," Journal of Interdisciplinary History, 2 (1970).

4. For the emphasis on family and household structure as the major unit of analysis, see Richard Sennett, *Families Against the City* (Cambridge, Mass., 1970). Sennett errs in defining "extended family" only within the household, thus ignoring the significant presence of kin outside the household.

5. See Tamara K. Hareven, "The Family as Process: The Historical Study of the Family Cycle," Journal of Social History, 7 (1974). For conceptualization and definition of the family cycle, see Paul C. Glick, "The Family Cycle," American Sociological Review, 12 (1947), 164–174; Reuben Hill, *Family Development in Three Generations* (Cambridge, Mass., 1970).

6. On the concept of "industrial time," see Pitirim A. Sorokin and Robert K. Merton, "Social Time: A Methodological and Functional Analysis," American Journal of Sociology, 42 (1937).

7. On the Amoskeag Mills, see Waldo Brown, *A History of the Amoskeag Company* (Manchester, N.H., 1915), a company history; Daniel Creamer and Charles W. Coulter, *Labor and the Shutdown of the Amoskeag Textile Mills,* Works Project Administration, National Research Project, Report No. L-5 (Philadelphia, 1939).

8. On classic planned New England textile towns, see Caroline F. Ware, *The Early*

New England Cotton Manufacture (New York, 1942); John Armstrong, *Factory Under the Elms* (Cambridge, Mass., 1968); Vera Shlakman, *Economic History of a Factory Town: Chicopee, Massachusetts* (New York, 1935). On the significance of the architectural design of the Amoskeag Mills and the relationship between corporate paternalism and control of the city, see Randolph Langenbach, "An Epic in Urban Design," Harvard Bulletin (April 15, 1968), and "Architecture and Paternalism: A Study in Social Space," unpublished manuscript. For the corporation's Welfare Program see Tamara K. Hareven, "Continuities and Discontinuities in Corporate Paternalism," unpublished manuscript.

9. In 1911, French Canadians constituted 37.6% of the labor force; native-born Americans (many of whom were of Irish and Scotch descent) constituted 18.6%; the Irish, 14.7%; the Poles, 10.8%; and the Greeks, 8%. By 1923, French Canadians constituted 46%. On the textile workers of Manchester in the context of other textile communities, see *Report on the Condition of Women and Child-Earners in the United States,* vol. I, Cotton Textile Industry (Washington, D. C., 1910), Senate Doc. No. 65, 61st Congress, 2nd session. Manchester was one of the communities investigated in this report. See also Ralph Vicero, "The Immigration of French-Canadians to New England, 1840–1900," Ph.D. dissertation, University of Wisconsin, 1966.

10. A reconstruction and mapping of the neighborhoods from the Manchester City Census of 1881, from the Federal Manuscript Census of 1860 to 1880, and from the most recently opened census of 1900, is now in progress.

11. This project utilized the following data: a 5% random sample of the individual employee files kept by the corporation from 1912 to 1936. The sample consists of 2,000 individual files. Individual workers' careers were reconstructed from these files over each worker's entire work period. They were subsequently traced through city directories, and wherever relevant and possible, workers' careers were reconstructed for the period prior and subsequent to their employment by the corporation, as well as during intermittent periods. The individual records were then linked with marriage records and were augmented by corporation records, newspapers, and a collection of oral history interviews of former employees. The records of French-Canadian workers were also linked with insurance records.

12. Recruitment before 1910 was carried out primarily through returning relatives to Quebec villages. From 1910 on, after the organization of the Association Canado-Americaine in Manchester, the corporation utilized the newspaper published by this organization for propaganda and recruitment of workers. The paper published major articles on the Amoskeag Mills, the copy for which was supplied by the Amoskeag Corporation. See *Le Canado-Americain* (1913–1915).

13. *Le Canado-Americain,* November 10, 1913. On corporation housing, see Langenbach, "Architecture and Paternalism: A Study in the Planning of Social Space."

14. The corporation published regular descriptions of the program in *The Amoskeag Bulletin,* 1–4 (1912–1918). The corporation's welfare and efficiency system is discussed in greater detail in Hareven, "Continuities and Discontinuities in Corporate Paternalism." On the strike, see *History of the Amoskeag Strike During the Year 1922* (Manchester, N.H., 1924).

15. On the French-Canadian background, see Phillippe Garigue, *La Vie Familiale des Canadiens Francais* (Montreal, 1967).

16. Compare with Smelser, *Social Change and the Industrial Revolution,* and Anderson, *Family Structure in Nineteenth-Century Lancashire.* See also Louise Tilly and Joan Scott, "Women's Work and the Family in Nineteenth-Century Europe," Comparative Studies in History and Society, 17 (1975).

17. This is based on oral history interviews as well as on an analysis of the women's employment patterns.

18. On the fluctuation of the textile market and its impact on the Amoskeag Company's hiring policies, see Creamer and Coulter, *Labor and the Shutdown.*

19. On the internal economic conditions of the family and their impact on labor market behavior, see U.S. Congress, *Report on Conditions of Woman and Child Wage Earners,* I; John Modell, "Family, Economy and Insecurity," paper delivered at the annual meeting of the Organization of American Historians, April 1974, and "Economic Dimensions of Family History," The Family in Historical Perspective Newsletter, No. 6 (1974). Tamara Hareven and John Modell are embarking on a study of family budgets in the early part of the twentieth century. The margin of poverty has been defined by early social investigators of the urban poor. See B. Seebohm Rowntree, *Poverty: A Study of Town Life* (London, 1922), and Robert Hunter, *Poverty* (New York, 1904).

20. On the role of kinship in migration, see Charles Tilly and C. Harold Brown, "On Uprooting, Kinship, and the Auspices of Migration," Journal of International Comparative Sociology, 7 (1967). On French-Canadian kinship see Phillippe Garigue, "French-Canadian Kinship and Urban Life," American Anthropologist, 58 (1956).

21. This is a recurring pattern described in the oral history interviews.

22. Labor turnover and patterns of migration are discussed in detail in Tamara K. Hareven, "The Laborers of Manchester, New Hampshire, 1910–1922: Patterns of Adjustment to Industrial Life," Labor History, 16 (1975). See also, *Report on the Conditions of Woman and Child Wage Earners,* I, 127.

23. It is now possible for the first time to reconstruct such patterns of migration, because the employee records actually state where individuals went on leaving the corporation. See also U.S. Department of Labor, Women's Bureau, *Lost Time and Labor Turnover in Cotton Mills: A Study of Cause and Extent,* Publication No. 52 (Washington, D.C., 1926), Part I, 109–113.

24. The overseer was the man in charge of production, management, and discipline in an entire department, which consisted of several workrooms.

25. The trace of the original 2,000 employee files gathered for the study turned up an additional 500 of their relatives who were also working in the mill. This does not represent all the possible kin combinations. It contains only the immediate ones that could be traced through vital records. If one allowed for second cousins and a variety of relatives that are not mentioned in the interviews, the number of kin could be considerably higher.

26. Evidence for kin clustering in the workrooms is derived from the reconstruction of kin groups by place of work. See also "Memo to Mr. Hagan," October, 1934, Amoskeag Files, Baker Library, Harvard University.

27. Based on oral history interviews and on a preliminary survey of the residential clustering in the corporation's tenements and boarding houses by Tamara Hareven and Randolph Langenbach. For comparison, see two significant studies of the social space of the urban working class, Pierre Chombard de Lauwe, *La Vie Quotidienne des Familles Ouvrières* (Paris, 1956), and André Michel, "La Famille Urbaine et la parenté en France," in Reuben Hill and René Konig, eds., *Families in East and West: Socialization Process and Kinship Ties* (Paris, 1970). On ethnicity and residential cohesion, see Herbert Gans, *The Urban Villagers* (New York, 1962). For a comparative experience in a textile community, see Donald B. Cole, *Immigrant City* (Cambridge, Mass., 1957).

28. Based on oral history interviews. See also Gerald D. Suttles, *The Social Order of the Slum: Ethnicity and Territory in the Inner City* (Chicago, 1968).

29. The reasons for leaving have been computed for the individual employee files.

30. Hareven, "The Family as Process," and Anderson, *Lancashire*. For an analysis of women's family cycles, see Peter Uhlenberg, "A Study of Cohort Life Cycles: Cohorts of Native Born Massachusetts Women, 1830–1920," Population Studies, 23 (1968).

31. *Report on the Condition of Woman and Child Wage Earners,* I.

32. U.S. Department of Labor, Women's Bureau, *The Share of Wage-Earning Women in Family Support,* Bulletin, No. 30 (Washington, D.C., 1923), 137–140.

33. Ibid.

34. Oral history interviews.

35. These patterns emerge from the reconstruction of the work careers of 1,000 women from the employee files, and from oral history interviews.

36. See *The Share of Wage-Earning Women.*

37. Creamer and Coulter, *Labor and the Shutdown.*

38. Wilson H. Grabill, Clyde V. Kiser, and Pascal W. Whelpton, *The Fertility of American Women* (New York, 1958), 404–406; J. Hill, "Fecundity of Immigrant Women," U.S. Congress, Immigration Commission, *Reports of First and Second Generations of Immigrants in the United States–Fecundity of Immigrant Women* (Washington, D.C., 1911), Senate Doc. No. 282, 61st Congress, 2nd session.

39. This is based on the reconstruction of the work histories and the computation of the number of times hired and dismissed for each worker. See also *Lost Time,* 29–32, 67–72, 84–87.

40. See John Modell and Tamara K. Hareven, "Urbanization and the Malleable Household: An Examination of Boarding and Lodging in American Families," in this collection.

41. Most of the interviewees still refer to the strike as the most traumatic experience of their lives. Some of them are still not on speaking terms with former friends and relatives.

42. See Talcott Parsons and R. F. Bales, *Family, Socialization and Interaction Process* (New York, 1955); Bernard Farber, *Guardians of Virtue* (New York, 1972); Sennett, *Families Against the City.*

43. For comparisons, see Susan Kleinberg, "Women's Work Patterns and the Occupational Structure of Cities," paper presented at the Brockport Conference, October 1974, and Elizabeth Butler, *Women and the Trades* (Pittsburgh, 1907–1908).

44. Compare with Anderson, *Lancashire,* and with Louise Tilly and Joan Scott, "Daughters, Wives, Mothers, Workers: Peasants and Working Class Women in the Transition to an Industrial Economy in France," paper presented at Second Berkshire Conference on the History of Women, October 1974, Cambridge, Mass. The study is based on data gathered and analyzed by Howard Chudacoff and Burr Litchfield.

45. See Michael Young and Peter Willmott, *Family and Kinship in East London* (London, 1957, revised 1962) and Gans, *Urban Villagers.*

Contributors

STUART M. BLUMIN is a member of the department of history at Cornell University. He is the author of *The Urban Threshold: Growth and Change in a Nineteenth-Century Community.*

LAURENCE A. GLASCO teaches history at the University of Pittsburgh.

SALLY GRIFFEN has taught at the State University of New York, New Paltz, and Dutchess Community College; CLYDE GRIFFEN is Lucy Maynard Salmon Professor of History at Vassar College.

PETER DOBKIN HALL is assistant professor of history at Wesleyan University.

TAMARA K. HAREVEN is associate professor of history at Clark University, where she is director of the History of the Family Program. She is the author of *Eleanor Roosevelt: An American Conscience*.

DEAN MAY is a senior historical associate in the historical department of the Church of Jesus Christ of Latter-day Saints.

JOHN MODELL is associate professor of history at the University of Minnesota.

DARRETT B. RUTMAN is professor of history at the University of New Hampshire. He is the author of, among other works, *Winthrop's Boston: Portrait of a Puritan Town, 1630–1649* and *The Morning of America, 1603–1789*.

MARIS A. VINOVSKIS is a member of the history department at the University of Michigan and a faculty associate of the Center for Political Studies of the Institute for Social Research.

Index